A Stranger to Myself

A Journey of Faith and Family

Kelly Spence Cain

with

Sandi Huddleston-Edwards

This book is a work of non-fiction. Some names, characters, places, and incidents have been changed to protect identities. Permissions have been obtained from those in the story.

Acknowledgements

When you come looking for Me, you'll find Me. Yes, when you get serious about finding Me and want it more than anything else, I'll make sure you are not disappointed. So to God goes all the glory for this story and this book.

Jeremiah 29:13 (*The Message)*

꧁꧂

It was 7:15 a.m. in the morning when I awoke with a jolt. It was like I'd heard a gun go off; my eyes were wide open, and I was sitting straight up in my bed with my mind on "high alert." I knew God wanted me to hear what He had to say, which was, "It is time to start our book."

I pretended not to hear God and questioned, "What was that?"

He replied, without hesitation, "It is time to start our book."

"But, dearest God, I'm not a writer. You know English was my least favorite class." But I also knew I was fighting a losing battle. To this day, I've never won an argument with the Omnipotent. I had so many thousands of people wherever I've shared my story of how God had saved my life from the grips of death, tell me, "You need to write a book." But that always seemed so overwhelming.

I remember telling what God had laid on my heart to my good friend, Cyndi Swartz, one night as she dropped me off. She looked at me with her big brown eyes and said, "Kelly, if you're going to do this, you have to do it with everything inside of you.

You've got to get serious about this. Once you start, there is NO turning back." So, thank you, Cyndi Swartz for giving me that encouragement and getting the ball rolling.

✤

God has helped me to climb mountains figurative and literally. He's assisted me in leading Bible Studies that started with six people and grew to twenty four people large. Who was the leader? Not me. First and foremost, it was Jesus Christ, but he allowed me to facilitate it.

There have been difficult times but so many more rewarding times. My point is that many people deserve gratitude for all He has accomplished in my life. If I were to name every person, it would be another book! I'm thankful for each and every one of you. You know who you are, and more importantly, God our Father knows, too. Some of you are not believers yet, but I hope you can come to realize that our "tragedies" are His "triumphs."

But there are a few people I do want to acknowledge.

Howard Cain, you are the love of my life. I'm so thankful for your constant support and belief in me and my story. Thank you for all of your support.

To my parents, Rod and Marilyn Spence, you know there is no possible way I would be the woman I am today if it had not been for the life-saving, God-given advice and support He gave to you to give me. I've always known I was blessed with wonderful parents, but until I saw how much you both sacrificed to get me back to a place where I could make it, did I fully realize it. I would have no other parents but you.

To my brother, Rod Spence, Jr., we don't get to pick our siblings, and I know how blessed I am to have you as my little brother. You've been the wind beneath my wings and had a much needed hug for me on days when I wanted to quit. But you would not let me. You have grown into a wonderful man.

Ellen Spence Smith, thank you sounds so trivial for all the blood, sweat, and tears I have put you through. Thank you for always being true to yourself and to me even when I did not like it. Thank you for being the sister I wish I could be.

To my friend, Dr. Elaine Osborne Harris, from the time I shared my "crazy" idea of wanting to write a book, your first response was one I will not soon forget. You said, "Well, it's about time!" Then the next set of questions just blew me away. You asked, "Do you have an editor?" I thought, "What is an editor?" Well you went on, "Well, if not, you do now. It's me. Email me everything you write, and I'll get it back to you, pronto!" And you did! Your support was so needed and appreciated. You are truly another gust of wind beneath my wings. Thank you!

This book would not be complete without thanking a man I admire, Chris McGee. Chris believed in my story since day one. He would come over after working a full day and help me edit what I'd written late into the night. What a great friend and mentor he is. My appreciation runs deep for Chris.

I could've never gotten this book to where it is, Sandi Huddleston-Edwards. When God gives out His crowns, I know He will have several extra ones for you. One will be for the act of giving so generously. Your time, resources, and wisdom will never be forgotten. I could have never gotten this piece of work to a finished product without you. You are the true writer of our book. I am forever indebted to you.

Many thanks to all the people who are mentioned herein and/or who have touched my life and helped me along the way. I wouldn't be here without you, and you know who you are.

To Those Lost Girls of Long Ago...
The Lighthouse

Oh, the beauty and the glory of the Lighthouse.
It symbolized safety and security in our perfect little world
two teenagers without a care in the world;
we were joined at the hip. Where you saw one,
you were sure to see the other. We had it all:
the ability to attract and our youth.
We were definitely going places! We would dance
down your long beaches,
dancing to the beat of our own drum, leaping and singing.
Sunning our bodies until, in our minds, we were perfect.
The sun was always shining.
We envisioned such amazing dreams for our lives.
Even though the Lighthouse was always there,
we were too preoccupied
to notice its beauty. We thought we were in complete
and utter control of our lives.
We felt like we held our destinies in the palm of our hands.
Life was perfect.

Then the tempest came, seemingly out of nowhere.
It took our lives by surprise.
We were just two innocent teenage girls.
Neither one of us was prepared to handle the cruelties
of adult life and here we were thrown into the worst storm
imaginable. Tossed and beaten down

by life's winds. We could not see the Lighthouse and
we were torn apart by the fiercest darkness.
We were whirling in the worst imaginable hurricane of life.
Where were our memories of the easy life?
We had weathered life's storms together for so long.
How could this happen to such an unbreakable bond?
A bond that was unbreakable now was shattered.
Years passed, life's changing tides moved us apart,
and happiness seemed to have shined on both of us again.
The Lighthouse could now be seen from different shores.
Once girls, now women,
we never forgot about our bonded dreams.
We were still connected.
No longer joined at the hip but still bonded at the heart.
We look forward to sailing new waters.
With the Lighthouse there to guide us,
we are sure to make it home…together.

Kelly Spence Cain

Table of Contents

Prologue
Introduction

My Journey of Faith Begins

A Physical and Spiritual Journey

A Journey of Giving and Belonging

Prologue

Weeping may last through the night,
but joy comes with the morning.
Psalm 30:5b NLT

Marilyn, Mom:

Distraught, shocked, and moving like a zombie in a bad "B movie," the hospital admissions clerk summoned me to complete the inevitable, ill-timed nuisance called paperwork. With the back of my wet hand, I wiped at the constant tears to clear my blurred vision. Empathetically, the primly dressed matron's perception caused her to withdraw the standard clipboard and pen from my outstretched but shaking hands. There was no way I could write.

"Please have a seat over here, Mrs. Spence. I'll help you complete the information. Okay, now. What is your daughter's name?" She asked with a raspy whisper.

"Kelly Anne Spence."

"Does she live at your address?" she gently prodded.

"No. I mean, yes. She's away at college, but she still lives with us."

"What is that address?"

My voice stammered the information using remote memory.

"What's her birthdate?"

"It's July 8, 1966."

I glanced towards the door, hoping to see my husband's face, while the litany of questions continued. What is her Social Security number? What is her blood type? Does she have medical insurance? If so, whom with? What is the policy number? My attention became easily distracted by the parade of passer-byes; this interrogation irritated me. When would this drudgery end and someone tell me Kelly's condition?

"Huh? What did you ask?" I feebly replied. "I'm sorry, but when will I know how my daughter is?"

The clerk began fidgeting in the creaky wooden chair. Were we finished, or was this a signal she was overtly agitated with my inattention or …what? Intuitively, my sixth sense deciphered her nonverbal as discomfort. She seemed reluctant to ask the next question. I focused on her faded, mauve-painted lips as they formed the next question. Instinctively, I braced myself.

"Mrs. Spence, is your daughter an organ donor?" she asked with a compassionate tone.

I hesitated; the answer was between my teeth, but I wasn't prepared to say it aloud – not when reality could be close. Earlier this morning when I'd left my daughter sleeping safely in her bed, I would have announced with pride to anyone that Kelly wished to be an organ donor. But these uncertain circumstances sobered me. No parent wanted to be faced with the actual results that saying "yes" could mean. But I found inner strength and pushed aside any thoughts beyond the affirmative answer.

"Yes," I stammered. "Kelly is an organ donor. It's stated that way on her driver's license. I'll show you. Wait! Do you know if the EMTs have her purse?"

"I don't know about her purse, but thank you, Mrs. Spence," she said with a smile.

I acknowledged her kindness with a slight nod. "That's a difficult question to think about at a time like this." This de ja vu moment seemed surreal; my earnest prayer and worst nightmare was that I'd never outlive my three children. Quickly, I said another silent prayer.

The admissions clerk nudged a box of Kleenex towards me. As I reached for a clean tissue, the automatic emergency doors opened, and Rod ran through the opening, appearing more fearful than I'd ever seen my husband. His ashen face was hard to bear, so I diverted my eyes downward towards the cold linoleum floor, which was worn, freshly polished, but slightly disdainful. I almost accepted the tempting urge to collapse onto its surface and grovel in my fear, but that's when my "fight or flight" instinct kicked in. I was a fighter, not a fleer; my faith in Jesus Christ was what I'd hold on to.

"Dearest Father, I need strength," I silently prayed. "Please bring Kelly and Lucy through this, and no matter what, please help me to have the assurance of your presence. Help me to be strong for whatever Kelly, Lucy, and our families must face."

God heard me and gave me the power to stand on wobbly legs to embrace my husband. As I smothered my face in his broad chest, I wished for nothing more than to close my eyes and awaken from this terrible nightmare. We held onto each other for a long while.

Finally, his cherished voice was husky and shaky as he whispered, "This can't be happening. It can't be Kelly. Are we sure it's Lucy and Kelly?"

Sadly, I nodded against his chest.

"Well, then. They're going to be okay. I know Kelly's going to be okay. Yes. Don't worry, Marilyn. Our Kelly will be okay. She's got to...." His voice trailed to silence.

Encouragingly, I responded with another nod as my mind retraced the previous few hours. Wasn't it just last night when Rod and Kelly had played tennis? Their good natured ribbing and laughter rang in my ears. Rod had beaten our competitive daughter once again on the neighborhood courts. But here we were, not even twenty four hours later, and we were wide awake but surviving in a slow-motion existence and enduring this harsh reality. Rod led me to a nearby vinyl sofa, the customary type you'd expect for a hospital waiting room. He pulled me down beside him and held my hands tightly as we bowed our heads, and I led us in a prayer of supplication.

Finally, after what seemed to be a thousand hours, a white-coated doctor entered the waiting room and whispered something to the admissions clerk. She nodded in our direction. My breath caught in my throat as I studied his grim expression.

"Hello. Mr. and Mrs. Spence?"

Rod nodded and said, "Yes."

"I'm Dr. Schlachter, chief neurosurgeon at this hospital. We've just finished scanning your daughter's brain. I'm sorry my news isn't good. Her injuries are critical." He stopped, easily noticing the immediate dismay shadowing our hopeful faces.

Trying to comprehend the full meaning of these difficult words, our four wistful eyes beckoned for more.

Trained and accustomed to maneuvering through emotional mine fields, he carefully chose his next words. "I won't sugar coat this. Your daughter has sustained one of the worst traumatic brain injuries that I've ever seen in my twenty-one years of practice." That's when my ears stopped hearing.

His lips continued moving, but I struggled to grasp his unfiltered words. A whirling tornado touched down in my head first, then in my heart. Then I heard his voice clearly through the turmoil: "Your daughter has a three percent chance of making it through the night."

The doctor swallowed hard a few times, allowing the impact of his words to bridge the huge divide of intellectual capacity and dreaded actuality that separated him from us. Ironically, all I could focus on was his Adam's apple that seemed to dance among the tendons of his throat.

"Mr. and Mrs. Spence, we've prepped for immediate surgery. We just need your written consent." Without hesitation, Rod signed the form that was simultaneously extended in our direction from the capable admissions clerk, who appeared and disappeared once the consent was given.

"Please have a seat." He motioned towards the couch.

As we robotically complied, I thought, "This can't be good."

"She's on a ventilator, which is the ONLY thing keeping her alive." He stressed the word "only."

Thankful we were seated, I began gleaning the meaning of his inconceivable words."

"She's in a comatose state – a deep, deep sleep."

When Rod audibly gasped, I squeezed his fingers. I needed to feel life penetrate my numb body.

"This means she's unable to respond, but you may see her for a few moments before the surgery. Please keep your visit as brief as possible because *time is of the essence*." He stressed the last five words.

He didn't have to say more; his stern elucidation had scored a "game, set, and match" as Kelly commonly said when something met her approval. In unison, we arose. I couldn't believe my breaking heart could break even more, but it was with every step we took towards Kelly's room. Dr. Schlachter's implied denotation and my inferred connotation was that Kelly was going to die. With only a three percent chance of making it through the night, he was giving us the last moments of our young daughter's life to say goodbye. I longed to drag my feet, but the urgency of the fleeting seconds drove me forward.

How could I express all the love in my heart and soul in just a few tiny minutes? How could I thank Kelly for all the beautiful experiences and all the happiness she'd brought to my world? How could I say goodbye to my little girl? Memories of seeing my infant daughter for the first time flashed before my mind's eye. What a lovely young woman she'd become.

Dr. Schlachter's voice interrupted my thoughts. "We had to shave her head, and she is extremely bruised and swollen."

But not a thousand warnings could have prepared me for the shock of seeing Kelly for the first time. Machines beeped and sounded alarms from every corner and wall of the brightly lit room. Tubes extended from every orifice in my daughter's basketball-sized bald head. It was hard to locate her eyes among the blue and black bruises and the dried red blood that still stained her limp body. I longed to touch the broken body, the broken face, the brokenness of this precious life. But the horror of her appearance seized my thoughts and actions, leaving me inept and paralyzed. Before I knew it, a nurse and Dr. Schlachter were rushing us out of the room.

As we stumbled down the hall toward the waiting room, the doctor warned us. "Once the surgery begins, hopefully, it will be a long time before we can come out and give you any news."

In spite of having a parched mouth and dry lips, I heard my feeble voice ask, "How long do you think KELLY'S surgery will last?" This time, I stressed a word – her name. I wanted this head of neurosurgery to know that our daughter was not just any patient. She was our daughter, and she had a name. It was Kelly. She was loved very much, and we knew her to be a fighter. Kelly would not let a severe brain injury take her out of this world. As convicted as my pathos was, my logic was not totally convinced.

The doctor replied without hesitation, "We're estimating a good seven to eight hours as a minimum. It could take ten. We won't know until we get started."

Rod and I nodded in acknowledgement. "Dear God, please let it take at least seven to eight hours," I silently prayed. "Anything less will mean...." The word was too devastating to even think. "We don't care how long the surgery takes. We just pray the surgery lasts as long as it needs to for Kelly to live."

I stared into this stranger's eyes. He seemed like a good man and a knowledgeable professional. My heart filled with compassion for him and the other staff, who had accepted and would endure this difficult task for the next few hours. When I spoke again, surprisingly, my voice sounded confident and not as shaky as I had expected. "We'll be praying for you and your staff, Dr. Schlachter, as well as for our Kelly. May God be with all of you and especially with our Kelly."

"Thank you, ma'am. Then your daughter will be in the best possible hands. We'll do everything we can for Kelly," he replied with a lingering smile. Then he turned away as we stared after him until he disappeared into an inconspicuous crevice in the hallway.

I breathed a sigh of relief because Dr. Schlachter had used Kelly's name. He now knew his patient's name and that she was our beloved daughter. And Dr. Schlachter knew we were believers who were praying for her and him. And I hoped that as Dr. Schlachter strode into the operating room to use his developed talents and acquired skills on his newest project, he had realized the weight of our hearts and the hope of our lives were too much for his mortal shoulders to bear and that he had whispered a prayer of reliance on our immortal God.

At times like these, we cannot understand why bad things happen to good people. Kelly was not perfect by any means, but

Kelly was good. On our own, we can never comprehend God's great love and compassion. But we can read about it and have it revealed to us through the Holy Spirit. As 2 Corinthians 4:6 and 4:9 says, "For God, who said, 'Let light shine out of darkness,' made his light shine in our hearts to give us the light of the knowledge of the glory of God in the face of Christ.'" "We are hard pressed on every side, but not crushed; perplexed, but not in despair; persecuted, but not abandoned; struck down, but not destroyed."

Satan will do everything he can to keep us from knowing the light of Jesus. But 1 John 4:4 assures us, "You, dear children, are from God and have overcome them, because the one who is in you is greater than the one who is in the world."

And we were about to discover this for ourselves.

Introduction

But what does it matter? The important thing is that in every way, whether from false motives or true, Christ is preached. And because of this I rejoice. Yes, and I will continue to rejoice, for I know that through your prayers and the help given by the Spirit of Jesus Christ, what has happened to me will turn out for my deliverance. I eagerly expect and hope that I will in no way be ashamed, but will have sufficient courage so that now as always Christ will be exalted in my body, whether by life or by death. For to me, to live is Christ and to die is gain. If I am to go on living in the body, this will mean fruitful labor for me. Yet what shall I choose? I do not know! I am torn between the two: I desire to depart and be with Christ, which is better by far; but it is more necessary for you that I remain in the body. Convinced of this, I know that I will remain, and I will continue with all of you for your progress and joy in the faith, so that through my being with you again your joy in Christ Jesus will overflow on account of me.

Philippians 1:18-26

My Journey
of Faith
Begins

Chapter One

Faith Journey

God blessed them and said to them,
"Be fruitful and increase in number;
fill the earth and subdue it.
Rule over the fish of the sea and the
birds of the air and over every
living creature that moves on the ground."
Genesis 1:28

Kelly:

I was asked, "When does a person's faith journey begin?" I believe every person matters to God from the minute he or she is born to the minute he or she dies. God loves each of us and longs for us to have a healthy relationship with Him. But I also believe it is up to us to realize His love and to accept His grace and forgiveness of our sins. While it seems easy enough to do, it is not.

Maybe this is why God allows difficult things to happen in our lives. Maybe this is the reason life is full of peaks and valleys with the peaks never lasting long enough and the valleys always seeming to last too long. Only God knows what highs and lows will get our attention.

I once heard a wise friend say, "God is always trying to get our attention. Sometimes He starts by throwing a tiny pebble.

When we bat that little nuisance away, He throws a stone. When we disregard that larger irritant, He throws a boulder. And when we narrowly step out of the boulder's way, well you better watch out because the brick wall is coming!"

Certainly, I can attest to each of these, including the brick wall. Not only did it take a brick wall, but it took a flat-bed, semi-truck, carrying a full load of cement blocks before He got my attention. A real faith journey doesn't begin until we admit we cannot do anything by ourselves. We need His constant help and the help He sends through other saints. I would not be the person I am today had it not been for all of the faithful souls, who paused their steady paces to lend me a guiding hand along the journey where I realized that I not only mattered to them, but I mattered especially to God.

One of my favorite radio disc jockeys is Joey Deese. This astute man used to say, "Whatever God brought you to, He will bring you through." Isn't that good stuff? I think so. I believe I have always been on some sort of faith journey with God, but I didn't realize it or acknowledge my need for Him until my misapplied security blanket was stripped away during a horrific accident. In a matter of seconds, I no longer had good looks, an athletic ability, popularity, intelligence, or anything else in which I'd defined who I was. I became a stranger to myself.

Once I was left with no other choice but to dig deep and find the not so pretty side of myself, I discovered how selfish, proud, arrogant, and basically sinful I was. Did my discovery surprise God? Not at all. Even before I took my first breath, He knew just what I needed – and what I lacked. He yearned for years to wash me clean and give me a new start with a new heart. And He provided the companions I'd need along my journey of faith.

A Stranger to Myself

My enduring companions have been my family, who represent a multitude of blessings to me. My family has stuck by me during my elations and during my darkest hours. But not everyone is as blessed as I am to have a supportive family, who has multiplied in numbers and care over the years. So if you don't, cry out to God to bless you with godly mentors and Christian sojourners, who can become your family. He will never fail you. And it is comforting to know that our Christian brothers and sisters can become members of our families, whom we can depend upon and admire, as well. They may come into our lives as coaches, teachers, friends, friends' parents, or ministers. They may take us under their wings or may invite us to live under their roofs for a while.

Before I accepted Jesus Christ as my Lord and Savior, I believed I was living my glory years and my nuclear family was my greatest blessing. At that point in my life, family consisted of my two parents, my older sister, Ellen, and my younger brother, Rod, Jr. And even though I knew all four of these wonderful people were blessings, it wasn't until I accepted Christ's mercy and love that I came to fully realize and recognize how important my family was and would become for the rest of my life. That's when family was redefined as Jesus Christ, my two parents, and my two siblings – my life-long companions. It took me eighteen years to authenticate and begin to internalize the profound meaning of unconditional love as my newfound faith and their unwavering love supplemented the hardest days of my life and still does. My family continuously gifts me with incredible, countless blessings. But if you are like me, it is hard to truly comprehend and fully value the meaning of family.

Just the other day, I was travelling to work on one of Charlotte's special transportation buses. This transportation system is designed specifically for people with disabilities who

3

cannot drive. As the jovial driver dismounted the bus to guide me up the steps and escort me to a nearby seat, *Earth, Wind and Fire's* song, "September" was blaring on the stereo. The beat was infectious!

"You're bringing me back to my glory days," I yelled over the music. But before I could finish my next sentence, God stopped me, arresting my thoughts.

I heard Him say, "Kelly those were not your 'glory days.' You did not even have a relationship with me back then. Your glory days began the day you accepted me. They are right now and will continue until I call you Home. You're living in your 'glory days.'"

So, obediently and thankfully, I realized this was an opportunity to share my faith, so I asked the driver to lower the stereo's volume, replacing the '80s song with my joyful voice. The driver and three other passengers received my testimony that morning – a story of survival because of Jesus Christ and His healing mercy for me.

Chapter Two

New Beginnings

"Anyone who says sunshine brings happiness has never danced in the rain."

Anonymous

Teenage years are full of peer pressure and rebellion: Sometimes experimenting with drugs and alcohol; eating from the trees of stupidity, naivety, and pleasure; testing established constraints and flimsy limits; questioning authorities; and seeking a place to belong amidst the random detours and hazy directions on this journey called life. Hopefully, we come to realize we are lost and return to the places where we ran from initially to regain our composure and sense of direction. Maturity and teachable mistakes are our rescuers, discovering our whereabouts and steering us towards the safety net of the *right* path. Our values, morals, and Biblical lessons quicken the pace and enlighten our courses. But we certainly can lose our way if our quest for individuality, irresponsibility, and freedom becomes obsessive and incessant. This thirst for knowledge and experiences can overshadow our parents' instructions and childhood innocence when the desire to control our own destinies becomes fixated and compulsive. Teenage years are a time when possibilities and button pushing can seem deceitfully right but can become treacherously wrong. And it's a time when raging hormones, the desire to fit in, and inexperience are too eager to take control of the wheel and steer through the huge gap before adulthood. High school was definitely what I believed to be my *glory* years. Having just moved to Marietta (a suburb of Atlanta) at the beginning of my freshman year, I loved it from day one because it was a great area, I loved challenges, and I enjoyed meeting new people and making friends. Of course, the first week at a new school can be the scariest because you know no one, and you are an outsider to a lot of established *cliques*. I can admit that being the new girl prior to Marietta had never been what I'd call fun. Even so, with my sanguine personality, *I had never met a stranger.* Thankfully, I met some really nice girls in fourth period before lunch on the first day. One of them, Pam, invited me to join her and her friends for lunch, which I eagerly accepted because there is nothing worse than having to eat alone on the first day of school. I quickly made friends, lots of them. By my sophomore year, I had made the cheerleading squad, was a leader on the cross country team, and the tennis team. In fact, my tennis skills were such that I could beat some guys on the boys' tennis team.

Being a fierce competitor and excelling in my chosen sports, self-confidence oozed out of every pore. My sophomore year continued to be an awesome one when I was one of two young women who were elected to the Homecoming Court. I felt like a real celebrity, riding on the back of a fancy convertible car and waving to the people in the stands. It was exciting.

At the end of that year, I was awarded the "Most Outstanding Sophomore Girl" out of a class of five hundred. The award was presented in front of the entire student body; even my parents were able to attend the ceremony. Life was good.

As a sophomore and junior, the popular upper classmen were always asking me on dates or to attend different events or dances. Not long afterwards, they'd ask me if I wanted to "go steady." So I usually did. After going steady with Jeff, the basketball star, for maybe three months, I'd be bored, and we'd break up. By the end of the next week, I'd be dating someone else and heading towards "going steady" again. That was up until my senior year when I fell madly in love with Kurt.

Kurt was a wrestling state champion; he played on the varsity football team and wore a pair of jeans and cowboy boots like nobody's business! He was known as one of the leaders of the *bad boys,* which was not really *bad* by today's standards. It meant the boys thought they knew it all, and anyone who told them differently may have gotten beat up after school. The dichotomy is I was a *good girl* looking for a way to defy my parents. Rebellion became my middle name, and what better way than to fall in love with a bad boy? But this rebellion had been festering for a while. During my sophomore year, I obtained my first fake ID when the legal drinking age in Georgia was still eighteen. Then to my dismay, the legal age was raised to twenty one, making me have to use the fake ID for a while longer. Ellen lucked out by being the exact age when it was raised. But with all the craziness we did, it is amazing none of us were killed.

In the summers, our family would always go home to Michigan for a week or two to visit family and friends, but when Ellen and I got a little older, we convinced our parents to allow us to stay home by ourselves. Almost as quickly as their car was out of sight, we turned our home into the Spence Party House. Every night our friends would come over, and someone would go and buy us alcohol. So you could say we were acting like teenagers. We would do things like playing tennis on the public courts at 2 a.m. After drinking a large quantity of alcoholic beverages, my friend, Billy, got on our Vespa (motor scooter) and almost wrecked it. Once again, it is amazing that so many of us made it to adulthood.

But in my senior year, Kurt became my hunk, and he told me over and over, "I love you more than any other woman I have ever met. I've never felt so much love for a woman before." And he pressed me to lower my convictions and have sexual intercourse by saying, "If you truly love me, you will take the final step and have sex with me. That will consummate our love forever."

But I repeatedly told him, "No, no, no, no, no!" I was committed to wait until my wedding night to have intercourse even though a few of my closest friends had begun sleeping with their boyfriends.

Finally, spring came. I was proud not to have succumbed to the peer pressure, but it was becoming more difficult to resist. I can remember being confused and torn about losing my virginity when I learned that other friends had surrendered to the temptation and were having sex – not always protected -- with their boyfriends. But as each of my closest friends – the "good girls" – started having sexual relations, I began questioning myself. Then I would think of my parents and how they would be disappointed. After all, my parents had been good role models for me. Even though they had dated six years, my parents had waited. Besides, I fantasized about the first time, reestablishing my principles to lose my virginity to my husband. Now don't get me wrong. I'm not painting a picture of me with a halo and silvery wings. By that time, I had engaged in heavy petting because of my raging hormones. At seventeen, my body was waking up to another world that I knew nothing about.

Finally, spring break came during my senior year at Wheeler High School. A group of us headed to Daytona Beach, Florida, where the first real week of freedom from parental supervision started off great! We spent the days playing Frisbee, tossing footballs, and jogging on the beach. I tanned so easily that people teased me about being a "California Girl" or even being a partial race. My best friend and I shared one Sony Walkman with two headphones connected to it, so we could run up and down the beach dancing. Of course, these shenanigans were created to attract boys. And we did! Many guys completely stopped their football games to turn and stare at us. Boy, those were the days!

At night the group met in someone's room to party. Most of us were innocent to what serious partying meant, but we thought it was a big deal whenever we had a bottle or two of Cella wine. Fortunately, no one in our group did drugs or smoked cigarettes. Basically, we were good kids alone in a paradise without adult supervision. So we went a little overboard at times.

On our second to the last day in Daytona, Kurt asked me to take a private walk on the beach that evening. Immediately, my naïve thoughts were, "Oh, how sweet! He wants to be alone with me under the stars. Oh, how romantic!"

But during the day, I noticed Kurt drinking way too much, but I'm sure I did, too. He reminded me several times about our clandestine rendezvous later that evening. At 2:00 a.m., he rapped softly on my door. When I opened the door, I noticed he had a blanket slung over his shoulder.

"What's the blanket for?" I asked.

"I just want a dry place for us to sit and talk for a while," he explained.

Once again, his romantic gestures thrilled me. How innocent I was! So out to the beach we went, walking just far enough to be out of ear shot or eye sight of anyone. Kurt spread the blanket on the moist sand, squatted down, and offered me his hand. I sat beside him. But when Kurt laid down on the blanket, I immediately felt a gnawing in the pit of my stomach combined with a quick onset of light headiness. I dismissed both feelings

9

and attributed them to the large amount of alcohol I'd consumed that day, that is, until he pulled me back until we were lying on our backs, side by side. I focused on the billion stars above me and tried to remain calm. I pointed to the Big Dipper; he ignored me. That's when Kurt rolled on top of me, pinning me down with his weight. I couldn't move. His mouth was pressing hard on mine as he kissed me, pausing long enough to whisper how he had waited for this moment all of his life.

That's when I stammered the most important words I could say, "No Kurt! We aren't doing THAT!"

Sadly, he didn't listen, and I became a sexual object, no longer his cherished girlfriend who he cared about. My dreams of romance were crushed in a few selfish moments. Shaking, disheveled, and ashamed, I cried. This was not at all what I thought making love would be like. There absolutely had been no love in this forceful act. My thoughts were raging and screaming the words, "I've been raped! Kurt raped me!" I was in so much pain – physically, emotionally, and mentally. I felt so dirty and violated. Disgustedly, I grabbed my torn clothes and put them on as fast as I could to cover up what had been stolen from me. Somehow, I grabbed the blanket, covered myself and went running down the beach on shaky legs with Kurt following closely behind. He was yelling for me to stop and shouting apologies now.

"Kelly, come back. I'm sorry. I thought you wanted it as bad as I did."

How could he think this was okay? I just kept running even though the pain was worse than I had ever experienced in my life. I remember thinking through my tears that my dreams were now shattered. What I had wanted all of my life had just happened, but I did not feel loved or special. Instead, I felt abused and full of shame. I asked myself, "Is this what sex is all about? If so, then why would people want to do it?" I felt so betrayed, lost, and confused.

When Kurt finally caught up with me, he had to all but tackle me. I was crying so hard and could not control my emotions. "Get away from me! I never want to see you again." I screamed furiously.

His cheeks were wet from sweat and tears. He repeated the same worthless apologies that he had shouted all the way down the beach.

I stopped and faced him. I screamed, "None of that matters. When I said, 'NO, we aren't doing THAT,' that should have been enough. You've made me feel dirty, disrespected, and used. I want nothing more to do with you." I felt the anger spewing from my lips.

I left him there sitting in the sand, crying as I sought a safe, private place to be alone and weep. Never had I felt so helpless in my life. I wanted my mother. She would know how to make things better. But Mom was hundreds of miles away.

That night, the inevitable questions pounded my temples. Why me? Did I do something to make him think this was okay? Was it because we both drank too much? Was it the way I was dressed in shorts and a tank top? Was I asking for it? What had I done to deserve this? Self-blame and self-shame were my conscience and my accusers that night. With Mom in Georgia, I needed a substitute. It would have to be my best friend, Lucy. She would understand. I knew I could trust her with all the sordid details of tonight. Lucy would listen to me and console me. So I woke her and sobbed my heart out, sharing my awful humiliation. But I was right. Lucy was my best friend because of all the things I knew she would do: listen, understand, comfort, and become my protector. She assured me repeatedly that I was not at fault. Then Lucy became angry and as fierce as a pit bull.

I don't remember getting much sleep before sunrise; Kurt tried every tactic he could to earn my forgiveness that day. He brought me roses, wrote me a letter with the theme "I am so sorry," and even sent his best friend to soothe my anger. But to no avail, because I was not forgiving him. That night, Kurt grew desperate and got stinking drunk. He even drove his precious Jeep into the ocean, thinking his feigned suicide would prove his love for me. The one thing he loved more than anything was his Jeep, so this pitiful stunt resulted in a messed up vehicle and him more in debt when the wrecker service charged more than $100 to tow it out of the water. I couldn't sleep that night; I was disturbed by the betrayal from the night before. One thing was for sure: I had broken off my relationship with Kurt.

After we returned home from spring break, my parents were eager to know how the trip had gone. I masked a smile and replied, "Great! We were all well behaved, and it was really fun." They expected we had sewn some wild oats like all kids do, but my soul's ambition was to never break their hearts with the truth. Never would I disclose what had happened that awful night on the beach. So life returned to *nearly normal* until time for my menstrual cycle, which I did not have that month. A few days later, I panicked when my panties were stained with spotted blood, so I went to Ellen, who always knew how to handle a crisis. After all, it was her job as the eldest sister. Right away, Ellen drove me to the drug store to purchase a pregnancy test. Not knowing how to administer the test, Ellen read the step-by-step instructions aloud; I did exactly what she said. Reluctantly, I handed it to her; my fear rose. When she didn't smile and looked concerned, I knew this was not going to be good news. She didn't have to say the words; I already sensed what the results were.

"Okay, Ellen. Tell me what it is! I need to hear you say it!"

A Stranger to Myself

Not one to mince words, Ellen's stare was penetrating. "Kelly, it's in the pink. You're pregnant." Tears filled her eyes before she looked away.

"This is incredible. Are you sure?" I stammered. "I've only had sex one time in my life."

"Yes, I'm sure. It's clearly in the pink. No doubt, you're pregnant."

Her words impacted my chest as if a sledge hammer had struck me. This was surreal; it could not be happening to me. I'd only had sex one time, and I was raped at that. How could I be pregnant?

"No, no," I shook my head. "This cannot be happening," were the only words in my vocabulary. I longed to go for a run; the shame that I felt was overwhelming, but my legs wouldn't move from the side of the tub. The bad memories returned in vivid color as if it were still happening. The intense pain and horror of having loved and trusted someone, who could force himself on a virgin, ripping her world apart, was too much to accept.

Again, self-blame and self-shame became my accusers. My mind raced with the self-condemnation facts and self-doubt questions I'd experienced when it happened. *I should never have gone to the beach with Kurt that night. I should never have gone to the beach with anyone at 2:00 a.m., especially when they were carrying a blanket. I should have taken more precautions. What did I think would happen? What did I really want to happen? Had I asked for it?*

We sat in silence while an hour transpired before Ellen took control of the moment and brought me back to reality. "Kelly. Don't worry," she assured me. "I know what to do. A friend of mine knows a good doctor. . . ." Her voice trailed off.

13

Suddenly, I felt relieved. "My friend will know what to do. We'll schedule the appointment for you, but you'll have to tell Kurt. He needs to pay for the abortion."

My heart leapt at the pronunciation of this word. It was hard to bear. I didn't like the word at all and never thought I'd experience anything close to it. But Ellen assumed a matter-of-fact mode and continued whispering her advice. Scared and confused, I felt like a robot, nodding in response to her parade of statements sprinkled with a few questions here and there. I never wondered if an abortion were the right thing to do. I never considered the millions of couples who were infertile and would love to adopt a baby. I never considered myself a mother. I just knew being pregnant because of rape was wrong.

Another friend of mine had gotten pregnant the year before and had an abortion. I never condoned nor judged my friend when it happened. I was just there to support her anyway I could. So that's when I turned to my friend, Lucy. I needed her compassion and advice.

"Lucy, do you think this is the right thing to do? Should I tell my parents?"

Without a moment's hesitation, Lucy said, "It's the right thing to do. And no – don't tell your parents. It would crush them."

So with her unwavering affirmation and Ellen's, I allowed them to take care of all the arrangements. Ellen consulted with her friend and found out the name of a clinic. Then she telephoned the clinic to obtain the current cost. Lucy and Ellen researched the procedures and explained them to me. And they assured me that Mom and Dad didn't have to consent or ever find out. That had been my greatest fear. I felt like a liar and a failure. My parents would be so disappointed and hurt if they knew. Suddenly, I felt like a little girl again – alone and frightened.

That next day, I telephoned Kurt and requested a time to talk. He excitedly invited me to his home after school. Then he added, "Mom won't be home, so we'll have plenty of privacy to talk." I hung up, newly disgusted and nervous.

When he answered the doorbell and saw me standing on his front porch and Lucy waiting in the orange VW bug behind me, he immediately could tell something was terribly wrong. My face hid no secrets.

He asked, "Kelly, what's wrong?"

Before bursting into tears, I managed to blurt out, "I'm pregnant!"

Without hesitation, he reached for me and pulled me inside the door; surprisingly, I allowed him to hold me and tell me everything was going to be all right. I literally sobbed and sobbed and sobbed some more. The tears just kept flowing on the same day when I should have been smiling and laughing. My "letter of acceptance" to the University of Georgia had arrived in the mail that day. I was actually going to become a member of the freshmen class. We'd known before spring break that Kurt had been accepted to Georgia Southern College. Here we were. Two young kids with our whole lives in front of us. Kids having kids could never be a good thing. What would happen to us after all of this was over?

When my cries slowed down, and my hiccups began, Kurt gently grabbed my shoulders and made me face him. To his credit, Kurt said, "I'll marry you tomorrow, Kelly, if that's what you want to do. We can raise the baby together."

Depression, anger, fear, and confusion crowded my mind. Everything seemed cloudy and foggy. Why was the foyer spinning? What made him think I could make a major decision about getting married in a few minutes, especially to someone who had raped me? I did know that two wrongs didn't make a right.

"I'm not ready to be a mother, Kurt, and I doubt you are ready to be a father. Besides, I know I don't want to get married. We have college and our whole lives ahead of us."

He seemed saddened, but he continued to listen.

"My sister has contacted an abortion clinic. I can get an appointment for next Saturday. The cost is $287. Will you to pay for it?"

"Of course," he said.

"Thanks. I'll need the money in two or three days. Can you get it by then?"

"No problem, Kelly. I have it saved up in my account. But you're not going through this alone. I want to be there to help you get through this."

"I'd rather you not, Kurt. Your part is just to help with the money."

He seemed disappointed, but how could he have expected anything else? I told him goodbye and left. Two days later, Kurt brought me the money. I politely thanked him for it, and we exchanged small talk for a few minutes before he left.

I handed over the $287 to Ellen, who was so sweet and gentle with me. I welcomed her compassion, confidence, and sympathy. She assured me her friend had said the procedure was not that bad, and this nightmare would soon be over.

Ellen said, "Life will be good again, I promise."

I wanted to believe her. I tried to believe her. Apparently, I did believe her because on the next Saturday, I found myself going through the motions of having an abortion. And true to his word, Kurt sat with my sister and Lucy in the waiting area until I was discharged. Afterwards, Ellen drove me home, steered me up the stairs, and tucked me into bed. Then she went downstairs and convincingly explained to Mom, "Kelly has a terrible head cold; it might even be the flu."

One week later on the following Saturday, I drove to our Catholic Church to confess my sin. I sat in the closed part of the confessional and cried warm tears while I poured out my heart to the priest and explained the horrible thing I had done.

The priest told me that God was very disappointed in me, but I could be forgiven if I took my rosary and said ten "Our Fathers" and ten "Hail Mary." After leaving the confessional, I knelt in a pew and said my prayers. I cried about being raped. I cried about disappointing my parents. I cried about having an abortion. And I cried for the baby – my baby – who I'd never hold. Then I told God Almighty that I was finished and was locking this secret in my soul. No one would ever discover what I had done. In my mind, I watched as I wrapped huge steel chains around a box and double pad-locked it. When I walked out of that church, I felt relieved and as if I had placed it all behind me. I had confessed and was assured God had forgiven me, so I was ready to return to my happy-go-lucky perfect life. But I never considered the reality of not being able to forgive myself.

There is so much about this traumatic time that I have purposely blocked from my memory. When I told God that I was locking it deep down in my soul, I wanted to forget about it. I never realized I was literally placing myself into bondage by doing so. It saddens me to realize I missed out on having my first and only biological child because of my selfishness and immaturity.

Chapter Three

Sorority Rush

I have come that they may have life, and have it to the full.
John 10:10b

At the beginning of the summer, my best friend, Lucy, and I purchased red heart-shaped sun glasses that we always wore when riding in her convertible orange VW bug. We thought we were something else and were ready to shake the high school dust from our feet and start the greatest time of our lives.

Lucy and I were sharing the same dorm room, so we were excited to finally be going off to college and freed from our parents' control. We'd gone shopping together throughout the summer months and had gotten matching rainbow bedspreads and mirrors for our rooms, so we could look at ourselves constantly and admire our beauty. We had chosen desk lamps in case we spent time studying when it didn't cut into our full college experience – boy time.

But our greatest plans were to go through sorority rush together. We had each purchased four or five perfect dresses because we had to feel like the belles of the ball. Happily on our last day home, we packed up her VW bug, Mom's van, and her mom's car with all of our new college stuff. It was surprising we didn't rent a U-Haul for that trip. Remember, we were "all girls."

Sorority Rush was to happen two weeks before school began, so when we arrived on campus, our excitement was ready to burst. We painted smiles on with our favorite colored lipstick, and the sorority girls from each house came out to meet us as we walked onto their property. They were happy we had arrived and had chosen their house to visit. At each house, young women took us around and campaigned all of the advantages and plusses for becoming a member of that sorority. We were treated like royalty. My sister was going through Rush at the same time Lucy and I were. This was an uneasy feeling I tried to dismiss from my mind because I was one of the top five girls in my graduating class; Ellen was just another girl and was not the most popular in high school as I had been. I wanted Ellen to do well at Rush and be accepted almost more than I.

On the following day, the second day of Rush, Lucy and I were asked back to every sorority we had visited the previous day, and we had narrowed down our hopes to three or four. As we revisited these homes, Rush got more intense. The girls in each sorority pressured us more to join their particular sorority. When we returned to the dorm, we wished we could be flies on the wall at their meetings to hear what sisters said about us. The Rush Process can make or break you. I remember one particular young woman, who was not invited back to the sorority of her dreams and committed suicide that night.

Ellen had already decided she wanted to be a Zeta, so she had befriended many Zeta's during her freshmen college year and was convinced this was the sorority that would make her dreams come true. When Lucy and I went to see the list of who had and had not been invited back to Zeta, my sister's name did not appear, but Lucy and I had been invited back. This was devastating to my sister and spoke volumes to me about true sisterhood. Secretly, I wanted to be a Zeta and had preferred it, but because of Ellen's denial and pain, I'd never become a Zeta.

Lucy preferred two sororities who wanted her and where she wanted to return – one was Zeta. So I joined the other sorority, Alpha Delpha Pi, which I thought was the best one on campus. During the last Pref Party, the sisters had brought out the Bible and stated they were a home that believed in Biblical principles and were followers of Jesus Christ. Mom later reminded me that was the reason I'd joined ADPI instead of Zeta because of their Christian belief, whereas Lucy had chosen Zeta as her final choice.

During our first pledge group meeting, we were introduced to one of the most cheerful people I think I've ever met named Susan Cheeley. Susan was excited to have us and was appointed our Pledge Trainer. With her bubbly personality exuding from her eyes and mouth, everything about her looked like a picture of Jesus Christ. She was a true Southerner from a small town in Georgia.

After the winter quarter, Susan invited fifty of us to her home. Her father worked in government and was extremely wealthy. Every one of the fifty girls slept on a bed in their mansion in Beaufort, Georgia. Susan was modest; you'd never known she was from such wealth. Susan took a special interest in every one of the Pledges but especially in me.

Chapter Four

The Accident

To keep me from becoming conceited because of these
surpassingly great revelations, there was given me a thorn in my
flesh, a messenger of Satan, to torment me. Three times I pleaded
with the Lord to take it away from me. But he said to me, "My
grace is sufficient for you, for my power is made perfect in
weakness." Therefore I will boast all the more gladly about my
weaknesses, so that Christ's power may rest on me. That is why,
for Christ's sake, I delight in weaknesses, in insults, in
hardships, in persecutions, in difficulties.
For when I am weak, then I am strong.
2 Corinthians 12: 7-10

Saturday, March 18, 1985, was like any other Saturday
morning except it was the weekend before final exams for the
winter quarter. Even so, this was my favorite time of the year
when cherry blossom buds were on the verge of blooming. At
eighteen, I was in love, about to complete my freshman year of
college, and participating in a cheerleading camp for young girls.
Danni, was my friend and mentor, who had asked me to help
with the camp when I came home from school. I was happy and
excited to take part.

Mom rose early to spend the morning running errands,
leaving my younger brother, Rod, Jr., and me sleeping soundly
upstairs. Ellen was living on campus now and didn't plan to

21

come home on this particular weekend. Over the years, I had memorized Mom's familiar morning pattern. She'd savor a hot, steamy cup of decaffeinated coffee while flipping through the newspaper – especially the sales pages. Absent-mindedly, she'd devour a small sweet breakfast muffin, smacking her lips as she licked the crumbs from her fingers. Then she'd shower, dress, and rush out the door to begin a day of running errands and grocery shopping before we'd even gotten out of bed – usually by 9:00 a.m. But Mom was returning even earlier today because she'd promised me a new tennis outfit to wear to the try-outs for the University of Georgia women's tennis team. Of course, I'd procrastinated, leaving less than a week to purchase the *perfect* outfit.

My best friend and college pal, Lucy, and I had been friends throughout high school. We shared many secrets and were practically inseparable. Shortly after noon, Lucy banged the brass door knocker, interrupting my pleasant dreams of Chris. Finally awake, I winced unbelievably at the clock's time and almost tripped rushing down the stairs to open the heavy oak door.

Lucy barged past me and looked frustrated. "Hey! I thought we were going shopping! Were you still in bed?"

"Yeah. I can't believe it's after 12:00. I went to bed late last night." I yawned. "Dad and I played a tennis match, and then we all watched the late movie."

"Who won?" Lucy asked nonchalantly, following me to the kitchen.

"Need you ask?" I responded with a frown, while pouring myself a glass of milk.

"Where's your mom?" She poured herself a cup of Mom's leftover coffee.

"Probably out shopping and running errands – like she does every Saturday morning."

"Where's your dad?" she probed. "Where's Rod, Jr."

"At the office. You remember. Dad works half a day on Saturdays, and Rod is still probably asleep unless you woke him up with your banging."

"I didn't bang," she sneered.

"Yes you did," I countered.

"No I didn't. Come on. Hurry and get dressed. The day is wasting away. I thought we could go to Cumberland Mall to shop for your outfit."

Cumberland Mall, located in Marietta, was a popular hangout for teenagers. This was a great idea until I remembered Mom.

"Mom's going with us, remember?" I asked.

"That's right. I forgot. Will she be long getting back? If so, can we go by ourselves?" Lucy asked.

"I have no idea. She had to go to the drycleaners, get her car washed, pick up a package at the post office, buy groceries, and... I can't remember what else is on her to do list."

"That's okay. I'm worn out listening to you. Well, do you think your mom would be upset if we shopped for your tennis outfit without her?" Lucy asked. "Besides, she'll probably be tired with all that running."

"I don't know. I wouldn't want to hurt her feelings. She seemed excited to be asked."

"She probably wouldn't care. Do you think?"

"I don't know. Probably not," I agreed. "Let me go and get dressed. If she's not back by then, we'll leave her a note."

Lucy and I had finished going through Sorority Rush together, and although we had pledged different sororities, we knew we'd always be the best of friends. Besides, Lucy was right. Mom would probably welcome a chance to sit down and put her feet up when she got home. We could go shopping for the tennis outfit and give her a break. After all, we were adults and could drive ourselves. Firmly convinced I was giving Mom time for herself, my excitement about finding the perfect tennis outfit grew. I scribbled a note and hurried out of the house, followed by Lucy.

The temperature was pleasant. This was the first warm day of the year when we could lower the convertible top on Lucy's bright orange Volkswagen Bug. We threw on our matching hot, red heart-shaped sunglasses, and without a care in the world, we slid into the 1964 VW Bug's seats. The car was old; its previous owner had removed the seat belts without bothering to replace them. Luckily, the mandatory seat belt law had not gone into effect yet. The car stereo was blasting out our favorite '80s songs as our heads bobbed in time to the beat. Before we knew it, we were on our way, heading toward the busy intersection not quite a mile from my home. I lifted my face towards the sun and closed my eyes. Big smiles were plastered on our young, carefree faces. We had everything going for us, so what more could we ask for? Maybe a great-looking tennis outfit. Unfortunately, fate responded to my question with a different answer. Lucy pressed the accelerator to the floor as she rushed to beat the yellow caution light to turn at the approaching intersection.

Tragically, we entered the intersection at the same moment as the eighteen-wheel flat-bed semi-truck entered it. The heavily laden truck was carrying a full load of cylinder cement blocks. As I looked up, I saw the truck barreling through the intersection, heading straight towards us. The truck driver seemed determined to make it through the light, no matter what. That's when everything slowed down, as if it were happening in slow motion. Lucy's eyes widened as her mouth opened to release a high pitched scream. Her sandaled right foot slammed the brake, hoping to slow the VW and miss the truck. But the realization of doom contorted her face in a horrible way. Before I could turn my head from Lucy, our vehicles collided with hair-raising force and an earth-shattering impact. Mercifully, everything faded to black as the vehicles' metal grinded and scraped and came to an abrupt stop -- directly adjacent to the park where I'd won many tennis tournaments.

My mom and dad were extremely diligent in journaling their experiences for the next few months. Their tear-stained pages and heartfelt entries would later become the missing links that filled in huge, dark gaps for me. It is with my deepest gratitude for their disciplined way of chronicling these events that I am able to share their memories with you.

Mom said she'd just returned home and was unpacking her groceries when she recognized Pat Henslee's face in the driver's seat of an unfamiliar vehicle. It took her a few minutes to process who she was. Pat was Joe Henslee's mother. Joe was one of my high school friends. Mom had met Pat several times and seemed to like her. Sitting beside Pat in the car was her friend, Jackie, whom Mom also had met before. When Mom turned to smile and wave a friendly welcome, she quickly saw Pat's drawn, white face staring over the steering wheel, her *mother's instincts* kicked into high gear. Instantly, she knew this was not a friendly visit. Pat slung open her car door and half way stood in the opening. Her voice was steady, firm, and extremely serious when she almost commanded, "Marilyn, leave your groceries where they are. Get your purse and come with us. There's been an accident. It's Kelly and Lucy." When Mom saw Pat's stricken countenance and heard the severity of her voice, she realized this was not just a fender-bender.

Mom asked Pat one question, "Is she alive?"

"Yes, I think so." That is all Pat could tell her.

I can visualize my mother as she gained control of her senses and pushed her way into the backseat of the car, probably slamming the door behind her. As Pat hastened out of the driveway, she explained that she and Jackie had come upon an accident and recognized it as Lucy's orange VW Bug. There was an injured person in the passenger's seat, who she had no other choice but to assume was Kelly. She'd asked a few questions of one of the EMTs on the scene. That's when Pat said she had turned her car around and headed towards our home.

At the risk of getting a ticket, Mom urged Pat to speed toward the Emergency and Trauma Unit at Kennestone Hospital. Mom later recounted, "And thanks be to God the hospital was in another direction, so we didn't have to see the accident scene. Based on what I've heard and the pictures I've seen since, I don't think I would have survived the trip."

For Mom and her chauffeurs, the seven miles stretched to what seemed like a hundred miles because they somehow were stopped by every traffic light on the way.

"Suddenly, I experienced an empty feeling in the pit of my stomach," Mom shared later. "I began shaking and crying uncontrollably as I realized I was living the worst nightmare any mother could ever have: the nightmare that your child is injured or even killed. Like all mothers, there had been many times over the years when I'd awakened during the night, filled with unbridled fear and rampant panic due to a nightmare or an inexplicable sound. I'd hurry to their rooms to check on them, ensuring they were okay. Relieved, I'd return to my bed and thank God that all was well. Only this time, it wasn't a dream -- it was true – it was real – and my daughter wasn't okay."

When Pat's car rounded the asphalt driveway and the hospital came into focus, Mom regained control of herself, and the three women became silent as Pat stopped the car with the engine running at the entrance to the emergency room, dreading what they'd find inside.

Mom said her two companions were extremely supportive. Pat urged Mom and Jackie to go ahead while she parked the car. She also offered to telephone my dad at his office and break the news. With Mom feeling a surge of adrenaline and with Jackie following closely behind, they ran through the automatic doors.

Marilyn:

Mom wrote in her journal these questions: *What news was waiting for me on the other side? Would Kelly be alive or...? I couldn't finish the sentence; it was unimaginable.*

Chapter Five

At Death's Door

Trust in the Lord forever, for the Lord, is the Rock eternal.
Isaiah 26:4

Trust in the Lord with all your heart and lean not on your own
understanding; in all your ways submit him,
and he will make your paths straight.
Proverbs 3:5-6

Kelly:

I'm told the impact was hardest felt on Lucy's side of the vehicle. She was ejected straight from the car and landed between a sub-division sign and moving traffic. Incredibly, Lucy, energized by nothing more than adrenaline and fear, noticed a deep gash to her right arm, which was bleeding profusely, and bounced to her feet. Slowly, she turned toward the car in search of me. That's when she saw a horrific sight.

I had been thrown straight through the front windshield, causing a major blow to the right side of my face. Dark crimson blood was spewing everywhere. Lucy's first thoughts were, "Kelly is dead."

She later stated, "All of a sudden, there were people gathering around me. Sirens could be heard coming from all directions. There were people in uniforms surrounding Kelly.

Most of them, if not all, were shaking their heads, aghast by the tragic remnants of the accident they were witnessing. From the murmurs that could be heard, I surmised Kelly was already dead or one shovel from the grave."

From the notes in my parents' diaries, I know that Lucy watched as EMTs and firemen sprang into action, reacting with the remoteness of their training that was now kicked into high gear because every second counted. Initially, they observed that the impact had destroyed my nasal and oral airways. Without hesitation, they performed all too common procedure for them: They cut a hole in my throat and placed a ventilator into my windpipe, so I could breathe. It also appeared that every bone in my face had been crushed, and my brain was swelling at a rapid speed. I was hastily wheeled into the back of the ambulance and rushed to the Emergency and Trauma Unit at Kennestone Hospital

On the day after the accident, Mom wrote: *As I hastened through the emergency doors, I glimpsed a limp hand hanging off of a stretcher, which was quickly being pushed into an examination room; instinctively, I knew it was the hand of my daughter. The unrecognizable person on the stretcher was Kelly. Fear gripped me; the hand had been so lifeless. During that split second, I questioned whether I would ever see my daughter alive again. Some of the EMTs were leaving the stretcher in an examination room. Their faces were sullen, as if they had lost their best friend. Their blank stares and shaking heads were more confirmation that Kelly was critical or even dead.*

Mom said she felt utterly helpless, so she turned away from the gurney and recognized Lucy, who was lying on another stretcher, who seemed to be in a state of shock. When Lucy realized it was Mom rushing toward her, she began crying out in gut-wrenching, uncontrollable sobs, "I'm so sorry! I'm so sorry!

Please don't hate me; please don't hate me!" she pleaded over and over.

Mom began crying as she grabbed Lucy's shaking, blood-stained hands and stared straight into her scared eyes to calm and focus her. That's when she decided to say a prayer before she spoke. She asked God for the words needed to convey a mixture of courage and compassion and reassurance to Lucy.

"Lucy, look at me. Look at me," Mom told her. "I do not hate you. I love you! Both you and Kelly are going to be all right!" Mom later shared that even though her voice sounded passionate when she stated those words, she questioned whether she truly had spoken them. She even wondered if she believed them herself. But somehow, Lucy stopped crying and wiped her eyes and runny nose with the white sheet covering her and became calmer.

Jackie and Pat appeared at Mom's side and guided her limp-like legs toward a waiting admissions clerk who needed her to complete the necessary paperwork for admission. Mom wrote, *I began to release my fears and weep aloud, but my friends stood by, waiting in silence, whispering audible prayers, and crying their own muffled tears. My legs felt limp, and my stomach felt empty.*

When a nurse appeared, she asked Mom, "Are you Kelly's mother?"

Without hesitation, she said, "Yes."

That's when they received *an ounce* of good news. The nurse confirmed they were working on me, which had to mean I was alive, so Mom probed for more details. She said my vital signs were good at the moment and that my age should work in my favor. And after gifting some optimism, she curtly smiled and disappeared into the corridor. Mom said she clung to her smile and good news.

A Stranger to Myself

Mom told Pat and Jackie that I was strong and in the best shape of my life; after all, I was going to "walk on" the tennis team. But Mom wrote, *Even then, I could not escape the pervasive feelings of helplessness and vulnerability.*

When Dad came running through the entrance, Mom wrote that he looked more distressed and lost than she had ever seen him, so she prayed, asking for strength before they grabbed each other. *Our tight embrace provided strength and the ability to stand on spaghetti legs. After a while, we sat side by side, holding each other's hands to squelch our nervous shaking. Then we turned to God in prayer.*

Dad later admitted that when he saw Mom's face, his initial reaction was to turn around and run as far away as he could. "Grief was written all over Marilyn's face. So I braced myself for the unbearable news. When she didn't say anything but came and hugged me, I began crying with her."

Mom whispered to Dad, "Kelly looks barely alive, Rod. It's awful. But a nurse came out a while ago and said her vital signs were okay and that her age should work in her favor."

Dad said he only heard two words: Barely alive. That's when his hopes began to mount and is what he clung to until my surgeon, Dr. Schlachter, entered the waiting room, wearing white scrubs and a "too stern" face. Dad's heart sunk because he knew this man was the bearer of bad news. And even though the news wasn't great, it was the only good news he gave: I was alive, but my injuries were critical. With his trained voice, the doctor dreadfully informed my parents I'd sustained one of the worst brain injuries he'd encountered in over twenty years. I had broken every bone in my face, and my brain was swelling progressively. The prognosis was so bleak. Dad later wrote in his journal: *I wanted to melt into the creases of the linoleum and disappear. And if that feeling wasn't enough, his next words*

31

made my heart and breathing stop instantaneously. "Your daughter has a three percent chance of making it through the night." Pausing long enough to allow us to absorb this nightmare, I was brought back to reality by my numb hands from Marilyn's squeezes. "She is injured about as badly as I've ever seen. Her brain is what we're most concerned about."

My parents play a lot of amateur tennis and excelled, often winning tournament championships. So I can relate to Dad's admitted feelings of this being like an extremely competitive tennis volley for game, set, and match. *This was too real. I watched as the doctor's lips mouthed incomprehensible words, but there were only muffled sounds. I wanted to scream why are you speaking so quickly? Slow down. I can't handle all of this. Marilyn's trembling interrupted my silent temper tantrum. My arm clutched her shoulders even tighter. Was I holding her up, or was she holding me up? At that moment, I wasn't sure.*

Dr. Schlachter told them, "I'm sorry. It doesn't look good."

Dad said he was afraid to ask this question because he feared the answer would be no. "Doctor, are you, are you going to operate?" So when Dr. Schlachter sighed and answered "Yes." Dad and Mom immediately felt relieved. This meant I had a chance.

The doctor provided more details: "We know there is a blood clot, but we're not sure of its size until we get inside, and removing the blood clot is our first priority, or your daughter will not survive another hour. She's already been prepped for surgery, so I need your signed consent."

The admissions clerk materialized almost magically with a clipboard holding a single document. She began reading it aloud and stressing the importance of some of the caveat phrases to my parents. "Do you understand?" seemed to be the only question she knew to ask.

A Stranger to Myself

Dad said he wanted to scream, "What kind of a fool do you think I am? Of course I understand. Where do I sign? My daughter doesn't have a lot of time." So without hesitation, he grabbed the clipboard and scribbled his signature at the bottom of the page, thinking, *My daughter will have every chance possible to live.*

Dr. Schlachter told my parents they could see me for a few minutes. As the nurse and doctor hustled them down the hall towards my room, they learned from his carefully articulated litany that a ventilator was the only thing keeping me alive. God bless ventilators. Dad told me later that even though he was an educated man, he still had a difficult time deciphering and comprehending all the words that were being hurled towards them: "Comatose state." "Can't respond." "Time is of the essence." But when the doctor said, "But based on the severe trauma to her brain, the best we can hope for is a vegetative state," they stopped moving. Mom recalls seeing big tears running down Dad's newly-chapped cheeks, while her mind was screaming, W*hy do you keep belaboring the bad news? Don't you have any good news? How about something positive? Isn't there anything optimistic at all to tell us?"*

She remembers having to tug at Dad's hand, so his cemented feet would begin moving again. She remembers asking the doctor questions but can't remember what they were.

"You have two minutes," Dr. Schlachter warned. "And I need to caution you. You probably won't recognize your daughter due to the brain's swelling. We've shaved her head, and she has lots of tubes running in and out of her body." Then he said the dreaded words their minds had resisted conceiving: "If she were my daughter, I'd take this opportunity to say whatever I need to say to her now."

Dad wrote these heartfelt words in his journal: *My heart was pounding as we entered that sterile curtained room. I saw a tiny form lying on a bed in the midst of hovering machines and liquid-filled vials and a labyrinth of translucent tubes. The words, "This can't be Kelly!" became a scratched record, repeating themselves over and over again in my mind. But even though I was able to sob the words, "I love you," I knew I could never tell Kelly goodbye.*

Before they realized it, my parents were ushered out of the room and back towards the waiting room. They turned to watch while several orderlies and nurses wheeled me out of the room and headed in the opposite direction. That's when Dad said he was amazed at the strength in Mom's voice when she told the doctor, "We'll be praying for you and your staff, Dr. Schlachter, as well as for our Kelly. May God be with all of you and with our Kelly."

My parents' night was filled with prayer. Dad still smiles as he tells me over and over again, "I don't believe I've ever prayed as much as I did that night."

Chapter Six

Waiting for God

*The gatekeeper opens the gate for him. The sheep listen to his
voice. He calls his own sheep by name and leads them out. When
he has brought out all his own, he goes ahead of them.
His sheep follow him because they know his voice.*
John 10: 3-4

Mom said that she and Dad retreated into the little visitation
room, broken and trying to find solace in each other's arms. Pat
and Jackie were there to support them. Mom said she didn't
know what she'd have done if Pat and Jackie had not been there
to drive her to the hospital and stay afterward to offer prayers.
Later, that night when Pat had to leave to go home, Mom and
Dad's newfound friend, Jackie, stayed; she was a comfort to
them, never leaving their sides except to fetch coffee or water or
to grab tissues. Mom later wrote in her journal: *Looking back on
this, it is easy to realize that Jackie was our personal angel sent
from God to remind us that we are never alone; God is always
with us even in the embodiment of a stranger even during the
longest night of our lives.*

My parents are blessed with lots of friends. After the
surgery began, Harry, a marathon friend of Dad's, hurried into
the waiting room. He seemed anxiously resigned. After giving
them hugs and awkward words of comfort and encouragement,
Harry sat with the group – Mom, our Priest, Jackie, and Dad --

while they waited and prayed during the long night. The strong, hot coffee was like an infusion of tranquilizers to them.

Harry explained how he had been a few cars back when the truck and VW collided. He described the horrific noise that split the otherwise beautiful, tranquil Saturday afternoon. Being the first on the scene before the EMTs could arrive, Harry ran to help the two victims until the professionals could take over. The driver of the VW had looked dazed, but she was standing and nursing a gash on her arm. It was not until later that afternoon when Harry learned the other victim was Kelly Spence. He had cradled her in his arms until the EMTs arrived. His wife had broken the news of my identity to him. Harry had been unable to recognize me, but he had easily realized the blood bathed girl had been thrown through the windshield of the VW convertible and shouldn't be moved. Her face was shattered by the windshield and subsequent impact with the grill of the truck.

In addition, Harry told my parents about a fireman named Rick, who was the second person on the scene to arrive. Rick had ridden in the ambulance with me, praying all the way to the hospital that I would be okay. And when this "stranger" got off work at 11:00 p.m., he came to the hospital to meet my parents and to inquire about my status. He offered many words of comfort during his stay that night, praying alongside my parents, Harry, our priest, and Jackie.

Mom later told me, "As I looked into the eyes of this kind man, I hoped you would live to meet him one day and to thank him for his concern and prayers."

My parents were impressed when some of my high school friends, who had heard the news about Lucy's and my accident, came to the hospital that first critical night to offer support. One was Janice Smith, who spoke kind words and assured Mom that I would be all right. Although her intentions were good, they could not comprehend the magnitude of the moment nor could they penetrate the heartache and doubt that constantly echoed through my parents' minds.

Mom's diary has an entry regarding this visit. *Isn't youth wonderful? I remember thinking, they have no concept of anything tragic happening to someone they know. They think they will live forever. I wanted to ask Janice how did she know our daughter would be okay. She has a brain injury, I wanted to shout, that will more than likely change her entire life. Her world may never be the same as she once knew it. My family's lives may never be the same again. Will Kelly be able to care for herself? Will she be able to talk? Or will she just exist? These questions were on the tip of my tongue, brought about by a surge of anger and worry I was now beginning to feel. It seemed I had so many questions and not many answers.*

I had been blessed with an eloquent speaking voice. I could get a whole stadium excited and energized with my infectious enthusiasm. Mom said she wondered if I'd ever be able to talk or walk. Here I was, just days away from trying out for the women's tennis team at the University of Georgia. How quickly things can happen and change our life's courses. Here I was in the emergency and trauma unit on a Saturday night, when I normally would have been out on a date. My parents and friends were wondering if I would survive the night! Dad describes his feelings of being like a hamster in a wheel, running and running and not getting anywhere.

Mom's journal writing continued. *This tragedy was beyond me. I was not big enough or strong enough or wise enough to stop these overwhelming feelings. I could not do anything for her, and that is a terrible feeling for a mother. In recognition of my inadequacies, I called on God's power to take over. So I relinquished Kelly back into the hands of God who had given her to us in the first place. She belonged to Him whose grace and mercy surpasses all understanding. I left her future, if she were to have one, to God.*

As my prayer ended, the detective working the accident arrived. He came by to assure us that the traffic light at the intersection had been working properly. He also had found two eyewitnesses that said the truck driver had the right of way going through the intersection.

I could not believe what I was hearing! Our daughter was in surgery fighting for her life this very minute, and this guy wants to assure us that the light was working properly. How does that help us right now? How does that change the outcome? I was completely flabbergasted and steaming at the downright coldness of this man! Didn't he have a heart? We had "bigger eggs to fry," as the cliché goes.

My parents said that sometime during the night when my surgery had been ongoing for four hours, a shaken Lucy appeared in the waiting room and announced that she had been discharged. Gratefully, everyone cried together, thanking God for this blessing. It was at this point that a nurse appeared, bringing with her some bad news. They had discovered a blood clot the size of a large grapefruit lodged in my brain, which had started hemorrhaging, so the surgeons had no choice but to continue the surgery. They estimated it would take at least another four hours. Grateful for even this bad news, the nurse had relieved them by confirming I was still alive. Mom said it seemed like all they could do was to nod at the barrage of voices that were speaking to them at different times throughout the night. Any silent moments were spent in hushed prayers.

By 4:30 a.m., I had been in surgery for eight and a half hours straight. This is when an exhausted Dr. Schlachter appeared, bringing with him more terrible news. Every bone in my face had been shattered. As soon as the large blood clot was extracted, my brain immediately swelled to fill the cavity left by the clot.

"In all honesty," he told them, "The prognosis does not look good. The brain damage is extensive. Her other injuries are minor in comparison: one broken rib on her right side, a severely sprained right ankle, and some deep lacerations below the right knee." Then he sighed audibly before continuing. "I'm sorry, but the best we can hope for is a vegetative state." He stared sympathetically – and he said, apologetically -- into my mother's eyes and placed his hand on her shoulder.

Mom wrote… *What? I had to let those words sink in. I remember thinking. What exactly is a vegetative state? What does that mean for her future? But my mind was playing games, resisting comprehension. I knew. I turned to hide my terrified face against my husband's shoulder. Rod was trembling.*

Dad later penned these words in his first journal: *I have never kept a journal in my life, but I think it is important to begin. So I've decided to record my observations and ambivalent emotions while Kelly continues fighting for her life – what is left of it. I wonder how our close-knit family will live through this devastation and tragic event in our lives. I don't think she's going to make it, and I almost hope she doesn't.*

After eight hours, the surgeon appeared. He was rubbing his temples with one hand and his eyes with the other as he approached us, wearing a serious look on his haggard face. Somehow, Kelly was still alive. The blood clot had been removed and her skull was put back together. That was the good news. Then he began his litany of bad news: There was doubt that she'd survive recovery. Kelly's optic nerve in her right eye had been completely detached; therefore, she'd never see out of this eye again. And on top of that, there was strong doubt she'd have vision in her left eye. There had been considerable damage to the left side of her body. The right side of her face was pushed back several inches from the left side of her face. Many of her teeth were loose and dislocated. If she survived, a special orthodontist would need to come in and put her teeth back in place and wire her jaws together to stabilize them.

Then he turned toward me and asked, "Do you have a lawyer?"

Before I could react to his last question, Marilyn answered him. "Doctor, I'm afraid that's the last thing on our minds right now. We don't believe now is the time to be considering legalities."

The doctor softened his gaze and took her hand in his, "I understand and am not trying to be insensitive. I'm just suggesting that you may want to get a good lawyer for Kelly's sake."

Mom said she was terrified and overwhelmed with negative thoughts. *What if I'm left with a vegetable for a daughter? Will I be able to take care of someone with severe disabilities? How supportive will my husband be? Will my husband leave me?* She knew she was way off base with these irrational, self-pity thoughts, but she couldn't help herself.

She later turned to her journal to record her thoughts. *I longed to relax. Instead, my stomach was churning with nerves. I could not get rid of the tension in my temples or shoulders. It would be easier to be held at gunpoint than to have my baby in an operating room, struggling for her life. I was living the cliché: "My heart was shattered into a million pieces."*

I prayed with my head bowed and my eyes tightly closed. God, I need You like I have never needed You before. I pray if Kelly is to be a vegetable, You will take her now. I do not believe

Kelly would want to exist like that. Oh, Lord, please take her and stop this nightmare for Kelly and for us, if it is Your will!

I felt like Rod and I were characters in the worst horror movie ever written. Before the surgery, as they had warned, Kelly was hardly recognizable. Her lovely face was extremely damaged; her tongue was hanging halfway out of her mouth, while a giant tube stuck out of her throat; that must have been the life support respirator. A large gash extended between her eyes and reached over to the end of her right eyebrow. And because of the size of her head, she looked like the alien character, E.T. When we had seen her before the surgery, I regretted not talking to her, not whispering words of love to her. More than likely, we'd never see Kelly alive again. I'd squandered any chances I had by not opening my dry mouth long enough to tell her I loved her. I would kick myself for the rest of my life for missing that moment.

After the surgery was over, my parents were informed that I was in a coma, which they defined as "a deep, deep sleep." The doctor confirmed that the ventilator was my sole life support.

As the bad news began to accumulate, my parents felt anxious. Mom said she wanted to run away because she'd gotten to the point where she couldn't take it anymore. But then she thought of tiny King David when he faced the giant Goliath. He didn't run. He stood and fought with only a stone and a sling shot. She was certainly facing her giant now, so with God's help, she would stand and face whatever came her way.

Dearest God, isn't there any hopeful news? Please give us some good news. We need to hear Your voice in all of this.

That's when she remembered His words, "Be still and know that I am God" (Psalm 46:10), so she waited silently for His reply.

Chapter Seven

Love of a Family

Be still, and know that I am God;
I will be exalted among the nations,
I will be exalted in the earth.
Psalm 46:10

Ellen was taking final exams at the University of Georgia, which was an hour and a half away in Athens. Rod Jr., now a sophomore in high school, was probably at home, frantically waiting for some news as to where everyone was. My parents tried to compose themselves before calling my siblings. When Mom telephoned Ellen's number, she received a disconnection message. "Great! What was that about?" Mom asked Dad.

She left a message with the apartment complex manager for Ellen to call the waiting room's pay phone number as soon as possible. Then she called Susan Sherrard for help. Her daughter, Lynn, was another of my best friends. Immediately, Susan took charge. Next, Mom telephoned our neighbors, the Masons, to have them break the news to Rod Jr. and bring him to the hospital. When Susan Sherrard arrived in the waiting room thirty minutes later, she assured my parents that her husband, Roger, was on his way to Athens to pick up Ellen and drive her to the hospital.

Their longest night continued. Whenever Mom tried to lie down on the uncomfortable vinyl couch and close her eyes, the slightest noise would wake her. Even her own rapid breathing startled her into awareness. She awoke, wishing she could be anywhere else and becoming all too aware she and Dad were living the worst nightmare of their lives. Mom continued to pray, "Dearest God, if she is going to be a vegetable, please take her now."

Always the organized planner, Mom even began to think about making funeral arrangements. Which funeral home should they choose? When would they have the funeral? What color casket would I want? What people should they be calling? A mother should never have to face these heart-wrenching questions. Her hurting soul cried out many times, "Oh, help us, Jesus!"

Mom wrote: *Of course, looking back now, I realize that Kelly's accident began the greatest test of my faith in God. My belief assured that Kelly's dying only meant heaven for Kelly. But would I be able to give God thanks if she should die? I missed my dad so much. Unfortunately, he had passed away when Kelly was in middle school, but oh how he'd loved his children and grandchildren. His life had been spent loving us as he walked a Christian path. Oh how I wished I could talk to him right now because he always had so much wisdom to share. But I knew what he would advise me to do, so I did it.*

I prayed, God, please help me to accept the outcome, no matter what. Please give me the unconditional love that my dad had for his children. Please give Rod and me the strength to face the future with or without our daughter. Lord, help Kelly to accept what she might be like if she makes it, and give Rod and me the courage to accept the Kelly that she becomes.

When Ellen and Rod Jr. arrived at different times in the wee hours of the next morning, Mom said that their collective strength and love radiated throughout the waiting room and replaced the dark despair of the hours before. My parents had desired to give them good news upon their arrival, and there was good news! Despite the litany of terrible news that had endured during the long, dark hours, I had survived and was still among the living, even if it were the respirator keeping me alive.

Months later, Ellen told me how she learned about my accident.

"I hurried home to my apartment after the final exam was over, thinking, *'One more exam to go, and I'll be finished for the semester. I can't wait.'* But immediately, I sensed something was terribly wrong. My roommates, best buddies, and the guys from downstairs gathered around as the apartment complex manager extended the receiver to me and gave me the number for the hospital waiting room. They deduced from the few comments the manager had made during Mom's call that something serious had happened. They were concerned for me."

"I dialed the unfamiliar phone number, allowing it to ring several times before Mom's voice answered on the other end. She quickly explained that Kelly had been in a serious car accident and was not expected to live through the night. She said that someone was coming to get me, but I didn't remember who it was until Mr. Sherrard arrived. I felt numb and barely heard the rest of what she was saying. My mind kept racing and hearing the broken recording over and over again. 'She's not expected to live through the night.' My friends said that I dropped the telephone receiver and collapsed on the floor. I don't remember that or anything about the silent ride to the hospital with Mr. Sherrard. I do remember walking into the waiting room where Mom and Dad were sitting with Father

Fogarty. I braced myself for bad news, but instead, Mom almost smiled, assuring me that you were still alive and out of surgery but that we could not see you yet. Rod Jr. and the Masons arrived moments later. I remember my little brother hugging me tightly, while he wiped his tears."

It wasn't until the following morning that we were allowed to see you for the first time. While I don't remember the details of what you looked like, I do remember knowing that I couldn't recognize you as my sister and thinking, *Her head is so much larger than it should be.* A white-coated doctor explained the current battle they faced was controlling your brain's swelling. Thankfully, you made it until the next day, when we were told you would live.

Rod, Jr.:

"The most defining time in my childhood and teen years occurred during my sophomore year of high school when my sister, Kelly, was in a tragic accident. When I walked into the small waiting room where my parents sat with Father Fogarty, I grabbed Ellen and hugged my eldest sister tightly. After our lengthy embrace, I looked at my parents who had risen to welcome me. That's when I realized I'd never seen my dad cry, but he was crying now. His eyes were swollen and bloodshot. I embraced him first for a long time; then I embraced my mother, who seemed to be holding it together for all of us. Mom explained the news they had received over the course of the night. My heart flipped somersaults in my air-restricted chest."

Marilyn:

When my children arrived at the hospital, we embraced and thanked the Masons and the Sherrards for helping our family. After an hour of bringing everyone up to speed with what we knew about the accident and the surgery, Rod offered excuses for us, leaving Father Fogarty, the Masons, and the Sherrards in the waiting room.

"Please excuse us for a few minutes," he said. "I need to be alone with my family. Please let us know if there are updates when we return." Confused, we followed him as he led Ellen, Rod Jr., and me down the hall into the small prayer chapel. That's when my husband displayed his faith more so than ever in our marriage. He prayed in earnest as tears streamed down his wet cheeks. I'm sure this was the first time our children had ever witnessed their otherwise jovial father crying and praying aloud except for asking the blessing before a meal.

Rod began praying a pious prayer. "Oh Holy Father, Thou art righteous and fair. Please, Lord, please let Kelly live! Please save her life. She's our child, and we love our children and are thankful to You for blessing us with Kelly, and Ellen, and Rod, Jr. Please heal her, Father, as the doctors continue to work on her. Please give them wisdom and knowledge, and please help them do everything to save her life! Please give her back to us. And please comfort that little body that is so broken and weak. Please help this family to remain strong and in Your care and mercy always." His despair stopped his words, and he lost his composure. It was like my husband's inner child was crying out.

That's when our fifteen year old son, Rodney, Jr., stepped up and prayed loudly, "Dear Jesus, we are so humbled by this accident. In one second, our lives have changed, and we realize how vitally important we are to each other. I love my sisters so much. I cannot imagine life without Kelly or Ellen. Please heal Kelly. She has always been my inspiration. Please rescue her, Jesus, and show the doctors who is really in control!"

As soon as Rod, Jr.'s voice stopped, Ellen began praying, "Please bring her back to us, Oh Lord. Please work through the surgeon's hands to restore my sister's life to us. We know Kelly is a fighter. Let her fight now! We cry out to You, Father, for her life."

At that moment, I knew I had never felt as close to God or to my children or to my husband in my entire life. My family had always been my greatest joy, my greatest blessings, next to my faith and salvation, and to know that my husband and each of our children had put their faith in God to heal Kelly made my broken heart joyful.

After twenty-four hours dragged by, we got our first bit of good news. Kelly was responding a little, and her brain scan looked good. As a family, we clung to each other in hope, in gratitude, and in praises to God!

Chapter Eight

Faith, Hope, Love

We could never learn to be brave and patient
if there were only joy in the world.
Helen Keller

Somehow, my family survived the days afterward as did I. It was March 21, 1985, Tuesday, and I had been deemed "in stable condition," so Mom left the hospital for the first time to spend the night in her own bed. By 6:15 a.m. the next morning, she was already showered and dressed. Her first bite of food since the morning of the accident was Raisin Bran cereal, a piece of wheat toast, and a fresh pot of decaffeinated coffee. She said that everything tasted so good. Until this morning, the huge lump in her throat and the sensitized nerves in her stomach had erased any appetite she'd had. But somehow, my parents had survived on the strong caffeinated hospital coffee and cups of water since Saturday afternoon.

As Mom left the house in route to the hospital, she thought about Rod, Jr. and how supportive he'd been of them and their need to be at the hospital with me, but she felt guilty. He'd received so little attention since Saturday, but this showed he was growing up.

Mom said, "In my eyes, he matured five years during those first three days after the accident. My son had always looked up to Kelly, almost placing her on the clichéd pedestal because of

48

her popularity and contagious personality. I knew he was doing everything possible not to be needy during this time."

When Mom arrived at the hospital around 7:30 a.m., she found my right eye was still bandaged from the extensive surgery, but the other eye was uncovered. I opened my left eye momentarily. She was thrilled even though I didn't track her face or hand movements. I nodded my head when she asked if I were feeling okay. So, she spent an hour happily scraping the dried blood and dirt from beneath my finger nails. Then she filed the broken nails and placed a coat of clear polish on them. After reviewing her handiwork, she conceded my nails looked much better. I would have been upset if I'd seen them in the condition they were in.

A physical therapist, Pam, arrived at 8:30 that morning to explain the importance of range motion exercises and to instruct Mom on how to administer these exercises throughout the day. They were designed to keep my leg and arm muscles from atrophying. Mom was feeling upbeat and positive, that is, until she spoke with Dr. Schlachter and three other doctors, who accompanied him that morning on his examination tours.

Excitedly, she explained what she'd observed. "She is getting better. While I was doing her nails, she opened her left eye, and when I asked her if she was feeling okay, she nodded."

"She's still in a vegetative state," Dr. Schlachter explained. "Even though she may seem awake, or open her eye, or even nod her head, she is still in a vegetative state."

Mom's return home that afternoon was full of dejection and depression. She wondered, *Why did he insist on using that word? Would the bad news never end and the good news ever begin?*

On Wednesday morning, the doctors and nurses had more decisions to make, like where were they going to insert another IV? Mom stared at the sleeping stranger's face that had been her gleeful daughter. She wondered, *Would Kelly want to live if she looked like this? Would Kelly want her life reduced to living on life-support machines?*

Sixteen days after the accident, I opened my left eye again. Of course, there was no evidence that I could see anything.

Years later Rod Jr. told me, "I remember how excruciatingly long the minutes and hours and days and weeks seemed while we waited for you to come out of the coma. Night after night, we prayed for you to return to us. We couldn't believe that our vivacious Kelly could be in an intensive care unit, fighting for her life. The house was too quiet without your laughter and good-natured ribbing."

"I know our parents love us very much. Our family has always been close and supportive of each other. During this rocky time in our lives, Dad opened up his heart to me, sharing how he had gone to the highest mountain that he could find. Being an outstanding athlete, he ran up the incline as fast as he could, and when he reached the pinnacle, he yelled in anguish and sacrifice to God, 'Please take me, dear God! Please don't take Kelly. Not her! Please take me instead!'"

I listened eagerly as my brother continued relating the story. "Kelly, you were not allowed to have visitors during the nighttime, so the many nights when we stayed at the hospital, I positioned a chair outside of your door, listening to the steady, repetitious beeps of the ventilator and other machines. Ironically, I found the beeps comforting because it meant you were still alive. I used this time for prayer and replaying memories of our happy times. And there were many pictures in my memory album for which I was thankful."

Rod, Jr. said, "One weekend night while sitting outside your door, I felt like there was more I could be doing for you, so I asked God to let me know what I could do, and that is when I heard His response. God said, 'Give her to me. You have done all you can.' Immediately, it felt like a huge weight had been lifted from my shoulders. What made me think I could take on something as big as this? So, in prayer, I did surrender your care to God, who is far more powerful than me and who knows what is best for you and for all of us. Afterward, I left the chair outside your door and returned to the stark waiting room where I quickly fell fast asleep."

For the first three days after the accident, Dad never left the hospital. But when I had been deemed stable even though I was still comatose, he decided to leave. His heart was broken from the never-ending nightmare of watching me struggle for my life. Out of habit, he kept a pair of running shoes in his car, and because the hospital was located in downtown Atlanta, he decided it was an ideal place to get in a short run. On this particular day, he had run about two miles when he arrived at the busiest intersection in Atlanta -- Peachtree and Colony. As he leaned against the street sign post, all of a sudden, he was overwhelmed with despair and grief. Uncontrollably, he began sobbing. With his body bent in half, he strengthened his grip on the street sign pole to break a fall. He said he was emitting no sounds even though the agonizing pain and anger was coming from his gut. With a reddened face, throbbing temples, and no air left in his body, he raised his sweaty fists to God and cried aloud, "How could you do this to my daughter? How could you let this happen to my baby?"

And God in His infinite wisdom knew this pitiful release was what he needed to go on. Immediately, Dad said he felt scared and ashamed. Who was he to question God? But he felt God was on His throne that day crying along with him and saying in the soothing words of a father, "It's okay, Rod. It's okay. Let it out. Let it all out. I already know what you harbor in your heart."

Emotionally spent, Dad regained his physical composure. Later, he said he thought it was surprising that someone didn't call 9-1-1 to report the pitiful man on the street corner that day!

On another such occasion, Dad detoured his running path from the sidewalk and ran into a nearby woods where he could be alone and pray to God. But in the midst of meditating, his anger rose and overwhelmed him as before. He began screaming, "God, you are powerful, and nothing is impossible for you. How could you let this happen to my daughter?"

Humbled, he began crying and crumbled to his knees, just pleading for God's help in all of this. With agape love, tender mercy, and a father's compassion, God heard his cries. Dad said he'd never felt as close to God as he did during that particular moment in the woods with his face to the ground. After sobbing for an eternity, he came away with renewed hope and reassurance that I would be okay. He knew my road would be hard, but he knew I could do it. My family would help me with the grace of God to guide us.

According to Mom, over the next blurry days, God displayed His presence and comfort through our friends, church, and community. There was an unbelievable amount of prayers said for me during those days. People whom we had never met offered up prayers. Churches got together at night, and their congregations were crying out for the Lord to help me.

Dr. Mike Mason, our dear neighbor, came to the hospital to visit me many times. Each of Mike's visits was somewhat of an amazing feat for him because he hated hospitals; he'd had bad experiences when his own parents were hospitalized. But instead of sitting in the waiting room with Mom and Dad, which is what he'd always done, Mike asked to see me, so they accompanied him to my ICU bed. The sight of seeing me for the first time overtook him; he cried. Before leaving my room, he whispered unabashedly, "Kelly, I love you. You have to live."

Mom had never heard Mike say anything emotional, not even to his own kids. A deeply private man, especially about his faith, he often read the Eulogy but Mike never prayed aloud. As they returned to the waiting room, it appeared to my parents that his knees were bothering him because he winced with every step he took. Mom said she told herself his knees were probably bruised from all the praying he and his family had been doing for me.

Over the next few days, Mom and Dad began wondering how they were going to manage their schedules on an ongoing basis. The hospital staff had "highly recommended" that a family member be present and available at all times. Neither Mom nor Dad had left the hospital at the same time since the accident. Besides, they wouldn't have dreamed of leaving me alone.

Mom wrote: *We loved this lifeless, frail little alien. We loved this little stranger, who had to be turned and changed every two hours.*

Our family discussed the necessary demands on their time and rearranged their four routines accordingly. Ellen would continue living at college. On the weekends, she'd come home and help out by being at the hospital. Rod Jr. was still a growing teenager, and that meant he needed guidance and support, too. So Dad began rising at 4:00 a.m. to drive the seven miles to the hospital to begin working with my legs and arms to preserve what little muscle tone I had left. Mom would wake Rod Jr., fix him a hot breakfast, and get him out the door for school before driving the thirty minutes to the hospital during rush hour traffic to spend what came to be predictable hours sitting by my bed, talking, singing, praying (anything to stimulate my brain and hers), and exercising my muscles repeatedly. Then Dad relieved her after he got off work, so she could head home to care for Rod Jr. Her routine became fixing supper for my brother, wrapping the food for my parents to eat later, flipping through the day's mail, and ensuring Rod Jr. had done his homework. They spent a few minutes talking about his day, his activities, and any issues he had at school. Then she'd return to the hospital and remain with my dad until visiting hours were over. Together, they'd return home, eat their late supper, too tired to discuss the trivial issues in their lives.

Mom said, "We prayed that our utmost hopes and deepest fears surrounding you would be met with God's ultimate mercy and fulfilling grace before tucking our numbed emotions and exhausted muscles into bed."

"On one such night, Rod was tossing and turning, finding it hard to fall asleep. So we talked, and it was a conversation that I'll never forget. He said, 'In the mornings, when I'm driving to the hospital, I talk with God. I beg Him to heal our daughter, Marilyn. But honestly, so much of the time, all I can do is weep. Then when I get to the hospital, I wipe away the tears, put on a fake smile, and greet each of the nurses by name and with a compliment or a joke. These ritual morning greetings and conversations ensure that when I shut the door to Kelly's room, no one will interrupt my time with her. And it works.' He continued sharing with me the following: 'Sometimes, I pray aloud, asking God, how could this have happened to Kelly? Sometimes, while we're doing the repetitions for the range of motion exercises and her muscles still feel limp, I scream at God. I ask Him why can't I take her place? Why can't I be the one on this bed? Why is this one of my children and not me? I have never felt so isolated or so helpless.'"

Mom said they wrapped their arms around each other and listened to their hearts beating. After a few minutes, Dad interrupted the silence by saying, "You know, I love all three of my children the same, not one more than the other. I just love them differently. They are all special in their own ways. Kelly is our star athlete; she's popular, a golden child. Then I find myself asking.... No. Maybe I shouldn't say it." She said he stared at the ceiling and shook his head.

"What do you ask, Rod," she prodded. "It's okay. We have no secrets. What do you ask?"

Dad reached over and covered her hand with his larger one before he continued. "Sometimes I ask...sometimes I ask, 'Would Kelly want her life reduced to living on a machine?' That's a question no father should ever ask."

"Its okay, Rod," she assured him. "I know, because I've asked that same question, and I felt guilty whenever I did. But we'll never know the answer to that question. Only God knows the answer and the reason, and only God knows what Kelly's future is going to be or even if she will have a future. We have to be strong and ask for God's will in all of this. But above all, we have to be prepared to accept whatever His will is."

Dad had agreed. "I know. But there are times when I don't think I'm strong enough to accept whatever it is."

"It's easy to feel that way," she assured him. "I certainly do – most of the time. It's a reminder that we are never in control of life even when we think we are. Before that Saturday afternoon, my life seemed so normal and so predictable. But now, well, now, it's all up to God. That's what we have to hold on to. No matter what happens. God will see us through all of this, Rod. He always has, and somehow He will again. Besides, He gave us to each other, and He has blessed us with three beautiful children."

In the dark, she saw my dad's eyes shining. "I love you and thank God for you, Marilyn," he said.

"And I love you. You're the strongest man I know – the most wonderful husband and father anyone could ask for."

I am so thankful for the love my parents share for each other and for my siblings and me.

One morning a few weeks later, Mike met Mom in our adjoining driveway as she was leaving for the hospital. Mike said with a concerned look, "Marilyn, Cheryl and I were talking last night. We think you and Rod have been running yourselves ragged. Why don't you take a day of rest? Let Cheryl or me go sit with Kelly instead."

"We're okay, Mike," Mom said with a forced smile. "I do appreciate your concern and offer. But we have to do what we have to do."

Even though she was bone tired, Mom was not tempted by his thoughtful offer. She was determined to remain on site and dedicated to my recovery. She looked Mike squarely in the eye and said as politely as possible, "Mike, today could be the day that Kelly comes out of her coma. And nobody – do you hear me – nobody – not even the Navy Seals are going to keep me from being there when she opens her eyes and sees for the first time. So if you don't mind, please get out of my way. I need to get to the hospital."

Mom said Mike just smiled expectantly and nodded his head slightly in acknowledgement before shrugging his shoulders in defeat. He ceremoniously bowed and moved to the side, allowing my determined mother to begin her morning's familiar trek to the hospital.

Chapter Nine

Awake!

That is why, for Christ's sake, I delight in weaknesses,
in insults, in hardships, in persecutions, in difficulties.
For when I am weak, then I am strong.
2 Corinthians 12:10

One night after an early supper, my parents returned to the hospital to learn that the afternoon nurse had exciting news! She informed them that I seemed to have responded to her voice when she came in to feed me, but she quickly added that I didn't respond when Dr. Schlachter had made his rounds. Their hopes were surmounting, so my parents agreed Mom should stay at the hospital that night. The rest of the world was sleeping as she laid on the portable cot beside my bed.

My mother's thoughts turned into prayers. She shared with God that the worst emotion she'd ever known was helplessness. *"Seeing my daughter in such terrible condition and knowing I was unable to do anything for her made me feel helpless as a mother. I prayed constantly that night it seemed, but I failed to feel any comfort. During the wee hours of the morning when light was peeping through the closed blinds, I felt helpless again, while I watched as the various machines moved liquids in and out of your body and pumped oxygen into your lungs. Feeling discouraged, I cried out to God, 'Why aren't you helping more?'"*

Six weeks after the accident, the waiting room was as packed by my visitors as it had been for the preceding weeks. My high school tennis coach; several high school friends who were home from college; a few neighbors; and, of course, my family, were in the crowded room. The nurse was tube feeding me through my nose when she asked me the same old question she had asked me so many times before but with no response: "Kelly, if you can hear me, lift your finger."

Well, I lifted my right index finger in response! Shocked, she had noticed the slight movement of my finger and immediately wondered if it had been a coincidental reflex on my part or wishful thinking on her part. So she asked me again, "Kelly, if you can hear me, lift your right index finger again." To her amazement, I did! You would have thought I had recited the *Declaration of Independence*. The nurse was so excited she threw the remainder of my lunch on the floor before running out of the room, down the hall, and straight into the waiting room where my family and visitors were hanging out. Mom said she came bursting through the door screaming, "She lifted a finger! She lifted a finger! Kelly is alive!" Mom said the entire room of people grew silent before standing on their feet, cheering, crying, and praising God.

Even though this story was related to me many times after my awakening, the first time I recalled hearing the story was about a year later. I asked my family to tell me the story again because I never tired of hearing it. I asked, "What is it I did again?"

Mom always smiled at this part. "You lifted a finger in response to her question."

The teenager in me laughed and teased, "Boy! You all were hard up for some excitement, weren't you?"

That's when Rod, Jr. chastised me. "Kelly, this was a huge moment. I remember all of us filing into your room, forgetting about hospital visitation rules. Everyone began asking you questions, all at once. I said, 'Move your finger, Kelly, if you can hear me!' And you did! That was the second miracle I've witnessed in my life. The first miracle was that you had made it through the first night. So you became my miracle, which you are to this day."

"Aww. That's so sweet," I cooed.

Ellen said, "I remember the nurse calling us into your room. She asked you again, when you did, what a glorious moment it was! What a glorious day it became! That's when we knew you were in that little broken body. You could hear us! You could respond! We hadn't known that until then."

So even though I was still in a comatose state and would remain so for many weeks to come, I did begin the process of coming out of my coma by raising my finger. Please fast forward with me temporarily. After working for over twenty years with trauma cases, I now can understand how a family holds out for the least bit of encouragement. It is the hope and the minutest glimmer of a promise that literally becomes the family's lifeline to the injured person.

Marilyn:

After Dr. Schlachter agreed the response was a good sign of Kelly coming out of the comatose state, the nurses began raising Kelly up, but her face would lose all color when she was in a sitting position. I think because she had become responsive, they were eager to put her in a chair to get her off her back. And sure enough, a day later, they had Kelly sitting upright in a chair for an hour. I'll never forget the very moment when I noticed Kelly moving her whole right hand! And in a short amount of time, she was using that hand in an attempt to remove the feeding tube from her nose. Fortunately, I was there to stop her, but my heart had leapt out of my chest with hopeful joy! My determined daughter was displaying her will to fight!

Once the staff fed Kelly breakfast in the mornings, they wasted no time in trying to put her on the tilt table. She tolerated it much better than she had sitting up initially, and she didn't lose all of her color. It was easy to see that she was improving day by day. But at the end of the tilting table therapy, her face would look extremely exhausted when she was returned to the reclining position, so she'd sleep the rest of the afternoon.

On top of all this, Kelly had started her period. At least that was normal.

The day following this monthly event, Kelly's temperature was 102 degrees F. The medical staff seemed concerned, so I prayed, "Oh Lord, please help Kelly, and please help the staff and us."

They reinserted the IV into her right hand to provide antibiotics. Over the weeks since her accident, Kelly had lost 24 pounds. With the onset of this fever, she lost another pound, weighing in at 125 pounds. The good news was that Kelly continued making scribbling movements with her right hand even though there still was no noticeable movement with her left hand.

The following morning at 7:00, Kelly's left eye was open; she seemed wide awake. Later that day, she reached up, and for the first time, she felt her face. Her hand was shaky and swollen from all the complications she'd had with the IV. I held my breath and wished I could have read her mind and know her immediate thoughts. To me, it seemed she wanted to scratch her face, but because of the uncontrollable shakiness, she was unable to. In no time at all, movements had finally begun in her left hand when we noticed that she was moving her fingers along the bedrail. What we didn't know in the beginning is that because Kelly's brain had been injured most severely on the left side, the opposite side of her body began to respond first. This is why she could lift her entire right hand before her left hand moved.

With her many improvements, we began to relax a little more and feel less anxious. One afternoon when I thought she was sleeping, I whispered in her ear that I was leaving for the afternoon. Kelly quickly opened her left eye and appeared frightened, so I stayed until the nurse returned.

Two weeks after the initial finger raising and the subsequent improvements, my parents were standing beside my bed as usual, telling me goodbye. Visiting hours were ending in ten minutes. Dad admitted to me months later that he'd been contemplating asking me *the question* all night long, so he finally did.

"Kelly, what is 2 + 2?"

Well, based on my mother's startled reaction, he may as well have asked me to recite Einstein's *Theory of Relativity*. "Rod, don't ask her that question; that is too hard for her! Do you want to put her back in a coma?"

Dad said my timing was perfect. As soon as Mom finished ranting and raving, I lifted *four* fingers off the bed, just like that. Immense jubilation ran through the walls of that room; I could still add the simplest of equations! Hey, we all have to start somewhere. That is considerably more than the medical professionals had given any hope of me accomplishing. I can just imagine the exultation that had to fill my parents' hearts that night.

And what was Dad's response? Simply, "That's my girl!"

Understandably, it was quite a feat for me to stand for the first time. The medical staff had been positioning me on a "tilt table" to begin inching me up from a horizontal position. According to Mom, they could only go so far, and then they'd have to put me back down because my face would turn as white as a ghost, and my blood pressure would sky-rocket.

I was able to respond to basic commands, but because of the severity of the injury, I had absolutely no short-term memory. Mom said I kept pulling out the tubes going up my nose. The medical staff finally had to restrain my arms because it caused me and my family so much pain to see the nurses attempt to reinsert them.

I don't remember those first couple of months after my awakening. This is true for most survivors who experience a traumatic brain injury, such as damage to the different lobes and the brain stem. The brain is somewhat like a bowl of *Jell-O*, so whenever an injury is sustained at the speed and force like mine, it reverberates throughout the brain cavity. One thing that injuries to the frontal lobe can cause is a lack of short term memory. In my current practice, I've learned this is the most common deficit people experience.

Most of my long term memories were still there, such as knowing my friends and family, reciting my childhood memories, high school years, but some of the tasks you perform on a daily basis were gone, such as tying your shoe laces and reciting your ABCs. These tasks, I had to relearn. What I had eaten for breakfast even minutes afterward was forgotten. People who haven't lived through a brain injury can't identify with what it's like to learn to swallow again.

The brain is the most complicated organ in the whole body. Things that we so often take for granted like how to get dressed, how to walk, how to balance yourself, how to go to the bathroom, how to eat, how to drink -- things that were easy and done automatically -- now took a lot of effort and strength and brain power. I was a disaster in the area of table manners, which prior to the accident had been impeccable. I felt like I was climbing a steep mountain all of the time; the sequencing of the steps to perform these actions was very challenging.

I had lost thirteen years of education, how to hold a fork, how to tie my own shoe laces, how to crawl, how to walk, and how to balance to be able to stand. The medical professions explained my lack of motor skills resulted from my vision loss. But I was off and running (no pun intended) to improve my motor skills and to relearn the many things I'd lost. My family had absolutely no experience with or had lived with anyone who had sustained a brain injury. At that time, I don't think we knew anyone with a disability. It is amazing how we all live a sheltered existence within our cocoons in our comfort zones. My family and I, through no fault of our own, had awakened abruptly in uncharted territory.

I often wonder about my younger brother Rod during all of this. He had to have felt neglected, and I would have assumed a little "ticked off" that he was getting so little attention. I think he took on responsibilities that propelled him into manhood during this unstable period of time in all of our lives. As a result, Rod, Jr. became more self-reliant. He never has said much about those years being hard for him; maybe I need to ask him; and again, maybe I don't. But I do believe I have the greatest brother of all time. He never has stopped believing in me even when I couldn't believe in myself. Rod, Jr. became one of my greatest cheerleaders up and down the long road called "recuperation journey."

Chapter Ten

Why Me?

Where can I go from Your Spirit? Or where can I flee from Your
presence? If I ascend to heaven, You are there;
If I make my bed in the depths, behold, You are there.
Psalm 139: 7-8

Even though dim memories gradually began returning, I felt
helpless, hopeless, and just like an infant again, except I was five
foot, eight inches tall. I wore a diaper or a "clothing protector"
that had to be changed on regular intervals. As I progressed, my
bladder had to learn how to hold its contents all over again.
Every time I needed to use the bathroom, I had to ring for a
nurse to assist me and that meant I'd have to wait for her to
come. I hated having to go in a bed pan at night because they
thought "It is too much trouble to transfer you to the wheelchair,
roll you into the bathroom, and transfer you from the wheelchair
to the toilet." After I'd finished my business and pushed the
"help" button, I'd have to wait again. The nurses thought they
were saving time and energy by bringing the bed pan, but when
urine would spill all over my sheets, they would have to do a lot
more than just transferring me; they would have to make up a
new bed with clean sheets and redress me in a clean gown. This
was humiliating – a person's worst nightmare. When I did get
transferred to the wheelchair and taken to the bathroom, I felt

privileged to be rolled to a sink where I could actually wash my hands.

The accident brought about a lot of changes in our home. One modernization was the purchase of our first answering machine. Mom and Dad took turns recording my daily progress so that when people called, they could listen to the update message. It is humbling to know I was so loved. My organized Mom was keeping a list of friends and family members who visited, when they visited, what gifts they brought, and who was bringing food to the home and hospital on a regular basis. My family and I were well-supported. Today, my parents *pay it forward* by being the first to respond whenever their friends or family experience a *tragedy.* Believe me! They realize how precious these kind gifts were when they had walked around like zombies, were always exhausted, and had a child in critical care. Mom has been known to bring food, mow lawns, or even do a couple of loads of laundry for someone. Mom said they tried putting a hat on my bald head, so it would not be so *uncomfortable* when my friends came to visit. She said as soon as it went on, I reached up and pulled it off.

My temporary residence had seven floors. The first floor was the Intensive Care Unit (ICU) where I'd spent quite a bit of time. The second floor was the step-down unit to the ICU called the Intermediate Intensive Care Unit (IICU), where I also spent considerable time. Can you guess which floor I was able to skip? Yes, the third floor, one for which my parents breathed a huge sigh of relief. You probably guessed it: The Maternity Ward.

I was not able to eat solid food until I progressed to the seventh floor, rehabilitation. Not only did I have dental braces again, but my mouth was wired together so that my teeth would stabilize in the correct locations. Finally, the day came when they removed my braces and took out the wires. I was eager to feast my teeth and taste buds on a delicious cheeseburger – my favorite. But after taking my first bite, I instantly experienced an excruciating pain. As it turned out, the truck's impact had cracked two of my molars in half. No one had discovered them before I did. After the dentist was called in to fix them, it was another week and a half before I could eat solid food. You can only imagine how good that first bite of *real* food was.

My first memory of the Rehabilitation Floor is an unusual one: Mom and one of my best friends, Lynn, were washing my hair in some sort of tub. I'm not even sure that is completely accurate. My maternal Grandmother Hart came to visit for two weeks during the fourth month of my hospital stay. Even though I supposedly communicated with her in a lucid manner, I don't remember anything about her visit. But the scary part that I do remember was not being able to do many things because of my *zero* balance.

There are not enough words to express my appreciation for the exceptional group of therapists, doctors, and nurses that went over and above the *call of duty* for me. It takes a tremendous amount of patience to perform this type of work because what used to take minutes to accomplish now took hours to do. An example of this is getting dressed. It would have been easier and quicker for someone just to dress me, but instead, the medical professionals knew I had to learn to do this on my own. They would wait painstakingly for me to sit down, raise my leg, lean over, put a pant leg on, pull it up to the knee, and then start with the other leg. Most mornings by the time I was finished dressing, I would be exhausted and need to lie down for a nap.

My frustration was remembering these tasks had once been easy for me to complete, but I might as well have been trying to climb Mount Everest. I had never felt so lost, even a stranger to myself. I had never felt so abandoned by God. Where was He when I desperately needed Him? He was silent during my steepest hills and lowest valleys. I remembered hearing a verse about the Lord being close to the brokenhearted and rescuing those who were crushed (Psalm 34:18). Well I was broken hearted, and I can't imagine anyone being more crushed in spirit than me. "Where are you God?" I cried out.

So I learned a coping mechanism, it is called *denial*. When I once asked my current support group what is *denial*, Mr. Charlie Wisecrack stated, "I think it is a river in Egypt!" While we all laughed in response to his silliness, I knew firsthand how *denial* could injure your soul. So I kept pushing myself to return to *normal*. It took me many years to learn that *normal* is only a setting on a clothes dryer! My friend, Robert, used to remind me, "Kelly, you have to accept it and live with your *new normal.*" I realized I had somehow taken a detour in my life and had taken a new path, but I longed to return to the familiar one that had been easier. Unbeknownst to me at the time, I was futilely travelling down a rocky road.

Chapter Eleven

Normal in Five Years

And we know that in all things
God works for the good of those who love him,
who have been called according to his purpose.
Romans 8:28

When I was first admitted to the ICU, the medical staff
followed protocol for a person with a traumatic brain injury by
immediately administering Dilantin to help prevent seizures.
Never before had I experienced an allergic reaction to any type
of medication, but they finally discovered Dilantin had stopped
the production of my red blood cells (RBC). If you are not
producing RBC, you die! Thankfully, upon discovery, they went
into *Plan B* quickly, switching me to Phenobarbital, which put
me into a *trance-like* state. I never felt really happy or really sad.
Don't get me wrong; I was sad and depressed. I thought for the
rest of my life all I had to look forward to was being depressed
because there seemed to be no end to my dismal feelings. If I had
seen a light at the end of the tunnel, I would have expected it to
be an oncoming train. But gratefully, I never became sad enough
to think of suicide. The reason is because God gave me life, and
I was raised to believe that God was the only One who was able
to take it away.

My family always set goals and found them important, so I
was raised to become a "goal setter." This meant practicing or

working frequently and during long sessions that interfered with other activities. I worked diligently to accomplish whatever goals I set, and prior to my accident, I had always achieved every goal I set for myself. I wanted to be in the top twenty tennis players. Check. I wanted to be on the cheerleading squad. Check. I wanted to be elected to the Homecoming Court. Check. Thankfully, I didn't lose my desire to achieve goals. After the accident, my goals increased in number and certainly changed in perspective and relativity. My number one goal now was learning to crawl.

My days on the Rehabilitation Floor were long and exhausting. My allergic reaction to Dilantin had begun daily rituals of prodding both arms and hands to draw blood. My body did not like to give blood without a fight! I remember it taking two nurses and eleven needle sticks to get the minimum blood required to check my levels. I had to be awakened two or three times during the night and early hours to have blood drawn. That is a memory I can't erase. Needless to say, I developed a high pain tolerance. But my favorite time of the day in those early months of *memory- retention* was when Dad got off work and relieved Mom, so she could go home and cook dinner for Rod, Jr. When he walked through the door, life seemed better, much less depressing. He'd immediately transfer me to the new four wheeler (wheelchair) to escape the pokes, prods, and "time to take your medicine" rituals.

I will never forget the day Dad and I were on one of our daily walks when I got up the nerve to ask him a question that had been replaying in my mind. "Dad, how long do you think it will take me to get back to *normal* again?"

I wished I could have seen my father's face because I'm sure he didn't know how to answer that question. His thought process probably went something like this: *Should I be honest with my eighteen year old daughter and tell her that her carefree days are over and whatever she called normal is now history? No, that will crush her hopes; she is too tender to be told the truth. Let me go with this approach.*

After a pause, he said, "I think it will take about five years." It seemed to me he had picked a number out of the sky.

"Five years?" my mind exploded. I thought, *are you crazy, Dad? Are you out of your mind? How could it possibly take five years?* But audibly, there was no response; inside, my heart was breaking.

Five whole years to an eighteen year old might as well have been one thousand years or eternity! Although deeply hurt, I never forgot his response. Everything was different from normal. I looked different, my brain worked differently, my athletic ability was over, and my quick wit that everyone enjoyed was gone. My voice was different – no volume, no power -- due to the tracheotomy. When I spoke, it was a whisper. I had begun noticing differences with my hearing; it was acute. I heard everything from the man yelling curse words down the hall to the ticking of the clock in my room. Even the florescent light bulbs drove me crazy! In my condition, having complete silence to sleep, read, or do anything else that required concentration was critical for me to function. The night nurse came in around 1:00 a.m. to give me a pill or take my blood pressure, and she would constantly forget to close the door upon leaving. Then I'd hear the nurse's medicine cart rattling or the third shift's laundry bin shuffling up and down the halls. This was the beginning of many more things to come.

Being dependent on others was most unfamiliar to me. But this became a *too familiar* nightly conversation that was initiated by me pushing the call button.

"Yes? May I help you?" The pleasant voice would ask.

"Yes! Please. My door was left open, and I cannot get back to sleep due to the noise. Can you please come and close my door?" I'd ask in my loudest whisper.

"We'll send someone right away."

Then I'd wait and wait and wait; it took someone forever to come.

Well, one night when the nurse had left the door open again, I was fed up! I thought to myself, *This is ridiculous; I am going to walk to the door and close it myself! I'm not calling or waiting on anyone to do it for me!*

Then it dawned on me that I couldn't walk yet. But my determination (and frustration) got the best of me. I lowered my feet to the floor and was elated to be taking one step, two steps, but on the third step, I lost my balance and came crashing down upon the cold, hard linoleum floor, landing with a "smack" on my tail bone! What horrible pain it was! As I lay on the cold, hard floor and cried, I accepted the truth: My life would never be the same again.

Two nurses finally rescued me from drowning in a puddle of tears. I was mourning the loss of the life and girl that I loved so much – I was gone forever. One of the nurses wiped away the salty tears with a cool rag. When they left me alone in my bed, I became angry. My life would never be *normal* again. My recovery was going to take a lot longer than my naïve expectations. I had not planned on any of this happening to me. I was mad at God for taking away *everything* I had once loved and leaving me with nothing – or so I thought at the time. A lot of people believe it is wrong to be angry with God. Some parents discourage their children from ever placing blame on the Almighty. But God has taught me differently by showing me truths about my anger.

God understands our emotions and can see the sources. He saw through mine and knew that I was a very broken young woman who had just lost everything in this world in which I had placed my security. In His omniscience, God read my heart and understood the devastation I was feeling just as Job had felt. In the Bible, Job questioned God and was angry at the endless fallacies he experienced. Job witnessed many cruelties and losses, just as I had. With the hands that life had dealt him, why wouldn't he be mad? And why shouldn't I be mad? Anger is a natural, human reaction when we lose hope and are frustrated and hurt. After all, God gave us human emotions; anger just happens to be one of many. Now, by looking at my devastation and anger in hindsight, God has shown me that He can even use anger for his glory. And this has helped me to become a better counselor or friend to someone, who may be going through similar circumstances, who may have felt cheated by life, or who may have experienced great losses in life. And I've learned that we experience many of these human emotions because we have the misinterpretation that we are in control. The unequivocal truth is that we are in control of absolutely nothing. We own absolutely nothing. God is in control of everything – even our next second on earth. He ordained our birth, and He ordains the appointed hour of our death. He knows the number of hairs on our heads, and He knows the number of tears we have shed because of disappointing earthly treasures for which we have placed our focus and worry.

I had no idea how true Dad's answer of five years would turn out to be. Because we live in an instantaneous society, we want things *now*. And back then, I didn't know what I know now: Overcoming a brain injury is a life-long healing process. Every brain injury is different. Even now, there isn't a moment that I can say, "I'm not going to deal with my brain injury today.

I'll deal with it tomorrow," because every time I leave my home, I fear being lost. It takes a great deal of determination and focus for me to remember where I am going, how to get there, which way do I turn, who am I meeting, do I have everything I need. The moment I don't ask myself these questions, I'll walk out in front of a speeding car coming from the left – my blind side. My daily journeys begin with prayer and then one step of willpower and two steps of courage.

"I would be nothing if not for God!"

Chapter Twelve

Joni!

*May the God of hope fill you with all joy
and peace as you trust in Him,
so that you may overflow with
hope by the power of the Holy Spirit.*
Romans 15:13

Shock? Dismay? Disbelief? I don't recall my exact thoughts
when I saw my reflection in the mirror. It was like having a
monster-like image looking back that couldn't have been me!
Even so, I'm glad my parents didn't hide the mirrors in my
hospital room. To them everything was beautiful because I was
alive. As you can imagine, changing from a homecoming queen
into someone with dark bruises and swelling, severe facial
injuries, and a shaven head was frightening. How could I ever be
happy again? Confusion and anger consumed my every waking
minute. Why had God forgotten about me? Where was God
when that truck driver hit our car? I had been a pretty good
person. Actually, I had been a *damn good person* – never doing
drugs, never getting into really bad trouble. Whatever sins I had
committed in my short life, in no way did I deserve this
punishment.

The truck driver's name was unknown to me, but later I
would learn of his three DUIs and an outstanding warrant for his
arrest. Where was God when that man chose to get behind the

wheel of that huge truck and drive? Could God have stopped him from going through the light at the same time we were turning? Why couldn't we have turned a second faster or later? Where was this magnificent and awesome God that I thought I knew? He was nowhere around while I was feeling so alone. He had been silent while my whole life was ruined.

My dreams of marrying and having children – much less having a boyfriend – evaporated. Who would want me now? God had turned His back on me. God had forsaken me. I was irate, mixed-up, and lost. The only one I had to blame was God. Why had He forgotten me? I was completely broken in more ways than one: my heart, my mind, my body, and my spirit for starters. Even my soul was shattered. In desperation and at one of my lowest points, I considered making a deal with the devil, whatever that meant.

What happens to people when they lose hope? I found out, but thankfully, I never lost the will to live as some do. You find yourself in a dark place without any light. What do you do when you're in this place? You can give in, roll over, and die. Or you can scrape, dig, and claw against the dirt and mud until you emerge from the pit. Once in the light, if you're smart, you realize you couldn't have handled this exhausting struggle by yourself. You admit your incompetence and reliance on another power – a supernatural power named God.

It was at this lowest point in my life that reading became my solace. It was one of the few things I could do independently, allowing my imagination to free me from my torturing thoughts and immediate surroundings. I read everything I could get my hands on, Lee Iacocca's biography and *The Thornbirds,* among others. And this was the time when Dad placed a book in my hands that would change my life forever: ***Joni, An Unforgettable Story***, by Joni Eareckson Tada.

When I began reading Joni's book, it led me to read verses like Roman's 8:28, which has become my life's verse. I'd never read the Bible in my life. True, I'd heard a lot of the Bible stories or had them read to me but never had read them for myself. Joni Tada wrote about this, too. When Joni was injured, her friend, Steve, would come to the hospital on a daily basis and would sit and read his Bible in her room. When Steve found a verse that was meaningful for Joni's situation, he would share it aloud with Joni.

As I read her story, I could easily relate to all that she went through. In a split second, a diving accident had transformed Joni's life from that of an active young woman to that of a quadriplegic, who would face every day in a wheelchair. It was a story of God turning her tragedy into the most remarkable story I had ever read. Finally, someone could empathize with me, and I could empathize with her. This woman understood what it was like to have your security blanket with all your hopes and dreams stripped away in a split second. And believe me, reading what she went through made what I was going through look like a walk in the park! Her book put my life in perspective. No, I could not walk at that time, but at least I had the hope that one day I would walk again, whereas, Joni had broken her spinal cord; there was no cure for that.

Reading Joni's story did a much greater thing for me than put my life into perspective. She introduced me to JESUS, someone I had never known before. Even though I had been raised by Catholic parents, had attended church almost every Sunday, and had been a good girl, I did not know where my soul would have spent eternity had I died that first night. I did know the after-life offered two choices: Heaven or hell. I looked deeper within myself and asked some tough questions. Did I have a personal relationship with Jesus? No. Did I know Jesus as a friend? No. Jesus, to me, was an authoritative parent, who was just waiting for me to do something bad. Then He'd zap me, which He had done!

Church had never been something I enjoyed. I was not even sure why I went to church besides Mom didn't accept "No" when it came to attending services. To me, church was a punishment for the sins or wrongs I had committed the week before. It was just something I did once a week. But this Jesus that Joni's book discussed intrigued me. Was He actually the right one to blame for my automobile accident? Or did the accident happen because two young girls thought they were indestructible? Could it be that we live in a fallen world, and people do drive while intoxicated?

But of all things, I will never forget reading *how Joni thanked God for her injury*. Yes, she thanked God for her injury. Now, wait a minute. Did I believe I could do this? Could I ever thank God for allowing my whole life to be destroyed in a matter of seconds? Could I ever thank Him for leaving me with a broken-down body and three fourths of my vision gone? How can anyone be thankful for tragedy? So I kept reading.

On page 184 of her book, Joni talked about "welcoming trials as friends" and "in everything, give thanks, for this is God's will for your life...." And how "He worked all things together for His good and the good of those He loves and are called according to His purposes." This completely blew me away! I was completely astounded, but at the same time, I was mesmerized and baffled. Instead of asking, "Why did my accident happen to me," I started asking, "Why not me?" That is when I became completely humbled and realized that every one of us has experienced trials and tribulations. Jesus talked about it when He said, "I have told you all this so that you may have peace in me. Here on earth, you will have many trials and sorrows. But take heart, because I have overcome the world" (John 16:33). And in James 1:2-4, we read, "Consider it pure joy, my brothers, whenever you face trials of many kinds, because you know that the testing of your faith develops perseverance. Let perseverance finish its work so that you may be mature and complete, not lacking anything." I kept reading some of the verses Joni pointed out in her book. In James 1:12, I read, "Blessed is the one who perseveres under trial because, having stood the test, that person will receive the crown of life that the Lord has promised to those who love him." Had God written the Bible for me? It sure seemed that way. All of these verses began speaking to me personally.

Joni wrote how out of all the millions of people in the world, she felt like God had specifically chosen her to have a true purpose and meaning in her life. This purpose was to go out and help others who have been afflicted with heartache and disabilities. It involved reaching out to others with disabilities and helping to carry some of their burdens. She referenced 1 Corinthians 1, which talks about "comforting others in the same comfort you have been given." Wow! This woman continued to amaze me!

I read about the many people she had touched and helped to transform their lives. Joni had even started a program called "Wheels for the World," where they collected old and abandoned wheelchairs and took them to prisons to have inmates refurbish them. The wheelchairs were then taken to third world countries by a team of volunteers, physicians, physical therapists, occupational therapists, nurses, and lay people who just wanted to be used by God. In these countries, people with no use of their legs had learned to walk on their hands or with their hands, pulling the dead weight of their legs behind them. Can you imagine their faces when they were given a wheelchair for the first time? I, personally, want to go on one of these trips in the near future. (You can find out much more about this program at *Joni&Friends.org*. It is truly a world-wide mission.) I learned about wonderful camps Joni had developed for families with members who have disabilities.

When I finished digesting Joni's book, I did two things that changed my life forever. First, I cried out to God, asking Him to help me. I asked Him to make me the kind of person He wanted me to become. Next, I asked Him if He could do the same thing in my life that He had done in Joni's life. Could He mend this broken, shattered life, and turn it around to make something good out of it? I asked Him if this was what He had in mind for me. Could He use this tragedy to turn me around and use me for His good?

"Help me," I cried. "I cannot do this on my own. I need your help. Please take this awful nightmare and make something, anything good out of it. Lord, I am broken, and I need a doctor, and I know you are the Great Physician. Can you help me to turn this tragedy into a triumph like Joni's story?"

That night was the night when my "real" relationship with Jesus Christ began, and I took the first baby steps toward my journey of faith. Finally, I had made a decision to surrender it all to Jesus Christ and it was "my" decision. It took me losing everything I had put my security in to realize He was all I had ever needed.

"I would be nothing if not for God...!"

A Physical and Spiritual Journey

Chapter Thirteen

Surrendering to God

Blessed is the one who perseveres under trial
because, having stood the test,
that person will receive the crown of life
that the Lord has promised to those who love him.
James 1:12

After I asked God to help me become the person He wanted me to be, I thought I was finished, so I said a prayer, and that was it. I had no idea where to go from there. Having been raised in a Catholic church all of my life, I found I had little resources on how to start a relationship with my Jesus.

I started asking myself questions like, "How does one grow as a Christian?" "How do I start this whole *saved* thing?" I was not even sure what I was being *saved* from. I had never seen anyone in my life open up the Bible except for the priest and the church readers. I was completely clueless, but, thankfully, God had a plan for me.

I made another decision that was inspired by Joni's book. I would have no more pity parties. *Pity helps no one, especially yourself.* Do you get that? You may want to reread that sentence. Let me help you. *Pity helps no one, especially yourself.* Pity prevents you from growing as a person, artfully refraining you from asking self-discovery questions. When you experience a loss of any type, you need time to grieve. Some people's grief may last longer than others. Some people never get over their loss. But when it becomes pity, it only reaps anger and bitterness. This is when I began to realize there were plenty of people right outside my hospital room, down the hallway that were a lot worse off than I was. So I knew my plan. I'd begin by helping myself and then them. I'd discovered a new path; my journey had begun.

Every night when I was not totally exhausted from speech therapy, occupational therapy, physical therapy, or visitors, I made it a point to ask a nurse to transfer me to my wheelchair. Afterward, I'd go and seek out someone to encourage. This became a huge turning point in my own recovery. No longer was I focused on how miserable my life was. My determination to find someone who needed a friend became my focal point. Why? I needed one myself.

During my *four-wheeler travels*, I met some of the most amazing people on the Rehabilitation Floor. One such person was a fifteen year old young man named Christian. He'd had a stroke. I'd never heard of anyone so young having a stroke. He was a shining example of determination, a true reflection of me. Christian had learned how to crawl and had just taken his first five steps. His mother, his younger brother, Almonza, and I had a party in his hospital room to celebrate his achievement. Together, we learned to celebrate the least bits of improvement.

Reading Joni's book definitely impacted my life. All of a sudden, I saw the world differently. I focused on what others were going through first instead of me. I began to read Bible verses that Joni had referenced in her book. I asked God different questions than early on. My questions evolved from "Why me?" to "Why not me?" Now, years later, I can recall those dark days and see how selfish my thoughts were. Why not me? After meeting the "real" Jesus, I realized I did not deserve anything but to spend my eternity in hell.

I had learned goal setting from my parents. For example, when Dad began running marathons, his first goal was to finish. His second goal was to place. Reading the Bible and goal setting became two of the things that helped me to discover my own ineptitude and learn more about God's omnipresence and omnipotence. My first goal was to read my Bible every day; my second goal was to crawl independently; my third goal was to move to the walking bars; and my fourth goal was to walk on my own. And so I began my spiritual and physical journeys.

Chapter Fourteen

Crawling

*Surely God is my salvation; I will trust and not be afraid. The
Lord, the Lord himself, is my strength and my defense;
he has become my salvation.*
Isaiah 12:2

The first time I crawled, I was exhausted by the time the
therapist wheeled me back to my room and transferred me back
to bed. I collapsed and napped away the afternoon under my
Mom's faithful and watchful presence until Dad came to relieve
her, Dad got me into the wheelchair, and asked the anticipated
first question: "Kelly, where do you want to go today?"

I always got excited by this question and especially loved it
when I could reply, "I want to go to the gym. I have something
to show you, Dad."

I can remember this day as if it were yesterday. Today, I'd
show him I could crawl. So Dad wheeled me to the gym, parked
the *four-wheeler*, and transferred me to the mat. Wobbly, I
pushed myself up onto my hands and knees and stopped. Then I
alternatively slid a hand and a knee forward. Next, I slid my
other hand and knee forward. I willed this move three more
times. When I turned to look at Dad, he was crying. An alarm
gripped my chest. This is how Dad and Mom had reacted when I

moved my finger the first time.

"What's wrong? What's wrong?" I cried. "Aren't you happy?"

Dad wiped his face and asked me, "Kelly, do you realize they told us you'd be a vegetable if you ever came out of the coma? The doctor said the best we could hope for was that you'd be in a vegetative state, and here you are moving both your arms and your legs. You are crawling! I'm so proud of you," he almost yelled it because he couldn't contain his jubilation. Dad crawled over to me and we sat shoulder to shoulder on the mat and cried happiness tears together. My big, strong dad who had cheered me on during many of the cross-country races and who had been at every victorious tennis tournament was once again cheering me on because I was able to *crawl* four steps. Finally, I looked into his eyes and said, admitting to myself as much as to him, "Dad, I have a long way to go."

He replied, nodding his head. "I know, Kelly. I know. One day at a time."

That became my new theme: "One day at a time."

What does *one day at a time* mean to the rest of us? Maybe it means to be able to pay our bills or pick up our kids from their school activities on time, but *one day at a time* for me meant I couldn't do anything about the past or what had happened as much as I wish I could have changed it; *one day at a time* was going to be my reality. I had no idea what the future held for me, but I accepted I could not control what would happen the next minute, hour, day, or week. I was not in control of *anything*. But the one thing I could do is to live in the present moment: the here and now.

Charles Swindoll says, "We have a choice every day regarding the attitude we will embrace for that day." Staying in the mindset of *one day at a time* reminded me (and still does) to live life to the fullest every moment of every day. He explained attitude and how important it is. He puts it above events of the past, education, money, circumstances, failures, successes, and even what people say or do. Your attitude can make or break you, and each of us has a choice of attitudes to make each day. Will we wallow in self-pity or be encouraging to others. Will we share with others or turn away? Swindoll said, "I am convinced that life is 10 percent what happens to me and 90 percent how I react to it."

I embraced this notion that my spiritual and physical journey would become a matter of changing my attitude.

A few days later, Dad put me in the *four-wheeler* and asked, "Kelly, where do you want to go today?" With Atlanta still in bloom and my love for the outdoors, I longed to go outside. So when Dad wheeled me outside to the hospital's garden for the first time in weeks, the grass never looked so green, the colorful flowers never smelled so aromatic, and the warm, humid air never seemed so refreshing. I savored a quick breeze on my face and inhaled fresh air into my nostrils. On the days I didn't have some new feat to show him, I'd choose to go outdoors, especially on the beautiful days. The breeze cleared my nostrils of the clingy ammonia and alcohol smells and erased the sounds of clinking and clunking medicine bottles and the shouts of brain injured patients. Being outside became magical; I was glad to be alive.

The time of day I hated the most during my rehabilitation on the seventh floor was when my family left at night, and I was alone. All alone. I can remember many nights of fear, listening to a man rant and rave, as he stomped up and down the hallway yelling and screaming profanities until sunrise. It was quite disturbing and scary. I'd bury my head into my pillow and focus on my *four-wheeler* trips with Dad.

A Stranger to Myself

I've since learned that screaming profanities is a customary behavior for a brain injury and is most commonly experienced in the fourth and fifth stages of healing according to the Ranchos Los Amigos Scale, which "measures the levels of awareness, cognition, behavior and interaction with the environment." According to the Web site, *TraumaticBrainInjury.com*, the scale is shown below.

Level I: No Response
Level II: Generalized Response
Level III: Localized Response
Level IV: Confused - agitated
Level V: Confused – inappropriate
Level VI: Confused – appropriate
Level VII: Automatic – appropriate
Level VIII: Purposeful - appropriate

Over the years, I've since cared for ministers, who were the most mildly mannered people before their brain injuries, but afterwards, their cursing could make a sailor blush.

The afternoon when I took my first steps was another magical moment. I asked Dad to wheel me to the gym and the parallel walking bars. Using my upper body strength, I slowly pulled myself up onto my feet. My arms strained against the parallel bars, dragging my feet to form short steps. Proudly, I only went down once. Finally, exhausted while exhilarated, I stammered, "Dad, you have to bring the wheelchair over here to me." When he did, his face looked like a Christmas tree. His pride beamed through the wet cheeks and audible sniffles.

After graduating to a walker, my parents added to their number of *funny stories* about my hospital months. When they returned to the hospital after dinner to stay until visiting hours were over, they could never find me in my room. They'd trudge up and down hallways, searching for me. Upon finding an available nurse, they'd ask, "Have you seen Kelly?"

Of course, my evening walks and occasional disappearances exasperated the seventh floor nurses. Each would quickly respond, "Yeah, we had to search for her, too, to give her meds. The last time we saw her, she was down on the east wing, trailing behind that walker as fast as she could." One nurse even volunteered to them, "I asked her, 'Kelly, when are you coming back to your room?' to which she replied, 'Where is my room? That's okay, don't tell me. I'll find it. I'll be back in a little while. I was just taking a walk. But which way is my room?'"

Unfortunately, many of my rehabilitation memories are cloudy. I just remember the highlights of demonstrating my newly-developed skills for Dad. And I do remember being returned to my room around 3:00 or 4:00 each afternoon from countless therapy sessions. Mom would always be there to greet me with a big grin. Progress was exhausting. Life was tiring but good.

Chapter Fifteen

Preparation for Reality

I have come that they may have life, and have it to the full.
John 10:10b

I was allowed to leave the Rehabilitation Floor for a weekend or two to prepare my parents and me for our new lifestyle once I got home. From these two weekends, we knew it was going to be a *big job*. But the day I was finally released from the hospital was a huge day for me. It was my release from captivity.

I'll never forget the trip home. As we neared my parents' subdivision, I couldn't believe my eyes when I saw a large banner that read, WELCOME HOME, KELLY! Neighbors lined both sides of the streets and were holding up smaller signs reading, "We love you, Kelly" or "Welcome home!" Little kids that I recognized from the pool lined both sides of the street and were banging on pots and pans with metal spoons. It was great to have this heartwarming welcome and to be back in the world.

But all too soon, reality set in. While in the hospital, I'd gotten a lot of attention. I'd had a steady stream of family, friends, and fellow patients around to keep me company. Now, it was just *me*. I always had a call button within reach where someone on the other end would answer, "How can I help you?"

There was no call button at home.

Most people who sustain an acquired brain injury encounter times like these of feeling lost, isolated, and even abandoned. According to the *Better Health Channel* Web site, acquired brain injury (ABI) is any damage to the brain that happens after birth. The specific symptoms or losses of functioning depend on which brain areas are affected. Some of the causes include alcohol or drugs, which can poison the brain; disease, such as AIDS, Alzheimer's disease, cancer, multiple sclerosis or Parkinson's disease; lack of oxygen – called anoxic brain injury (for example, injury caused by a near drowning); physical injury, such as an impact (or blow) to the head, which may occur in vehicle or sporting accidents, fights or falls; stroke – when ablood vessel inside the brain breaks or is blocked, destroying the local brain tissue (retrieved August 6, 2015).

According to *Traumatic Brain Injury.com,* The number of people with Traumatic Brain Injury (TBI) is difficult to assess accurately but is much larger than most people would expect. According to the CDC (United States Centers for Disease Control and Prevention), there are approximately 1.5 million people in the U.S. who suffer from a traumatic brain injury each year, 50,000 people die from TBI each year and 85,000 people suffer long term disabilities. In the U.S., more than 5.3 million people live with disabilities caused by TBI. Patients admitted to a hospital for TBI are included in this count, while those treated in an emergency room or doctor's office are not counted.

The causes of TBI are diverse. The top three causes are: car accident, firearms and falls. Firearm injuries are often fatal: 9 out of 10 people die from their injuries.Young adults and the elderly are the age groups at highest risk for TBI. Along with a traumatic brain injury, persons are also susceptible to spinal cord injuries which is another type of traumatic injury that can result out of vehicle crashes, firearms and falls. Prevention of TBI is the best approach since there is no cure (retrieved August 6, 2015).

So for a brain injured person, this is where the hard work begins and the realization that this is not going to be a quick fix sets in because the truth of the matter is healing from a brain injury is a life-long process. People come and visit in the hospital, stay for an hour or so, and leave. But when the patient gets home, the friends don't come around as often. The phone calls are not as frequent as they once were. Friends see you more as a liability than as a companion. Life is not fair, but no one promised it would be. And for a lot of people, this is where depression takes a huge bite out of your hopes and dreams; depression is something most people are not expecting. I was fortunate that my two parents refused to see my hospital release as being the end and knew it would be the beginning. My parents became my greatest advocates.

Mom sought out the lady who lived next door, Mrs. Walton. She had just opened a computer lab, so I could work with her to *relearn* how to read, write, and do arithmetic. She had helped me with my SAT score in the past. Mrs. Walton had such a sweet and encouraging demeanor. I looked forward to going to see her and always knew when I left, I was better off than when I'd come. I saw her three times a week in the mornings, while squeezing in time between speech therapy, occupational therapy, and physical therapy from the outpatient center at Kennestone Hospital. She helped me learn how to read again and then to increase my reading speed. She helped me learn how to add, subtract, and multiply again and helped my cognitive processing speed, which was very slow. Due to my loss of vision, it now took me about three to four times longer to do simple tasks compared to a person with good eyesight and no brain injury.

Remember, I could not drive, so I was dependent on my mother. Her new, full time job was carting me around to all of my therapists' and doctors' appointments. By the end of each day, I was exhausted, but when I tried to sleep at night, I had terrible insomnia. I was on a high dosage of Phenobarbital, which they gave to me in two doses. Phenobarbital is a depressant in nature and was supposed to put me to sleep. But when I had a difficult time sleeping through the night, the doctor changed my prescription to be given all at night before I went to bed. Even so, I still had insomnia six out of seven nights a week. The following days when Mom would wake me, I'd be exhausted before I even put my first foot on the floor.

I continuously wanted to take naps during the day, but at night when I laid down for bed, my eyes would pop open and my brain would say, "Here we go again!" I'd lie awake all night long, thinking about how bleak my life was. Those nights were painful and exhausting.

Chapter Sixteen

End of a Relationship

Do not be yoked together with unbelievers.
For what do righteousness and wickedness have in common?
Or what fellowship can light have with darkness?
2 *Corinthians 6:14*

After I'd gotten out of the hospital, I was walking, but I still had to ring the bell for Mom to come and change the television station (this was before the time of remotes), or if I had to go to the bathroom, I still needed assistance. I wore a *transfer belt.* A transfer belt was placed around my waist and held by my mother so that she could steady me if I lost my balance.

During the hospital months, my parents and Chris established a close relationship. Every night when they returned home from the hospital, like clockwork, they'd receive a call from Chris, wanting to know the latest updates. "Did she move anything today?" "Did she make contact with the real world today?" "Did she open her eyes today?" "What did she do today?" They realized what a good man Chris was and what a good husband he would be to me.

Later in the summer, Chris came home from Lubbock, Texas. His father had just moved from Roswell, Georgia, to Lake Lanier. Chris telephoned me, and we set a date to see each other. Mom, Ellen, and I worked all morning, even overtime, trying to make me look as close to the old Kelly as possible. I can imagine how far away from that old Kelly I was, having already had four or five of the seventeen surgeries on my neck and face. My hair was not in good condition, having grown unevenly in splotches on my scalp. I felt sorry for Mom and Ellen, who had worked so hard on me. Mom had even purchased me a new outfit for our reunion.

When Chris came to get me, we embraced as he greeted me with "Kelly, I'm so glad to see you." We even kissed, but it was all different. Even though I'm sure I was shocking to Chris, he was very gracious. But because I knew him, I could easily read his face. Although he had tried hard to cover up his reactions, he was very taken *aback* with the differences. After all, my face was still swollen from going through the reconstructive surgeries. Maybe it was I who felt so different. After all, I was a stranger to myself and didn't love this new Kelly. There had not been enough time or healing.

So we drove to his dad's new lake house to ride on the boat. I remember announcing, "I want to ski!" One thing about a person with a brain injury like mine is we live in a lot of denial. I wanted to be that old Kelly so bad, and thankfully, Chris had the wisdom and foresight to know that was impossible.

He gently promised, "Kelly, next time we'll try skiing, but the lake is very rough today, and no one is skiing."

When he dropped me off at home, he explained he was still in transition. "The Air Force is moving me from Lubbock, Texas, to Seattle, Washington." Then he promised, "Kelly, when I get to Seattle, I'll be sure to write you or call you with my new phone number and address."

I happily replied, "Great! I'll look forward to it."

Well, as you can probably guess, I didn't hear from Chris. Unfortunately, this is very typical in a relationship where one of the people has had a brain injury. It's not like a broken leg where

your leg will be like new in two or three months. It's not like
you'll be able to run like you used to. I think he realized during
our date that this was going to be a life-long healing process, and
if he was honest with himself: He couldn't handle it. He couldn't
handle this stranger. He was used to the homecoming queen
version of Kelly. He was used to the bubbly personality. I call
those years my *zombie years* because those pills totally knocked
out any affect, any happiness, or any joy that I was to feel.

Chris was a good man, but I had to let him go, along with
any hope of marrying him. Even though he had graduated from
college, and I was only eighteen, he had been ready to propose
before the accident. At times, I wonder how different my life
may have been had the accident never happened, and we had
married.

--------◆--------

Fast forward seven years when I returned home from a
summer weekend trip. Upon arriving home, Dad greeted me.
"Kelly, you won't believe who we heard from while you were
gone." Curious, I asked, "Who Dad?"

"Chris. He was visiting his father and called us. He said
when he drove by our exit, he thought about you and wanted to
find out how you're doing. He left his phone number. Why don't
you give him a call?"

During our special summer of falling in love, Chris had
confessed that one of the things that intrigued him was I was the
first woman to beat him at tennis. I loved beating guys in tennis,
especially cocky ones like Chris. So I telephoned him, and we
planned another date to go and play a set or two of tennis at
Terrell Mill Park and have a picnic afterwards. Terrell Mill Park
was the exact place where my accident had happened. On a side
note, there had been many previous wrecks before ours at Terrell
Mill Park. But apparently, our accident was the one that made

the city revisit that intersection. Today, it is unrecognizable. They reengineered and removed a number of blind spots.

Chris seemed delighted. "Kelly, don't worry about anything. I will get the food and come and pick you up." He confirmed the plans of our date. "We'll enjoy the park, and then we'll play a set or two of tennis, besides I want to play you in tennis. Now that you've lost some of your eyesight, maybe I'll have a chance to hold a candle to you. Afterward, we can have a nice picnic."

It was a beautiful summer day; the temperature was perfect. Chris spread a blanket on the grass, and we enjoyed catching up. It felt romantic until I asked him to update me on what he'd been up to over the past seven years. Chris related several stories that indicated no evidence of a changed heart. He was still the same old Chris, going to bars, meeting different women, and partying, partying, partying. When he graduated from flight school, he moved to California to serve in the Air Force. That's where he met a woman, married her, and stayed married for four years until they divorced, having no children, thank God. That was all he had to say about his life.

That's when I got to tell Chris what Christ had done in my life. I explained how I had come to know Christ even when I felt like God had stripped me of everything I once had. Everything had been taken away. I told Chris he still had his good looks, his athletic ability, and his intellect to be grateful for. I was on a roll and eager to continue.

"Chris, today I thank God for that accident because it brought me to know Jesus Christ. It made me realize that Jesus wanted a personal relationship with me. He wanted to know me as his child, and you know what? He wants to know you as his child also."

Chris looked at me and said, "Kelly, I'm so glad that you found this."

But what he was really saying was that he was glad this was working for me, but it wasn't for him. He was not at the same place that I was. Instantly, I recognized how much I had grown over the past seven years. I had grown from being a party girl to being a disciple of Jesus Christ. My mission was completely different than what Chris's mission was. His mission seemed to be party, party, party – the same as mine when I was eighteen years old. I pray that Chris will read this book and will have a "God incidence" and will realize that he has a God shaped void. And women will not fill it, partying will not fill it, drugs and alcohol will not fill it, only a relationship with Jesus Christ will make him complete. And that is my prayer for every person who reads this book. The overwhelming gift and blessing from my car accident has been my personal relationship with Jesus Christ. Through it, God has illuminated my knowledge that I cannot get out of bed in the morning without His help.

God had used the accident to bring so much more into my life – so much more meaning. John 10:10b says, "I have come that they may have life, and have it to the full," meaning a full and meaningful life. That is what Christ has fulfilled for me. I now have a purpose for living each day.

It saddened me to know that this would be our last date because we were not on the same page. So when he dropped me off that day, I said goodbye, never to contact him again. I was at peace and thankful God had brought closure to this relationship.

Chapter Seventeen

The Tragic Advice

The mind of sinful man is death.
But the mind controlled by the Spirit is life and peace
Romans 8:6

Lucy's mother called Mom after I was released from the
hospital and said, "Marilyn, I'm sure Kelly has been wondering
why Lucy hasn't been calling her or coming to see her, so I
wanted you to know that Lucy has been going through some
very intensive counseling services with a registered psychologist.
She's been taking this really hard, her psychologist has
recommended she stay away from Kelly. She is not to interact
with Kelly until Kelly gets back to looking more normal."

Well, my looking more *normal* wouldn't take place for
another five years. Lucy doesn't remember her mother
telephoning mine, but I'll never forget their conversation, which
my mother shared with me in detail.

I told Mom that my first reaction was that I wish I could
have met her psychologist and smacked the mess out of him. I
would have screamed into his ear, "Don't you ever encourage
two friends who were closer than sisters not to visit each other
because of a traumatic accident or because someone is having
trouble. Lucy could have come to the hospital and helped me
learn how to crawl or walk again. She would've realized that I

loved her. I have not blamed her for a millisecond. I've never thought the accident was her fault."

And truly, it wasn't until many years later when I read my dad's journal that I knew Lucy was given a ticket for running the red light. I think that was the worst thing the officer could have done. From what I've gathered, there were no reliable sources who came forward after the accident to say who was at fault. The only two witnesses I've heard about were an elderly man, who suffered from dementia, and an eleven year old boy, who was walking with the man. But it doesn't matter to me. Nothing will ever change what happened, but Lucy and I could have healed each other. Her guilt is something she has lived with for years when she shouldn't have lived with it for one second. It is called an *accident* because it was an *accident*. No one could ever plan such a horrific event if they wanted to.

Even though her mother forbade Lucy to visit me after the accident, Lucy had snuck and did it anyway – for a short while. But after she began seeing the psychologist, she stopped altogether.

But what blows me away is that my parents wanted to preserve Lucy's and my relationship, so they never shared that Lucy had received the ticket. That shows you my parents' integrity. And when they began going through the court case, you can imagine how many letters they received from ambulance-chasing lawyers. (They even had ambulance-chasing lawyers coming to the hospital.) In the end, my parents chose Yuhuda Smoler because he was the only attorney who employed an investigator, who uncovered that the driver of the truck had had three DUIs and an outstanding warrant for his arrest from another state. He was thorough, and that is why they chose him to represent us.

But my parents told Mr. Smoler, "We don't want any money from Lucy or her insurance company – not a penny."

Because of this and so many other things, I have nothing but respect and admiration for my parents.

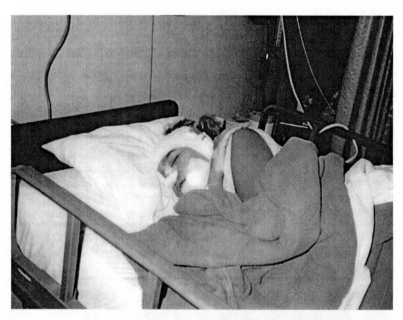

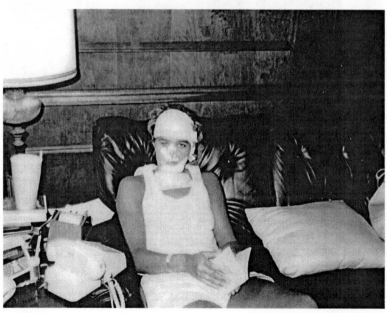

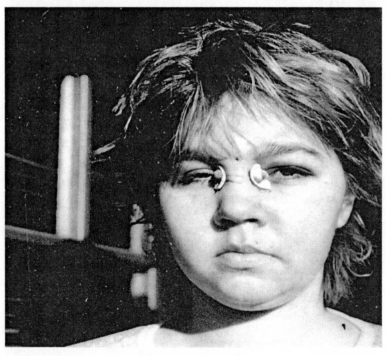

Chapter Eighteen

Lost

For the Son of Man came to seek and to save the lost
Luke 19:10

I was very much a perfectionist before the accident. Therefore, I had to completely re-focus.

Ellen will tell you, "Every single time Kelly walked out of our house [before the accident], her makeup was perfect and not a hair was out of place. She was just *it*. She was *perfection*. She was *a homecoming queen in a package*."

During my recovery, my family got upset with me when I wouldn't take a shower or get dressed up for anything. It was difficult for my family because they remembered who I used to be; they wanted me to get back to being *that person*. But that Kelly had died on March 18, 1985. Who I was now, and who I'd become was a person who didn't put all that much emphasis on her outward appearance. God had shown me that the inward state is so much more important.

That summer when I was discharged from the hospital, I wanted to return to college. As you read previously, one of the best things about people with brain injuries is that a lot of us live with denial. A lot of us refuse to face the truth or reality. I thought I could return to the University of Georgia, and life would become great for me again. I just wanted to be *normal*.

I insisted my mom drive me to Athens, Georgia, to meet with the Dean of Students with Special Needs. I remember this man; he was nice, very Southern, overweight, and a jolly type of guy. While Mom and I sat in his office discussing my wishes, I tried to convince him of how determined I was to return to the University of Georgia. regardless of a brain injury and four neuro-psychological reports in which the doctors were strictly against this. The doctors had written, "We strongly recommend that Kelly not attempt college again, period. Her scores are substandard to the level of a college student that failure would be imminent. And add in the social pressure...."

So to appease me, it was decided that I'd attend Kennesaw College to integrate back into college life with the sustained support of my family. But immediately, I began using my old study habits, which were lacking. While the professor was speaking, I would try to take notes, but I'd forget what the professor had just stated. I would read the chapter, highlight what I thought was important, and stay up an hour or two later, studying the night before the exam. My grades plummeted from being an "A/B" student to failing.

Mom didn't waste any time. She called Dr. Lindenbaum, my neuropsychologist at the hospital, and begged him, "Dennis, you have to help Kelly. You have to help her because she is failing college, and I don't know what it would do to her to fail out."

So Dr. Lindenbaum agreed, "I will work with Kelly" and asked her to bring me to his office.

One of my greatest fears since the accident was of being lost, not knowing which way to go, not knowing where I was, or not knowing where I needed to be. On one occasion as Mom was driving me to Dr. Lindenbaum's office, she inadvertently turned down the wrong street. In her defense, all the office buildings looked alike on three or four of the streets, so Mom stopped the car in front of a building where she thought Dennis's office was.

"Okay. Here you are, Kelly. I'll see you in a couple of hours."

I hopped out as she drove away and entered the office door, but the familiar woman wasn't sitting at the receptionist's desk. The entire waiting area looked different. The lady behind the desk looked up and asked, "May I help you?"

"Yes. I'm here to see Dr. Dennis Lindenbaum."

"Well, this isn't his office," she stated.

I froze. "Do you know where his office is?"

"No, I'm sorry, I don't." Then she returned to her work.

Panic gripped me. I was dismissed, so I walked out of the office and just stood there for several minutes, looking forlorn and all alone. The cement sidewalk seemed to go on forever in each direction. I almost crumbled, not knowing what to do. Before I did, I walked back into the office. One of the other nurses noticed my white face and trembling lips and hands. She easily recognized I needed some *TLC (tender loving care)*.

"Can I help you?" she asked. Her eyes were patient and kind.

"Yes. My mom dropped me off here to go to Dr. Lindenbaum's office, but this isn't his office, and I don't know where it is or how to get there."

"What is your name?" she asked, while reaching behind the counter for a phone directory.

"Kelly Spence."

She quickly located Dr. Lindenbaum's office address and phone number in the yellow pages; she dialed the number and explained my situation to the person who answered the phone on the other end. Before two minutes were up, a secretary from Dr. Lindenbaum's office had walked over to take me by the hand

and lead me to his office. He greeted me with a big smile. That experience was traumatic for me and, therefore, memorable. And thirty years later, I still fear being lost.

❖

Over the course of three or four weeks, Dennis helped me to develop a study style that would help any college student. When I received my new syllabus at the beginning of the quarter, he'd have me divide the assigned reading pages into the number of days until the first exam or next exam.

Kelly's Study Style

After receiving the syllabus, divide the assigned reading pages into the number of days until the first or next exam.

Read the pages, annotating (highlighting or taking notes) on the important parts prior to class lecture.

Work with Students for Disabilities group on campus, so during class, a note taker can be provided for each class. This is normally someone the teacher recommends, a volunteer, or a friend.

Note taker takes notes with carbon paper, so student has a copy and note taker has a copy.

While note taker is taking notes, tape the lectures.

After the class lecture, listen to the lecture tape(s) in the evening.

After the class lecture, re-read the annotations during the first reading.

Go to the library or a quiet place to concentrate and combine your own notes and the note taker's notes into a final copy.

Finally, transcribe the notes onto index cards, placing a term or clue on one side and the answer on the backside.

A Stranger to Myself

For the preceding days before class, review index cards, rereading these highlighted parts again.

On the night before the exam, I'd be on my knees, praying to God for just a C. All in all, I was grateful for the instructors at Kennesaw College. It was a gift to attend a community college because it was small enough where the instructors worked with me to learn concepts and provided me with a personal note-taker. After a brain injury, analytical thinking is absent for a lot of people; my trouble was indeed in connecting the dots.

Many people, figuratively speaking, *placed their hands over mine to help me* in my thirst for knowledge and normalcy. This included my parents, who drove me to and from the community college for all of my classes. I realized the burden this was causing them and recognized that parking spaces were sparse on the campus, so I placed a note on the bulletin boards, stating that I needed a ride to campus on certain days and times. I included the fact that I owned a *handicap placard*. Many offers began coming in. So my parents were relieved of this daily chore and only had to transport me if I had an early class or had to stay late. I attended the fall and winter quarters before returning to the University of Georgia. I felt at that time I was ready to return to the big dawgs – the Georgia Bulldogs.

Chapter Nineteen

Driving in the Dark

The Lord is good, a stronghold in the day of trouble;
and he knoweth them that trust in Him.
Nahum 1:7 KJV

Ellen returned to school after spring break but came home on most weekends to check on my progress and to help our family whenever and wherever she was needed. She was studying even harder in school, so she wouldn't add any undue pressures on our parents, and as a result, her grades had improved. And whenever she needed money, she worked at the theater in town.

When I announced to my family that I wanted to return to the University of Georgia and live off campus at the sorority house, Ellen was astonished – shocked isn't a strong enough word.

To help me with my dream of returning to the University, my parents learned about a lady named Eliana, who worked out of one of the hospitals and retrained people with disabilities on how to drive safely. When my parents and I initially met her, Eliana said, "The first thing Kelly is going to need is a new car," to which I screamed, "Yes!" I liked this lady already.

"She needs a Mercedes, a BMW, an Audi, a Volvo, or a Nissan Maxima." Was this lady for real? Was I dreaming? "It needs to be a four-door car and a dark colored car because in my opinion, people see dark colored cars before light colored ones. And don't get a Honda. Hondas are unsafe."

Again, I screamed, "Yes!"

So my parents took me shopping for a car, which was so much fun. As a result, we bought a brand new Nissan Maxima with a dual braking system installed; that meant I had a brake on my side, and my passenger had a brake of his/her own for emergency stops. Next my parents signed me up for drivers' lessons. I took either five or six lessons from Eliana, but she was a *no play* person, who took her job so seriously, I became afraid to step into her car. I'd tell myself beforehand, "Don't mess up. Don't mess up!"

I began driving with special glasses that had a prism built into the left hand corner of the lens, so I could look into it, and it would automatically move whatever was in my blind spot, so I could see it. The first model of these glasses had a dental mirror that went straight off the top of the bridge of the glasses. They were hysterical! But the glasses helped me see where my peripheral vision was missing.

Dr. Gottlieb, one of the world's premier technical experts for people with vision losses prescribed my second model of glasses, which had a small mirror right off the front. Boy, did I get looks when I wore those babies, especially when I ran or played tennis. I never planned on getting rid of them, but I have no idea where they are now.

Ellen couldn't believe our parents had relented to my constant pleas for a car, even against doctors' orders, and purchased me a car. Their rationale was that when I returned to college, my sorority sisters could use it to get me to and from classes and where ever else I needed to go. Ellen was adamant she would not ride or drive with me. She was the only one in the entire family to put her foot down. Her own life meant more to her than risking it riding with a woman who took twenty minutes to put on a pair of tennis shoes and was limited to less than half the vision she was supposed to have. My reaction time was incredibly slow; my thought processing was like watching a turtle cross busy traffic. Ellen thought our parents were definitely living in denial to think I was capable of such a responsible task. Ellen secretly prayed that I would not have to injure somebody like I'd been injured, or even worse, kill somebody else to make me realize that driving was not a good idea.

Bless my brother's heart, Rod, Jr. had just turned sixteen years old and gotten his driver's license. As my greatest encourager, he never wanted to tell me "No" or discourage me from becoming more independent. As a result, he became my favorite person to ride with, and Rod, Jr. always let *me* drive.

One day, as we were traveling on Terrell Mill Road close to my parents' subdivision, out of nowhere, a lady ran a stop light and plowed into us from the left-hand side. The lady had been distracted while playing with her cassette tape deck. Her dog was in the back seat but was okay. This was accident number one -- my first driving accident -- but we had the green light, and even though it wasn't my fault, Rod Jr., and I were scared really bad.

When I discontinued the driving lessons with Eliana in midstream, I couldn't help but to wonder if she ever would have passed me with her blessings. Either way, God had used her to get me a car.

"But I would be nothing if not for God…!"

Chapter Twenty

Cinderella

Consider it pure joy, my brothers, whenever you face trials of
many kinds, because you know that the testing of your faith
develops perseverance. Let perseverance finish its work so that
you may be mature and complete, not lacking anything.
James 1: 2-4

A year after the accident, I made it back to the University of
Georgia for the spring quarter and moved into an eight-girl room
at the sorority house. Did I return too early? In hindsight, I
probably did. But I had overcome great odds to finally make it
back.

I had discovered what an amazing Christian woman Susan
Cheely was. She was a senior and graduating soon. When I was
in the hospital, she would drive the hour and half journey from
Athens to Marietta, Georgia, just to sit with my parents when I
was still in the coma. My mother said she never came without a
gift, a smile, and words of encouragement and hope for the
family.

When I began rehabilitation on the seventh floor, my first
memories are of Susan arriving on a Friday night just to have
pizza with me and to shower me with love and hope that I was
going to make it. She continued doing this every Friday night
until the day I was discharged. Then she began visiting me

111

at home. I have journal entries of when she took me to a Sandy Patty concert at Six Flags over Georgia, which is the amusement park in Atlanta. Even today, I don't remember ever going to see Sandy Patty, but it is in black and white in my journal.

I do remember feeling the love and acceptance from Susan I'm forever grateful.

Before my return, my sorority sisters had been very sweet to me. I remember they had invited me up for a weekly meeting they had. I had persuaded Mom to drive me to the meeting, which was 1.5 hours from our home. As we approached the sorority house, we were delighted to find they had hung this humongous sign, reading "Welcome Back, Kelly." The sign and the Southern-style plantation home caught many a gaze.

My sorority sisters vied to sit beside me during dinner. They showered me with love and praises and told me how good I looked. And during the meeting that night, they awarded me a great bouquet of colorful flowers and a bronze plaque that read, "You are our inspiration." The whole night had been focused on me, the girl who still loved the limelight. That would never change. That's how God made me, so Mom and I were elated on our drive home. But I'd soon learn to my chagrin how superficial and fake these sentiments were.

An eight-girl room for me with my newly developed ultra-sensitive hearing, my easily distracted manner, and my complete inability to organize anything may as well have been me moving into hell. Everyone in this sorority had been a homecoming queen. Everyone had been super popular in high school. Everyone had been accomplished. But my appearance after the accident was the opposite of being a beauty queen. I needed plastic surgery on my face every six months. The operations couldn't be scheduled any faster because it took six months for the swelling to subside. All in all, it would take several years and seventeen reconstructive surgeries before I was finished.

After the accident, my sorority sisters could love me for a visit, but when I came back to actually live with them, they realized how different I was. They were not getting the old Kelly back. Instead, they had gotten an off-balanced, slow moving, slow thinking version, who was not easy to look at. My former processing speed had been like a cougar – going from one thing to the next without skipping a beat. Now it was more like a turtle. Kerplunk, kerplunk, and it only had moved an inch. I was disorganized most of the time. The sad fact was my sisters didn't know how to handle me. They could be nice to my face, but as soon as I turned my back, they were gossiping. "Did you see how Kelly ate her dinner tonight? You'd think she was raised in a barn." Almost immediately, I was ostracized. Unfortunately, Susan Cheely and her gang of mature Christian women had graduated and these women seemed selfish, self-centered, and unwilling to help a struggling young sister. They saw outward and not inward as Susan had done.

Mary McGuire, one of my sorority sisters, whom I am thankful for, was one of the only honest people in my sorority. She took me aside and confided, "Kelly, we don't mean to be ugly, but when the dinner was put on the table the other night, we had chicken, and you started eating it with your hands. That spurred a whole week of gossip about how bad your table manners were."

Jane, my counselor, helped talk me through why my sorority sisters seemed to distance themselves from me. She helped me understand what they couldn't realize on their own and what nobody had been able to explain to them. For my parents, having me was like having an infant again. They must have been overwhelmed by the magnitude of tasks I had to relearn, but you'd never have known it.

Once when I was showering at the sorority house, I lost my balance and fell against the side of the tub. Thank goodness there was a shower curtain there to break my fall, and as soon as my bottom hit the side of the tub, I bounced back up because I knew there were other women in there, and it scared me. Can you imagine how scared they were? It wasn't that they were bad people; they just didn't understand me or what I was going through. Through their immature lenses, I appeared more as a liability than an old friend. Everything was all well and good when they could keep me at seven arms' lengths.

One day while feeling neglected, I discovered a tiny room in the attic of the sorority house. It had one lonely desk, so I purchased a small lamp and converted this tiny room with the lonely desk and the little lamp into my haven where I spent at least eight hours a day because it was quiet – the only place in the entire house that was quiet. This haven became my escape, a place where I didn't have to acknowledge I had zero friends, zero dates, and zero men who wanted to take me out. Actually, I had zero life.

I felt so dejected. Once again, I asked, "Where is God in all of this?" I felt alone, isolated, abandoned. What was going to happen to me? Was I ever going to find happiness again? Why me, Lord? Is it right that one person should have to suffer and feel so alone? Where was my multitude of friends now? I used to be the leader of the pack. Now I didn't even know where to find the pack. "Are you hearing me, Lord?" I cried. "Are you hearing the cries of my heart?" I truly felt like a stranger to myself. I felt like my prayers were bouncing off the ceiling and not reaching His ears. I felt so much sorrow, doubt, and disillusionment. And on top of all this, I studied ten to twelve hours each day just to earn a C or D. As a result, I was exhausted most of the time because I had to study, and the only place I could study was in that little cubby up in the attic of the sorority house. That's when this Cinderella learned to use the alarm on my running watch.

I would study for thirty minutes. Then I would set my alarm for fifteen minutes, put my head down, and rest. Then I'd start over again with my homemade flash cards. At bedtime, I couldn't go to sleep, so I was pulling all-nighters – studying three or four nights out of the week. I'd go to class, take the test, and return home to crash, but I couldn't crash long because girls would be coming in and out of the room talking.

The University of Georgia's campus is spread out. They have six different bus systems that transport students from one place to another. This was overwhelming, too, because every day I would not remember what time my class was or what bus I needed to catch or where I needed to take the bus to or where I needed to transfer. It was a nightmare. Once when I transferred to another bus system, I realized that I had gotten off at the incorrect stop, so I had to get off that bus and take another bus back. I had a meltdown – crying because I was so scared. The other people riding the bus must have thought I was a little disturbed or a *whacko*.

I began second guessing myself. "What am I doing here? I no longer fit in with these people. I am not popular. I am more of an outcast. Will my life ever get better?" I asked God again, "Will I ever find happiness? Maybe this is too much for me. Maybe I am not ready to deal with a huge campus with my directionally challenged brain."

Today, I know I had to experience those challenging times in order to grow empathy to understand how hurting people feel. Today, I can see how God uses my weakness -- a lack of direction -- as a strength that allows others to assist me and get to know me. For the first years after the accident, I tried to cover up my weaknesses and challenges, meaning my loss of vision, my loss of direction – my brain injury. But the more I got to know God, the more I realized how He uses our weaknesses to show His strengths. It is not about me.

In 2 Corinthians 12:10, we read "That is why, for Christ's sake, I delight in weaknesses, in insults, in hardships, in persecutions, in difficulties. For when I am weak, then I am strong."

"But I would be nothing if not for God…!"

Chapter Twenty One

Wanting to Fit In

Be strong and courageous. Do not be afraid or terrified
because of them, for the Lord your God goes with you;
He will never leave you nor forsake you.
Deuteronomy 31:6

While living at the sorority house, I allowed myself one
Friday or one Saturday night each week to go out and have fun.
When you're on an anti-seizure medication, the doctors tell you,
"Kelly, if you take one sip of alcohol, it will send you into the
biggest grand mal seizure you have ever seen or ever heard of
having."

When you are told that, you do not drink. And what do most
college students do on the weekend? They drink. And most of
my sorority sisters drank all throughout the week. It just blew me
away. Before my accident, I, too, had gone out at least four
nights a week and drank until I couldn't see straight. That is just
the thing you did as a college student, who was enjoying her first
time away from parents and rules.

So I'd go out and have fun, which really wasn't fun to me
anymore. How much fun could you have going out with all these
young people and watching them drink themselves to oblivion? I
wasn't able to drive them home because of my vision loss. It
wasn't fun at all, and being on the outside looking in was
terrible.

One of my heartbreaking memories was of me getting myself all dolled up and walking down the hallway where there were four or five of these eight girl rooms. Of course, my sorority sisters never stayed in my room to talk about their plans for the evening. I remember standing outside the door of one of these rooms for a moment, hearing them discussing their plans for the night.

Felicia said, "Okay. This is what we're going to do. Jodie, you're driving tonight."

Jodie replied, "Okay. I will."

Felicia had continued, "Good. We're going to TKs (a bar) first, and then we're going to the ATO house; they're bringing in three kegs and have the best band on campus playing there tonight. After that, we're going over to Joe's house for an after-party party."

I stood outside the door wanting so badly to fit in, to be accepted. It was ingrained in me. I was a people pleaser; I always had been. So I went "abounding" into the room (probably I didn't abound, but in my memory, I did). Immediately, they shifted in their seats. They had to be thinking, "Uh oh. What are we going to tell her? Look who just walked in."

So Felicia, the leader of the group, innocently said, "Oh hi, Kelly. How are you?"

They were sitting on the floor around a half-eaten pizza, having a big old time talking about the weekend.

And I replied, "Fine. I was just wondering if ya'll have plans for tonight." You could have heard a pin drop.

Felicia said, "Well, Kelly. You know, we're throwing around a couple of ideas, but we have not come to a final decision, but when we get our plans finalized, I'll send someone to come and get you; we'll let you know."

A Stranger to Myself

My heart fell from my chest to the pit of my bowels. I went back to my room and fought back the stinging tears. I tried to squelch my pain by reminding myself they were eighteen and nineteen year olds. Their world revolved around them just like my world used to do. In the end, I called Mom. I've always been a talker as you probably can tell. If I had kept all of my emotions pent up inside of me, I probably would have committed suicide.

"Mom, what's so wrong with me? Why doesn't anybody like me? What happened to my life?"

I had heard it before in my parents' voices. I think they would have cut off their right and left arms just for me to find my smile again. And my mom, week after week, would give me the best advice, and she did it once again. God clearly spoke through her.

"Kelly, I want you to listen to me. There is nothing wrong with you. You have been through a traumatic accident that has left you with not only one disability but two, and the problem is they are silent disabilities. You cannot see a brain injury. You cannot see a partial vision loss. It almost would be easier if you were in a wheelchair because then they could see what was wrong with you and deal with that. But they can't see a brain injury even though they know you are different. They don't know what to do with you. They don't know how to deal with you. They don't understand what you've been through and who you have become." And her next sentence is what turned the light bulb on.

Let me explain what my mother's words meant to me at that moment. When you see someone who is in a wheelchair or has cerebral palsy, instead of taking time to look in the person's eyes and get to know him/her, it is easier to walk by and pretend he/she is invisible or cross to the other side of the street. Maybe people actually think, "If I associate with this person, people may put me into the same category with him/her."

Mom's statement was what I needed to finally realize my dream of fitting in with my sorority sisters was a hopeless cause, and I needed to find a new group of friends who would accept me as I was. So my journey began that day to find a totally new group of friends. We ended the conversation with her saying, "Call your sister." And so I called Ellen.

Ellen knew, bless her heart, how superficial my sorority sisters were. It would have been the same if I'd pledged any sorority. My sister had a boyfriend who she thought was the "cat's meow" and who accompanied her everywhere. She immediately replied, "Henry and I will be by to pick you up at 7:00. Be ready."

Most days when she arrived, I'd descend the stairs after making myself as beautiful as I could only to hear my sister's usual comment: "Kelly, you're not wearing that, are you?"

I would say each time, "Well, I think I look pretty good."

And she'd say each time, "No you don't."

Then she'd grab me by the hand, lead me back up the stairs, go through my closet, and pick through my clothes to find something else for me to wear.

Do you realize what that did to my self-esteem? I went from being super confident to having no confidence at all. And she'd say, "Kelly, I say these things to you not to be critical, but you don't know anymore. You don't have that sense that you had before the accident. You are inappropriate 99 percent of the time."

When she told me that, I thought, "You mean I'm only appropriate 1 percent of the time? I wonder when that 1 percent happens? I better celebrate that 1 percent!"

Chapter Twenty Two

Barry

*The righteous cry out, and the LORD hears them; he delivers
them from all their troubles. The LORD is close to the
brokenhearted and saves those who are crushed in spirit.
The righteous person may have many troubles, but
the LORD delivers him from them all; he protects all his bones,
not one of them will be broken.
Psalm 34:17-20*

I didn't drive much after the lady ran the red light and
slammed into Rod Jr. and me. So Mom had taken me to meet
with Diane Wahlers, who helped students with disabilities at
UGA. She helped to find me tutors, got my textbooks on tape,
ensured I had more time to take tests, and was extremely
supportive and absolutely wonderful to me. Diane also got me
into a support group where she explained one member was
wheelchair bound, one had a service dog, and one student was
dyslexic.

I was relieved to finally find the correct room, which Diane
had given me. I was to participate in my first ever students with
disabilities support group meeting. I had eagerly anticipated this
meeting, maybe it was because I wanted a place to encourage
others with my great story. Or maybe it was because I needed an
outlet to tell people about how unfair and downright mean my
sorority sisters were treating me. No, I think it was because I

needed, in fact, I longed for a place where I could be accepted as the Kelly I was beginning to know for myself.

At the sorority house, I was constantly acting like I was happy and acting as if I were a part of this cool crowd. It was exhausting trying to be someone I no longer was. The weekends that I didn't go home were the worst for me because I was "supposed" to be going out on Friday and Saturday nights to get wasted. But drinking wasn't important to me and I wanted to make a difference. I wanted my life to count for something bigger than myself. God had found me as a helpless young woman in a hospital bed without an ounce of hope. Now I wanted to saturate myself with anything that moved about in the goodness of God.

My first observation while taking a seat in this group was I noticed a very handsome young man. I thought, "Well this can't be that bad. These folks look like compassionate people who are nice and who might accept me."

Diane was a great leader, probably because she was a good listener. She had kind eyes and a sweet smile and accepted everyone she met exactly where he/she was. She always asked, "How is it going? Is anyone having trouble? Is there anything the group can help you with?" We discussed things like the way you begin to like yourself again. What do you do if you never liked yourself? I appreciated how these people understood the disappointing pain from being left out of a group. They knew what it was like to be given a second chance to make a difference in this world. Our little group had big dreams.

Many people might mistakenly wonder how depressing a support group like this might be. "Do y'all just sit around and cry about your daily struggles and disappointments?" No we didn't. These people became more than just friends – they became an extended family. Finally I would be surrounded by friends who may not be going through the exact same thing as I was but would know how it felt to stand outside the circle they desperately wanted an invitation to enter. That's when I learned more about the dyslexic student – Barry – who didn't like himself. He was the handsome young man I'd seen first.

My friend, Barry, taught me that a friend loves at all times. He came into my life at a time when friends did not come easily. Barry had grown up in a middle class family but had always felt like he was on the outside looking in. His wonderful parents took him to church every week and every Wednesday night, but even at church, he felt like an outsider. He had a severe case of dyslexia and had difficult reading, comprehending, and articulating his thoughts and feelings.

But at that first support group meeting, I knew I'd found a life-long friend. We exchanged phone numbers and started hanging out whenever we had a free moment.

I remember Barry saying to me, "Kelly, one thing I admire about you is you know what it is to be at the top and to have lost it all. I believe God is going to bless you and give you everything that you lost and more. I've never had what you had. I never felt like I was a leader, and, in fact, I never felt acceptance in a group because I've always felt different from everybody else."

Barry was such a great encourager for me; he accepted me as I was. Sadly, he was not an encourager for himself. At one of the lowest points in his life, he shared, he'd sat with a loaded gun in his mouth. He asked God to give him courage to pull the trigger.

I told him, "Barry, there are others who have struggled with similar disabilities like yours. God wants to turn your weeping into rejoicing. He wants to use you for a great purpose."

Together, Barry and I found acceptance in a group called "Campus Life," which was similar to another group on campus called Campus Crusade for Christ.

The following summer, I was offered an opportunity to go on a summer missions' trip to Panama City Beach, Florida, There were seven of us who rented a house for the duration of the mission. Our goal was to move in and scout out Panama City Beach to find jobs where we could be used by Christ to win souls for Jesus. Inevitably, I lost touch with Barry during that time.

When we moved there, we all found jobs at different places. Shawn was a seminary student at Dallas Seminary and was home with his fiancé, Gloria, to lead this project. Shawn and I were the only ones working at the same place – the prestigious Waffle Iron right on the strip in Panama City Beach. He was hired as the cook, and I was hired as cashier. Because I needed a ride to work each day, Shawn told management he needed to come in at 9:00 a.m. rather than at 5:30 a.m. That is when my shift started. Our friendship grew that summer; he became someone I greatly admired. And because he is a good listener and I'm a good talker, you can guess who told the most stories on our drives to and from work.

In mid-July, Mom telephone me one night. "Kelly, I have some bad news."

"What?" I was alarmed, thinking someone in the family was hurt.

"Your friend, Barry, committed suicide," she stated quietly.

I was dumbfounded. You see, my teachings were that suicide was the unforgivable sin. Anyone who committed suicide was going directly to hell. I was completely devastated by this sad news and began asking myself, "Why did I lose contact with Barry? Why didn't I call? Why didn't I write to him?"

Mom continued. "Kelly, he'd been dating a young woman who broke up with him. The note he left said he couldn't stand the pain anymore."

Still in shock, I hung up the receiver and went to the small chapel in the basement of the house we were renting. I knew I needed to get away and find solace with my Heavenly Father.

Later, Shawn came and found me on this terrible night when I was grieving the loss of my dear friend. Shawn began by asking me a few questions.

"Kelly, do you believe Jesus Christ forgives sins?"

I looked at him quizzically and answered, "Of course I do. Jesus paid for all our sins – past, present, and future."

"That's right," he agreed. "Do you believe Barry was a Christian?"

Once again, I replied, "I just don't believe it, I know he was. He encouraged me every day to stay close to my Jesus. He knew that Jesus was the only way to God the Father. He most definitely was walking with the Lord."

"Kelly," he continued, "Do you believe God forgives you when you tell a lie?"

"Of course I do, Shawn."

"Do you believe God sees one sin as worse than another?"

"No," I said. "I believe He sees them all the same except for blasphemy of the Holy Spirit."

Shawn nodded his head, agreeing with my conclusion. Then he asked me the *ringer question.* "Do you feel that pulling a trigger is any worse than telling a lie?"

"No. God sees it all as sin."

Shawn assured me. "Kelly, your friend, Barry, is sitting at the feet of Jesus and is being welcomed by our Heavenly Father into the throne room of Heaven."

By this time, I was crying. "I had thought suicide was the unforgiveable sin."

Shawn held up his Bible. "Kelly, I've read this book from cover to cover six times. Nowhere in the Word of God does it say anything about suicide being the unforgiveable sin. You were taught a lie."

Shawn explained that Barry had suffered a lot during his lifetime. "Maybe it was just God's time to take him into His loving arms. Barry is not suffering any more. Barry has the largest smile you've ever seen on his face right now. He's dancing in the throne room of God's glory."

At this point, Shawn knew I needed the arms of my Heavenly Father, so he walked over and gave me a great big hug. I felt God's arms wrapped around me. My heart knew Barry was safe and finally home.

When I returned to school, I went to our support group. I remained a member throughout my undergraduate years.

Chapter Twenty Three

Campus Crusade for Christ

What, then, shall we say in response to this?
If God is for us, who can be against us?
Romans 8:31

I wanted to grow my circle of friends, but I didn't know where else to look.

Because of my brain injury, I had a hard time thinking outside of the box. But I had a friend from Wheeler High School who introduced me to an organization while I lived in the sorority house. My parents acknowledge that because of this organization, I found my smile again. Life had been crashing down like an avalanche, especially because of my isolation. Walt Murray, had gotten involved in Campus Crusade for Christ during his freshman year. He called me every Tuesday or Wednesday night like clockwork with an invitation to join him.

"Kelly, we're having the best meeting tomorrow night at 7:00 p.m. Why don't I swing by your sorority house and pick you up and take you? We can go together. I have so many people who want to meet you."

I'd always come up with some excuse like, "Walt, I'd love to go, but I have a big test coming up in two weeks. Thank you so much, but I really need to study, or I really need to do my nails." I never do my nails, but what I was really implying was, "Those are your friends, Walt. I'm over here in the sorority group, and I want my friends to be over here."

Memories of Walt always brought a smile to my face. I used to babysit for his younger sister with my main job being to protect and keep her two older brothers from killing her. Then something changed in me. Maybe I had gotten fed up with being utterly rejected by my sorority sisters, and Walt got an "A" for persistence. He hadn't taken no for an answer thus far, so I relented and accepted his next invitation.

When we walked along the top of the two hundred-seat lecture room at the University, I immediately felt God's embrace. Walt guided me down the stairs to a section where folks had gathered. He began introducing me to lots of his friends and acquaintances. A young woman named Cheryl stood out more than anyone else I met that night. Cheryl seemed genuine when she welcomed me.

"Kelly! I'm glad to meet you. Walt has told me so much about you. Are you sitting with anyone tonight?"

I replied rather dumbfounded at her friendly familiarity, "No."

She giggled. She was treating me as if I were a celebrity of some kind. "Then would you like to sit with me?"

Remember, for that entire school year, nobody had wanted to sit with me. In fact, everybody in my sorority house wanted to sit at any table minus me. My reception and Cheryl's acceptance just blew me away. My tension and anxiety relaxed. This is what all teenagers are looking for – to feel accepted, to fit in. That first night, we had so much fun singing happy songs, doing silly quacking motions with our arms, and having a blast.

Before attending this meeting with Walt, I don't know what I had expected. These were Christians – not monsters. But for whatever reason, I had envisioned people with huge black moles on their faces or with horns coming out of their heads or with three noses. I didn't know what to expect, but these people were nothing like that. They were really cool. The women were lovely, and the guys were handsome. God was good.

At the end of the meeting, Bill, the director, approached the microphone and asked for everyone's attention. He said, "We just got word that Andrea Campbell's grandmother has passed away. Let's remember her family in prayer. So with Andrea leaving for her grandmother's funeral, we have an open space for next weekend's fall retreat. I will remain standing here until the first woman who wants to take her place comes forward.

Suddenly, there was hope again. My life had been going down hill, and there was no telling what I would have done over the next couple of weeks if my life had stayed where it was. Get out of my way! I was a legally blind woman on a mission to get to Bill first. Honestly, I don't remember how many people I knocked out of the way. And I did.

The event was held outside of Athens, Georgia, at a retreat center. Among lots of activities, we had a square dance. Was it dosie-doe or one step to the right or one step to the center? People like me, who messed up, had the most fun, so I ended up having an absolute blast. While attending that retreat, I had found hope. I had found love. Finally, I had found acceptance by a group of people who cared about me and who were sincere.

When I went home the following weekend, which is where I spent many weekends, my parents saw that I was happy and my smile was back. They were like, "Hallelujah! Hallelujah! We've got Kelly back! We've got Kelly back!" They weren't sure whether I had joined a cult or what this Campus Crusade for Christ was all about, but they were for getting my smile back. God had led me to a place that gave me joy again.

———❀———

Cindy Sullivan became my mentor at Campus Crusade for Christ. I had begun keeping a journal after the accident, but Cindy taught me to journal in a new way. She wrote letters to God, telling Him about all of her complaints and misgivings. She even said it was okay to use curse words if you felt you must. "Kelly, let it all out because Jesus knows your heart anyway. He wants you to be honest with Him when you journal, so it's okay to get angry. And then, take it one step further. After you finish your letter, write a letter to yourself from Jesus. In the letter, state how you think He would respond to you. I challenge you to do this. I try to do it once every three months, but I probably need to do it every month. I don't do it nearly enough."

Her suggestion became a healing point. Through my journaling, God showed me that He never intended for me to feel the pain and hurt I had experienced. His assurance was that He is always with me and will never leave me nor forsake me. He encouraged me to hold on a little longer, so He could show me how He would use this ugly, nasty, hurtful time in my life for His good and for His glory. In reflection, time and time again, God has used my difficulties and challenges to help someone change his/her perspective. It is unbelievable how great our God is.

———❀———

On the fifth year anniversary after the accident, I found my journal writings from the day when Dad had wheeled me outdoors for the first time. That was the day I'd asked him, "Dad, how long will it take for me to get back to normal?" Do you remember his answer? It was five years. I sat on my bed and penned, I am proud of what the Lord has helped me to do, and for the first time, I can honestly say that I like myself.

A Stranger to Myself

It took five years for me to honestly be able to write that sentence. That statement of self-acceptance became a huge milestone in my recovery. Recovery is a process that is different for every person. You may have been sexually abused by a family member when you were young. You may have grown up in an abusive alcoholic home. Every person has experienced trauma in life. We just have to fight and struggle to make sense of and embrace our scars. I used to always try and hide my scars. I used to put heavy makeup on to disguise my scars and never would tell people about my vision loss, but today, I am proud of my scars. And I am proud to be a person who is legally blind and who uses a cane to walk in public. God has taught me that He can use our scars to point people to Him. Scars are things He can use when we testify about his miraculous work. They become a roadmap of where we've been and where we can go – if we allow ourselves.

Chapter Twenty Four

Ellen to the Rescue

For the Son of man has come to save that which was lost.
Matthew 18:11 NKJV

By this time, I should have been going into my junior year
of college, but because I'd missed a year, I was entering the
second half of my sophomore year. I was only taking one serious
course and a physical education class because that was all I
could handle. It was more than enough, it required me to study
twelve to sixteen hours a day for the one course. By that time,
Mary had informed me I was eligible to be in a two-girl room. I
didn't want to live in the sorority house anymore, but I didn't
know where else to live. Looking back now, I wonder why I just
didn't go back into the dorm. Anything would have been better
than living in that sorority house, but that was all I knew, and I
desired to fit in. People with a brain injury have a hard time
troubleshooting to find solutions and alternatives.

When the sorority posted next year's housing chart in the
common area, I was one of the first ones to put my name on a
line for a two-girl room. The other line I left blank. I went to the
little chapel and prayed to God for somebody nice, for somebody
that would be able to accept me for who I was. One of my
roommates had been cruel to me. I remember on this particular
day, Ellen called. She and Mom kept close tabs on me

because they realized how bad living in the sorority house had gotten.

Ellen asked, "Kelly, how are you doing?"

As usual, I was in my room by myself where I always was because no one hung out in my room.

I replied, "Not good, Ellen. Nobody has put a name on the line beside my name."

Ellen assured me by saying, "Well, just hang in there Kelly. You hang in there and don't give up. Don't you dare give up and try not to worry. Everything's going to be okay."

When our conversation ended, Ellen telephoned Mom and declared in a loud voice, "I'm tired of these brats doing this to her."

As I've mentioned, the homes at the University of Georgia are humongous antebellum homes where one hundred girls can live at one time. I was sitting in the middle of my bed, when I remember hearing squealing tires on the circular driveway's pavement. I heard a door open and then slam closed. I heard heavy footsteps on the concrete steps; the sorority house's front door slammed open. I heard stomping up the wooden stairs. Now keep in mind, there were huge doors on these eight girl rooms. Suddenly, my door was flung open, and my sister, as if in a super hero costume, valiantly burst into the room, and she threw a leather trunk onto the adjacent bed, and in a drill sergeant's voice, ordered me as follows: "Kelly, get up. Help me pack. I'm getting you the heck away from these self-centered witches."

My eyes couldn't get much wider. All I could do was stammer meekly, "Okay. Okay."

I stood up and started throwing things in the trunk while Ellen yelled,

"These bleeping bleeps have been nothing but bad to you. They don't deserve you."

She grabbed my books, and we walked out of that home – not speaking to anyone. That was the last time I stepped foot inside or outside of that house.

This was supposed to have been Ellen's first time of enjoying her own room at college. Needless to say, she never had her own room. She sacrificially shared it with her younger sister as a roommate. Ellen became my heroine – for sure. I am thankful my sister was a senior in the business school at that time. We became better friends during spring quarter, and I became better friends with Ellen's sorority's sisters than I ever did with my own. If I had it to do all over again, I would have sent a counselor, who was knowledgeable about people with brain injuries, ahead of me to explain all these things to them. But that is hindsight, and the road moves forward.

Ellen:

There were a couple of the sorority girls who tried to help with using the car to drive Kelly around, but it was just too much. The bottom line was this: Kelly was very hard to live with. Because Kelly could not see very well and had no short-term memory, she could not keep track of her things. On top of all this, noises bothered her – even Swatch watches. When these watches first came onto the market, they made very audible ticking sounds. And small repetitive noises drove Kelly mad, so by the second semester, it became apparent that Kelly should not stay in the sorority house because she was miserable. For the second semester, she moved into an apartment with me and two of my sorority sisters. My sister and I shared a bedroom where she studied all the time. It was difficult for her because she had to transfer everything into long term memory, or she could not remember it.

And we struggled with the new Kelly. She had no fashion sense, often wanting to wear the strangest things. She had no filter, often saying whatever popped into her head. She had no sense of personal hygiene, often not recognizing when an item of clothing was dirty or she was dirty. It seemed that all I did was criticize her, and she felt constantly picked on.

But after we got past the basic hygiene and appropriate dress issues, I learned to love her for the new person that she was. I realized I could not turn her back into the person she had been; that person was gone forever. Once I changed my attitude, life with my sister became easier.

So that left us with nothing to fight over except the car. I still didn't think Kelly should be driving, but Mom and Dad and Kelly thought she should. They were too afraid that telling her she could not *drive* would *drive* her to want to *drive* even more. She had kept her driver's license from before the accident, had passed all the DMV tests, and had taken lessons from a private instructor. The decision not to drive would have to be Kelly's.

Chapter Twenty Five

A Father's Love

Charm is deceptive, and beauty is fleeting;
but a woman who fears the Lord is to be praised.
Proverbs 31:30

While still in my zombie years, I knew with the attorney's help, we had won a settlement, but I had no idea if we had won $100 or $1 million. I remember us taking the attorney and his wife out to dinner on the day when we had finally settled. Purposefully, I believe my parents didn't want me to know the amount because of the horror stories they had heard over the years about teenagers being given large sums of money and blowing it all in a year's time. After the settlement was won from the trucking company, I purchased the Nissan Maxima. It was the nicest car I had ever owned even though I don't remember driving too much at college because I could walk or take the campus bus to any location, but Ellen and I shared the Nissan Maxima. Even though I failed to drive a lot, I remember thinking, *I cannot live without being able to drive.* It was a form of independence for me, but my sister wanted to take it away.

"What do you mean, Ellen? Don't you think I can drive?" I asked when she refused to allow me to drive her one day.

Ellen was straight with me. "I am not riding with you, Kelly." And she stuck to it.

A Stranger to Myself

In the end, Ellen was the only one out of the family who was right about this issue. But at this time, no one had explained to me that I was legally blind. I knew I had lost some of my vision, but because I could see out of one eye, I was raised with the mantra, "If there is a will, there is a way." I thought with the special glasses, the little mirror on my side mirror, and a concave mirror on my center mirror, I could drive and never would admit I couldn't. So I did drive *a little* at college. It was more about the *norm* that I wanted to hold on to.

Each weekend before I left the sorority house for good, I had gone home for solace from the living hell I was in. I had made friends with a couple of people who also were from Atlanta, so I'd ride with them, and Mom or Dad would pick me up at their homes. As a result of my weekly sorority hell and my desire to fit in, I became bulimic. According to most dictionaries, bulimia is an eating disorder where the sufferer eats excessively followed by self-induced vomiting or other unhealthy measures to avert gaining weight. I had wanted so much to be that sorority image, but after the accident, I had gained weight. When the braces were finally removed from my teeth and my molars were fixed, I had eaten everything and anything in sight, including all three meals at college and snacks, while my ability and desire to exercise had diminished.

But it was bulimia that put me in control again. I was able to decide when I wanted to binge. I was able to decide when I wanted to hide in the attic. I was able to decide if I wanted to visit the infrequently used third floor bathroom. I was able to decide how to deal with not having friends. That's why I decided to binge and purge.

When I left the sorority house for good and moved in with Ellen, my life had improved. I changed from being miserable to *almost* being content. When the fall quarter ended, Ellen and her two roommates were graduating, so I moved in with two new friends, Nicole and Megan, and finished the spring quarter.

Afterwards, Natalie, a friend from Campus Crusade for Christ, asked me, "Kelly, do you want to room together when we come back next year?" She was a new acquaintance and seemed tomboyish but cool and level-headed. Natalie had rented a two bedroom apartment, and her current roommate was moving out.

"Do you really want to room with me?" I asked.

"Yeah, I think we'd have a really good time," she said with a smile.

After about two months of living together, Natalie said, "Kelly, I want to talk to you about something. I wouldn't say anything to you if I didn't love you. You need help. I just followed you to the bathroom and heard what you were doing in there. You need counseling for this. You need professional help to get over this. Kelly, bulimia kills people and ruins your insides. I will go with you and hold your hand. I'll do whatever it takes to make you well again." Natalie had spent the previous summer working on a mission trip in Yellowstone National Park. Her newfound friend there had had an eating disorder – bulimia – so she was attuned to the signs.

I cried from embarrassment and hurt, and Natalie cried right there with me. And true to her word, she accompanied me to my first mental health appointment and even accompanied me two or three more times. It seemed I was always in counseling of some type. Natalie had researched this disease and was knowledgeable enough to talk with the counselor during my sessions. It was apparent that any counselor at a college with female students had to be an expert on eating disorders. The counselor explained to me that I had lost control of so much that bulimia was something I thought I could control. And this counselor helped me to realize that a big part of my bulimia was based on wanting to please my father.

Dad was a marathon runner and a triathlete, so fitness was important to him. He would run a marathon for 26.2 miles and return home with a first place trophy. In fact, he believed by his words and actions that "thinness is next to godliness." After the accident and the sorority house disaster, I realized my weight gain was out of control and had worked hard to lose weight.

There is no other man I respect greater than my father, so Sundays became our favorite day of the week because we could spend it together. He told Mom, "Marilyn, you know Kelly doesn't go to the Catholic Church anymore. I'm sorry but I want to take her to another church. I'm sorry to miss our captivating Catholic service." (He was being facetious; together, we had watched the heads bob during many a Catholic service.)

Dad was excited that he finally got to hear a real preacher like Charles Stanley and Andy Stanley. And later, we began attending Mt. Parrin, where Dr. Paul Walker was the minister. Soon, his phenomenal son took over Mt. Parrin North, which was closer to my parents' home. The church choir had one hundred members. I loved having Dad all to myself on Sundays. After service, we would go out for lunch. One Sunday I was especially proud because I had dieted hard all week long. I proudly announced to my father who was sitting across the table from me, "Dad, this week I lost four pounds on Nutrisystem."

But his reply broke my heart. "Oh well, that only leaves, what, twenty more pounds to go?"

Dejected and with a broken heart, I yearned to reply, "Dad, did you not hear me? I've lost four pounds in one week! Can't you say something encouraging?"

But that's just how my dad was. He didn't realize how different girls were from boys. Even when I'd make a bowl of popcorn and get ready to pour the butter on, into the kitchen my dad would come with a snide comment, "Kelly, you know what that butter does. It goes straight to your thighs."

"But, Dad," I'd moan. "I want butter on my popcorn."

So this counselor helped me to see that I would do almost anything to please my father, including losing weight. I thought that if I were skinny and a size six instead of a size ten or twelve, he would love me more. At five foot, eight, I tried to maintain my weight at 130 pounds.

The counselor suggested I write Dad a letter, which I did, and Natalie and the counselor read it. I wasn't even sure I'd send it to him, but it felt good – a catharsis –to write it. In the letter, I explained how deeply it hurt me when I had lost four pounds, and he immediately reminded me of how much more I needed to go. "Dad," I wrote, "because you prize thinness so much (he only had four percent body fat – that is how in shape he was), if I ever gained fifty pounds, I seriously would be afraid that you would not love me anymore. With all due respect, Dad, all I want you to do is love me as I am. Kelly."

I decided to mail it, and I'll never forget the phone call I received from him.

He said, "Kelly, I am sorry I hurt you. I don't know why I'm like that; maybe it's because of the way I was raised. My mother was always thin and a socialite, so she'd look the part of a wealthy person." And he didn't stop there. He wrote me a letter that stated, "I am more concerned about your sister's and your weight than I am about my own weight. I didn't realize it had such an effect on your sister and you. I'm sorry for causing heartache and pain in your life."

I prize that letter, which I stored away as a precious memento. It took inner strength for him to share his feelings. From that time on, my dad no longer spoke about Ellen's or my weight, at least not directly to us. With having Natalie to be accountable to, seeing the counselor weekly, and by finding peace within myself and with God, I quit being bulimic and took another step towards accepting my new *normal*.

Natalie was a devout Christian who encouraged me to memorize scriptures. I never realized how much the Word of God had to say about your body image. For example, in Matthew 15:11, Jesus says, "What goes into someone's mouth does not defile them, but what comes out of their mouth, that is what defiles them." Your body is the temple of the Holy Spirit. By reading the scripture, praying, and joining Campus Crusade for Christ, finally, I felt like I belonged. I was making new friends with people who accepted me and loved me for who I was and not what I looked like or what I could do for them. Unaware of the unexpected detours ahead, this is when my life became a lot happier – even joyful.

Chapter Twenty Six

My Hero

To the Jews who had believed him, Jesus said,
"If you hold to my teaching, you are really my disciples.
Then you will know the truth, and the truth will set you free."
John 8:31-32

It's not hard to comprehend that Dad is my hero. He's always been *the* six million dollar man in my life; there is nothing Dad can't do. He used to run 26.2-mile marathons with a mileage breakdown time of six minutes per mile and a body fat percentage of four percent; that is unbelievable; that is unheard of. Even now, I can't run an eight or nine minute mile. Dad had joined a running club, the Chattahoochee Road Runners years earlier, so he'd run with five or six of the members several times a week. If my dad didn't get a two-hour run in, he didn't consider it a work out. That was his *normal* run, as he called it, his "run of the mill" run.

When Dad entered his forties, he began having minor injuries. Even though his injuries were not major, he began thinking, "Now is the time I might need to transition into triathlons because they are much easier on the body." Once he made that decision, nothing was going to stop him. So he purchased a $1400 bike, which, in 1987 and still is, a large sum of money. His bike-riding began, and as *normal*, he became an outstanding bicyclist. Just like his running, his tri-athlete training became an addiction. After he started training for the triathlons, he'd bike a hundred miles each week. He began swimming; he swam a mile or two every night. Determination runs in our family. Every Saturday, he'd come home from marathons, half-marathons, mud-runs, or tennis tournaments with a first place trophy. That was just the *norm* for my dad. But he never boasted about winning, or thought anything else about it because he had a very competitive nature. So when he turned forty seven, he was really enjoying these triathlons and decided to enter the "Iron Man." In 1987, the only Iron Man event was held in Kona, Hawaii. It was the only one available in the world.

There were only three guys in the running club who could compete at Dad's level. So far he had always beat them. But on this particular Saturday's morning race, one runner beat him for the first time. Well that elevated Dad's competitive spirit a few notches. The following week, he trained and trained and trained. Whenever Dad remembers this time, he says, "My addiction led me to train excessively."

On the morning of July 22, 1987, on my brother's eighteenth birthday, just two long years after my accident, my family was hit with another tragedy. This time it was Dad.

As usual, Dad had awakened at 4:00 a.m., gone to the pool and swam for two miles, and headed to work. During lunchtime, he had thrown on his running shorts and running shoes and ran ten to fifteen miles. Dad was blessed to have Rex Wallin, a Christian man whom Dad respected highly, as his boss. He had no issues with Dad taking a two hour lunch because he knew the work would get done, and besides, Dad was good at what he did for a living. Afterward, he had returned to the office, took a shower, and went back to work.

That night at dinner, Dad said he felt a little tired because he'd been pushing himself, so he planned a night of relaxation.

But Ellen's boyfriend, Henry, had other plans. He was a good athlete, too, and enjoyed working out with Dad.

"Rod, come on," he suggested. "Let's take a short fifty mile bike ride. I think I can take you tonight," he teased. With such a competitive spirit, it was hard for Dad to dismiss the temptation.

So he said, "Okay, Henry. Let's take a short ride."

Now in the '80s, Atlanta was not a bike-friendly town, so after hanging their bikes on the Volkswagen Rabbit's rack, they headed to the outskirts of Atlanta. Once arriving at Highway 41, they unloaded their bikes and began their fifty mile ride towards Stone Mountain. This is no short drive even in a car, much less on a bike. Atlanta is a very hilly town – huge inclines – and this road was known for being tough.

Predictably, Dad had biked almost a whole hill ahead of Henry on his new Eddie Mertz bike in just a short while. As Henry topped a hill, he'd see Dad three quarters of the way up the next hill. Dad was riding down a steep incline at around fifty-five miles per hour. In other words, they were "whipping it" when Dad remembers seeing two large stones on the road that he could not avoid, so he braced himself for a fall. He hit one of the stones just right, and it threw him thirty feet off the road; he landed in a ten foot deep ditch off the shoulder of the road. He immediately blacked out.

Henry came over the crest of the hill, he didn't see Dad where he should have been, topping the next hill. With great intuition and immediate insight, Henry thought, *Wait, something must be wrong*. He began pedaling slower down the hill, looking at each side of the road for Dad. Initially, he didn't see him. So he sped up and topped the next hill. He turned and looked down the hill behind him and looked up the hill in front of him to ensure Dad hadn't caught a wind sprint and was farther away. He still didn't see anything. So Henry turned around, and retraced his previous distance. Once again, he found nothing. On the third time down the hill, Dad came to. As he was inching his back up off the ground onto his elbows, Henry caught the movement of a helmet deep in the overgrown brush. He threw down his bike, stumbled down the embankment, and screamed, "Rod! Rod! What happened? Are you okay? Are you okay?"

Dad, the eternal optimist, replied, "Yeah, Henry. I'm okay, but can you get this brush off my legs. I can't move them."

Henry glanced up and down the ditch. He was amazed at how far off the road Dad was. He carefully examined Dad's legs, and while there was a lot of loose brush on his legs, nothing was holding them down from being able to move.

He switched into cautious mode, and said, "Rod, this may sound crazy, but I need for you to lie back and stay as still as possible. I'm going to get some help!"

"Okay. Try not to be long," Dad yelled back.

Remember, this was 1987; very few people owned a cell phone. Were they even available back then? Yeah, I think so: The bag kind with the big heavy phones or walkie-talkie type radios. So Henry ran up the embankment and mounted his bike. Within fifteen or twenty minutes, a helicopter was buzzing over the exact place where Dad was lying on his back. While it blew up a lot of dust and dirt into Dad's face and the surrounding area, it landed nearby. The EMTs carefully placed him on a backboard, loaded him into the helicopter, and asked, "Mr. Spence. Where would you like to go?"

"Kennestone Hospital," Dad replied. That was the hospital he knew best, and it was where I had been taken two years earlier.

A "God incidence" occurred shortly afterward when the helicopter landed on the hospital's pad and the EMTs ushered him into the emergency entrance. The same surgeon that was on call the day I was brought in was the same emergency surgeon on call the night Dad was brought in.

My accident had happened right before finals week in my winter quarter of my freshman year at the University of Georgia. Dad's accident happened right before finals week in my summer quarter. I'd been on campus studying and going to class since 8:00 that morning. It was probably 8:00 or 9:00 in the evening and the library was going to close. I called for someone in my family to come and get me, but no one answered the home phone.

"That's strange," I thought. "Nobody's home." Something, call it intuition, told me to call our next-door neighbors, the Masons. They had become our closest friends, especially after my accident.

Cheryl Mason answered the phone, "Hello?"

"Mrs. Mason, this is Kelly. Do you know if anyone is home at my house?"

Cheryl's voice broke. "Kelly, it's your father."

I cried, "What happened? What happened to Dad? Please tell me."

She was crying, too. "Rod had a bad bicycle accident."

Oh Lord! I thought. We'd always warned him to be careful around cars; car drivers don't seem to care about bicyclists. I made up my mind that Dad had been hit by a car or had a run-in of some sort with another vehicle.

So I asked, "Mrs. Mason, did he get hit by a car? What happened?"

She said, "No, Kelly. It wasn't a car. Rod, Jr. is on his way to get you, so stay where you are. Your dad's at Kennestone Hospital. Your mom and Ellen are already there."

My head started spinning; my knees went weak. My dad was my lifeline.

Chapter Twenty Seven

Persistence

When you cannot stand, He will bear you in His arms.
-- St. Francis of Assisi

I experienced many emotions while I waited for Rod, Jr.
Dearest God, please don't take my dad away after all we've
been through. I can't imagine life without him. Please don't take
him away. He's my greatest cheerleader and inspiration. He has
truly been the wind beneath my wings, I prayed.

I stood on the sidewalk outside of the library with just a
streetlight shining on me. I had so many questions for God. In
fact, the first one was, *Where are you God?* I remembered
feeling those old feelings of entitlement come back. *How could*
you, Lord? How could so much tragedy happen to one family –
MY FAMILY? The self-pity took control. I had to remind myself,
Your dad detests self-pity.

I began crying because Cheryl hadn't shared a lot of details.
I didn't know if Dad was alive or dead. Surely she would have
said, so I prayed again, *God, this can't be happening. Wasn't it*
enough for my family to go through my accident? And now, my
poor mother has to go through another tragedy. God, we can't
handle it. God, you have to handle it for us! Please don't let my
dad die.

When my brother found me, I climbed into the car, and we began crying together. "Rod, I can't handle it. How are we going to get through this?"

My younger brother said in a matter-of-fact way, "Kelly, we're going to be strong for Dad." I'd forgotten how mature my brother was.

During the forty-five minute drive to the hospital, I composed myself and dried my eyes. When we entered the doors, we checked in at the front desk. Mom, Ellen, and Henry rose from their seats and came to embrace us. Some of Dad's running friends were sitting in the uncomfortable waiting room chairs. Almost immediately after we arrived, the assistant surgeon met us in the corridor.

"We're going to operate on your father; his life is not in danger, but it appears there may be spinal cord damage. We won't know the extent until we are further in."

"What is the likelihood of spinal damage or what we're facing?" Rod, Jr. asked.

The assistant surgeon cleared his throat. "We're not sure if the damage is in the neck or in the lower back. Depending upon the location, it may mean he is a quadriplegic or a paraplegic. We're not sure of anything, yet, so hold tight. We're going to do our best."

United, we stood as a family, watching the doctor disappear through the double doors; with his departure, I suddenly felt this overwhelming sense of being lost. I was completely and utterly devastated with sorrow for my father. I knew my father would want me and my family to think positive thoughts. Now was the time to be strong and resilient. It hit me that I was experiencing the same thing my family had experienced two years earlier after my car accident. Just as they had prayed and joined together to help me, I now needed to do the same for my dad. We had good news and he was alive. We all sensed God was holding him and us in the palm of His hand. Whatever happened, our faith in Christ would help us to make it through this tragedy just as He had helped us make it through my tragedy. And whatever the medical results were, it would be the beginning of a new life just as mine had been.

A nurse led my family to a cot where Dad was laying before they prepared him for surgery. Rod, Jr. reached him first. Wet tears clung to Dad's cheeks as he told my brother, "I can't feel my legs. I don't think I'll ever walk again." Rod said this was the second time that he and Dad had cried together. After hugging him and telling him we loved him, we left for the surgery to begin.

At 7:00 a.m., a nurse interrupted our prayers and the loud ticking of the clock. She led us to an office where two surgeons waited. Dad's surgery had lasted all night, so we were desperate for news – any news about his current condition and prognosis. But when one of the surgeons saw us, he was moved for words. So were we.

"Oh, my gosh!" he exclaimed. "I need a minute. I cannot believe this! Wasn't it about two years ago that we were in an all-night surgery with you, Kelly? And now here we are with Rod's surgery. I can't believe this is the same family!"

Dr. Schlachter explained his spinal cord had been broken at thoracic 11, which was the lower part of his back. Two steel rods had been inserted into his spine, and he had five vertebras fused together. Thank God for that blessing! As we exhaled and smiled to each other with relief, the doctor cleared his throat.

"Uh ah. This means Rod will have full use of his upper body." I held my breath as he continued. "But he will be paralyzed from the waist down. I'm sorry."

I couldn't imagine this prognosis for my dad. The use of his legs meant everything to him: tennis, running, swimming, skiing, biking. I looked at my mother, who was smiling in the midst of her tears. She thanked Dr. Schlachter and the other surgeon for all that they'd done. That was just like my mother: grace under fire. Isn't that the saying? Rod, Jr.'s bottom lip was trembling. Ellen was crying softly against Henry's shoulder. Henry looked perplexed, unable to comprehend how someone's life could change that quickly.

Dr. Schlachter noticed our individual demeanors and sought to change the tension in the room. "And son," he said as he stared into Henry's eyes, "You did a good job keeping him still and getting help as quickly as you did."

Acknowledging the physician's accolades, we all agreed audibly and took turns hugging Henry and thanking him for all he'd done for Dad the night before. Then we thanked the surgeon, who pulled me toward him and hugged me tightly.

"I do good work, don't I?" He asked me with a laugh.

"You sure do," Mom agreed and patted him on the back.

"Yes, you do, Dr. Schlachter. If it weren't for you and so many others, I wouldn't be standing here."

"Oh, well," he nodded. "I only played a small part. We all know why you're here. There's a greater physician than me."

"You're definitely right about that," I said. "And I'm glad to be here."

As we walked out of the office and back toward the waiting room, I kept telling myself, *It could have been worse. He could have been a quadriplegic like Joni.* Then I realized I hadn't thanked Jesus for answering my prayers and felt remorseful and ungrateful. *Thank you for giving Dad back to us. He's alive because of your mercy and ultimate grace. Thank you for bringing him through the surgery and for letting Dr. Schlachter*

*be his doctor. Thank you for guiding Dr. Schlachter's skillful
hands once again as they helped my family. And thank you for
this prognosis. It's hard to accept, but I pray that you please
help us to be strong, so we can be strong for Dad. He's always
been strong for us; he'll need our help with this adjustment.*

Most spinal cord injuries occur at the end of summer and
happen to men more often than women because men tend to be
more reckless. For every eight men injured, there is one woman
injured. The number one cause of spinal cord injuries is
automobile accidents; the second leading cause is diving
accidents.

Mom held Dad's hand as Dr. Schlachter explained the
injury and prognosis. She said Dad became very depressed the
following few days, reasonably so. His way of life for forty-
seven years had been shattered by a stone in the road; he went
into the ditch with legs that worked and left the ditch with
paralyzed legs that couldn't work anymore.

But God is good all the time, and His blessings are
bountiful and timely. One of the doctors in my parents' dinner
group was a surgeon at the Shepherd Spinal Center in Atlanta. At
the time, it was one of two hospitals in the world that treated
spinal injuries. And as it turned out, it was in our backyard –
only forty-five minutes from our home. Their surgeon friend
pulled some strings, and Dad was admitted into the Center
within a week after his accident where he remained for two
months, learning how to cope with his new life. And just as Dad
had been my inspiration during my hospital stay, I spent every
possible minute in his hospital room.

And while it seemed several windows were closing in Dad's
life, God was opening many double-doors. His old boss, Rex
Wallin, had started his own construction company while Dad
was in rehab. Mr. Wallin visited Dad at the Shepherd Center to

ask him if he'd work for him as an estimator. Dad had spent his "two legged life" in the field as a superintendent, owner's representative, and acted as a civil engineer on commercial projects. Even though he was computer illiterate and had little estimating experience, he knew how to read blue prints and realized this offer was a blessing from God, so he almost yelled his response, "Yes!"

George Murray, my good friend Walt's dad, came every evening while Dad was hospitalized. George was an ex-Vietnam Vet and a proud runner in the Chattahoochee Road Runners. George would enter the room and sit down in the chair beside the bed.

"Hey Rod. Good to see you today."

After they'd exchanged customary pleasantries, they'd sit for two hours in silence, watching television or just spending the minutes together in thoughtful solitude. Afterward, he'd stand and say, "Well, Rod. I'll see you tomorrow. Have a great night."

Then he'd leave. To this day, Dad says, "George Murray will forever have a gold star beside his name in my book because I just needed to know I had a friend who cared."

What is the name of that song? "Silence is Golden." Well that's the inspiration and motivation George gave to his friend, Rod. In addition, George and the other club members of the Chattahoochee Road Runners, sponsored a 10K race in Dad's honor. With the money they made, they purchased Dad his first racing wheelchair. Because of Dad's healthy life style, his rehabilitation went well, and he was discharged earlier than predicted. You can take a man's legs away, but you can't take his competitive spirit – at least not my dad's. Three months after getting released from the hospital, he immediately joined the Shepherd Wheel Chair Racing Team and began training in his new chair.

His boss, Mr. Wallin, had been extremely supportive of my family during my accident, and as a solid Christian man, he displayed his patience once again when Dad returned to work and learned how to use the estimating software, which covered up a lot of initial flaws that he made. Work became challenging yet rewarding, and he eventually became a pretty good estimator and project manager.

Dad has said many times over the years, "I will be forever grateful that he [Rex Wallin] reached out to me at the lowest point in my life and gave me the opportunity and blessing of working for him."

Before Dad's injury and my accident, everyone in the family except Mom had run in the Peachtree Road Race every July 4. Dad and I had run the race for eight years total, more than anyone in the family, my only miss being 1985. But I ran it the following year after my rehabilitation. The Peachtree Road Race is known as the world's largest 10K with about 60,000 runners. It's the most fun you can run anywhere. You see Army guys running in it with their fatigues and boots on, yelling cadences. Lucy and I always got behind these guys because we thought we were prima donnas and they'd enjoy having us stare them on. A little flirting never hurt anyone. Dad always finished the race as one of the top 200 runners out of a field of 60,000 and had received special medallions for his accomplishments.

After Dad's accident in 1989, that next July 4th, he ran the Peachtree Road Race the following year in his racing wheelchair and beat his best time ever when he had run it. There is a notorious hill known as "heartbreak hill." It gets its name honestly because that is just what people think about it. Runners have been known to have heart attacks climbing this hill, but it didn't deter my father in the least – not even in a wheelchair. *The Atlanta Constitution* and *The Marietta Daily Journal*, along with journalists from New York, wrote many articles about my remarkable father. *The Atlanta Constitution* actually wrote a series about his amazing feat.

The Sunday morning after the race, I had dressed for church and was coming down the stairs when Dad wheeled over to me and said, "Kelly, you may want to read this." He thrust a folded newspaper toward me.

Right on the front page of *The Atlanta Constitution* sports section was my dad's picture!

"Dad! This is the article you were telling me about," I squealed. "This is great!"

He said, smiling, "Yeah, and I want you to read it."

So I began reading the article, which discussed him being a civil engineer who built multi-million dollar buildings, who liked to be onsite rather than working behind a desk. It explained about his accident and how he'd become a bidder, which was beneficial to the organization because who would you rather prepare bids than an engineer who knew the ins and outs?

In the article, the reporter asked him point blank, "Rod, was there ever a point when you wanted to give up, throw in the towel, and say, 'This is too hard. I can't do this?'"

My dad replied, "Yes. There was a time."

"Tell me about that time," she probed.

He affirmed he'd been in the darkest depression he'd ever experienced. He continued, "That's when my daughter, Kelly, abounded into the room with a bright smiling face. When I saw her and remembered all she'd gone through and all she'd fought to regain, I knew the days of self-pity were over. Kelly overcame a major brain injury in 1985 and is back attending college at the University of Georgia. I thought of the days when she'd take me to the hospital gym and show me how she could crawl. Two weeks later, she showed me how she could pull herself up and walk on parallel bars. My clock struck twelve. When I saw her face and all that she'd overcome with such a positive attitude, I knew I couldn't quit. I couldn't give up. I had to press on. I had to get better."

Overwhelmed, I cried tears of joy and thanksgiving; God had allowed me to live and become my dad's inspiration just as he'd been mine. Our hearts were full of sunshine and love as we hugged each other that Sunday morning.

A few days later, he was interviewed on television and recited the same story. Today, I can think back to the time when Dad was hospitalized. We were told many stories by paraplegics who were receiving treatment at the Center. Too many of those young men told about their wives, who'd walked into their rooms, placed their wedding rings on the table, and walked out without another word.

I am so proud of my mother. She never faltered, not even one day. Mom never felt sorry for herself. She saw what had to be done for her family, and she did it. She's always been supportive and is the same today. As my brother so eloquently stated, "When Dad was able to run the Peachtree Marathon in his wheelchair, this is when I realized how true the cliché is that says 'Behind every great man is a greater woman!' My mom has carried us through. Thank God for my mom!"

Mom and Dad were invited to attend a four-day Christian retreat called "The Walk to Emmaus." Dad seemed reluctant to attend, but Mom really wanted to go. I guess her persistence and his need to pray after his mother's recent death, were the deciding factors. Finally, he agreed.

On the first day of the retreat, they learned about priorities when the leader asked the question, "Where do you spend your time, money, and thoughts?"

Mom said, "What an eye opening discovery that question was. When I answered, 'Playing tennis, shopping, running errands,' I realized these activities took up way too much of my time and money. God needed to be first in every activity of my life."

Dad agreed, "That retreat was the beginning of my formation as a Christian leader. Shortly after the retreat, I had my own *burning bush experience.* One night I was in bed reading the Bible. I began having uncontrollable leg spasms. While trying to calm them, I heard God's voice saying, 'This too shall pass. I'm going to use you in great ways.' That is when I opened my heart to Jesus and accepted Him as my Lord and Savior."

Afterward, my parents began to read the Bible daily. and thirsted to learn and know more. Dad joined a prayer group, taught Sunday School, and joined another Christian group at the church that performed charity work. Together, they joined a Community Bible Study as another step to grow their faith. Dad worked on many other "Walk to Emmaus" retreats and gave a few of the talks. He eventually became the leader of a "Walk to Emmaus" retreat for 120 men. "Talk about getting out of your comfort zone," he laughed. Dad also became a Grand Knight (leader) in his church group.

"It's amazing what you can do with the support of Christian men," he said. Marilyn was even amazed. She declared, 'You are finally the Christian leader of this house. This is a big change from when our kids were growing up.'"

"The Walk to Emmaus" retreat helped Mom deal with Dad's and my accidents and helped her see how God was working in our lives. The support of the friends they made on that retreat are still with them today. It changed my life and my siblings' lives too, because we saw our parents change to living out their faith -- not just talking about it.

When a child can witness her father on his knees in prayer, the child will take notice.

Mom says, "I can only give thanks to Him who strengthens and guides us. We certainly have done little to deserve the blessings that He has poured out on us."

Because Dad is still active and competitive, no little thing like paralysis was going to restrain his strong willpower and determination. He began enjoying his new life and was introduced to wheelchair tennis, basketball, snow and water skiing, and hand cycling.

Mom still accompanies Dad to his tennis tournaments, where he plays in wheelchair tournaments and is ranked in the Southeast as one of the top senior players in the country. They travel to places where these big tournaments are held like Hilton Head Island, South Carolina; Augusta, Georgia; and Savannah, Georgia. And as *normal*, Dad always returns with another first place trophy. In addition, Dad plays tennis with folks who have legs (he gets two bounces) and with other paraplegics.

"I have really enjoyed wheelchair sports," he tells everyone.

As I've said, he's amazing. He may have fallen off the "beaten path," but he's back on the road again!

Rod, Jr. proudly tells everyone to this day, "We were so proud to watch Dad reclaim his life. This was my miracle number two."

Chapter Twenty Eight

Mission Blessings

*Listen to the advice and accept instruction
that you may gain wisdom in the future.*
Proverbs 19:20 NRS

The year was 1990, and I had finally done it! I was graduating with my undergraduate degree in Educational Psychology. All of those late nights studying eighteen hours a day had finally paid off! What I had come to realize was the main reason I had studied so much was due to my lack of short-term memory. But the hidden reason of why I had *chosen* to study so much was because as long as I was focused on studying, I did not have to focus on the fact that I was "damaged goods." The reason why I had not gone out on weekdays or many weekends was because I had had no one to go out with. Studying had been my excuse to cover the pain.

With my newfound friends in Campus Crusade for Christ and my worst years behind me, I was feeling pretty good. I was elated and extremely proud of myself and my accomplishments. Imagine this! To this day, I can show you actual neurological reports written by leading doctors that stated, "Due to the severity of the brain damage, Kelly should not attempt college again." They deduced this based on the batteries of tests that I had been given after the accident. There were three or more such reports that stated the same harsh recommendation. These

158

doctors were only doing their jobs. They were writing their reports based on their education, their experience, and their own knowledge. I would like to point out something to every doctor that reads this book: *You cannot measure the God-given human spirit. The drive that God has put in a person to succeed and glorify HIM.* When I look at those reports today, I am so thankful my parents had the God-given wisdom to not allow me to put my eye on these reports. I never read what the doctors had written. There is no telling what reading or hearing those reports would have done to my spirit. I had enough things going against me. I certainly did not need their recommendations to defeat my aspirations. There was no doubt in my mind I was going back to college, and by golly, I proved them all wrong. A verse that helped me comes from Luke 19:14 and paraphrased is, "What may seem impossible to man is possible with God, for there is nothing impossible with God."

After graduation ceremonies were over, I heard how wonderful the Campus Crusade for Christ summer mission trips were, so without hesitation, I signed up. This was becoming a busy time in my life. While I waited to see if I'd spend my summer in New York with Campus Crusade for Christ, I was completing master degree applications for the next fall quarter. I even made time in my busy schedule to drive to Auburn University to meet with Dr. Keith Byrd, head of the Rehabilitation Counseling Department, to convince him why I had to be accepted for the fall quarter even though my Graduate Management Admission Test scores were hundreds of points below the average student's scores who were being accepted into the program.

It was easy to recognize that Dr. Byrd was a spirit-filled Christian man, so I shared my story of what God had brought me through, the healing that He had done, and the miracles He had performed for me. I told him what the four neurologists had forecasted about me in their written reports: "Kelly should never attempt college again" and how I had proved them wrong by graduating with my undergraduate degree.

By meeting Dr. Byrd face-to-face, I would become more than just another applicant. I wanted him to see that I was a real person and not just a name on a piece of paper. And when he heard I was running eight to ten miles per day, he would realize I'd become a woman that had overcome the great odds stacked against me. I wanted him to hear the passion in my voice that I wanted to attend no other school than Auburn University.

During our meeting, which became more about my testimony (story), I felt like I was talking to someone who understood what I had been through. He was a very compassionate man. At my first mention of how God had saved my life, he broke into a huge smile. I knew from that moment on that we shared a lot more in common than a desire to help hurting people; we shared the most important thing in life – a daily walk with Jesus. Dr. Byrd shared how he and his wife had come to know the Lord. In the end, it was a wonderful celebration we shared that day. When I left his office, I felt like I could walk on clouds. God had turned the tables in my favor. I knew that Auburn University was the place I'd attend to study for my Master's degree.

Soon after, I was elated to discover I'd been accepted to the New York City Mission Trip sponsored by Campus Crusade for Christ. This would be a whole summer living in New York City and serving people who were homeless. The only other person I would *know* was a young man named James with bright red hair. I was not really "friends" with him, but he knew who I was, and I knew who he was.

A Stranger to Myself

So James and I flew off to New York City on separate flights. This was the biggest thing I had done on my own since the accident. I had one goal: to fit in. I wanted this summer to be the season that I was a *normal* college student. James and I met each other and the other members at the LaGuardia International Airport – one of the largest airports in the world. Once again, I would learn that my *normal* days were over, and I would have to find a new *normal*.

My desire to be treated as *normal* was excessive, I didn't tell anyone about my challenges and limitations: loss of short-term memory, loss of sense of direction, and loss of memory for directions. Nor did I tell anyone that I was legally blind. Let me reiterate. I did not tell *anyone*.

On the second day of the mission trip, we took a whirlwind tour of New York City, including the Natural Museum of History and ended the night with a Broadway play. It was one of the best days I had enjoyed since my accident. For the first time, no one knew me as "Kelly, the poor woman who had lost her beautiful face and was different now." They just knew me as *Kelly*.

It was already dark when we were coming back on the subway. A seat on the right-hand side of the car became vacant next to a nice older lady. Without hesitation, I plopped down into the seat because I was fearful of losing my balance and didn't want to fall. And you know me by now. I've never met a stranger, so here I was on a Christian summer mission trip, wanting so badly to tell someone about Jesus.

The older lady had an accent that sounded like she may be from Holland. She readily told me that she and her husband read the Bible every night and prayed. In a matter of seconds, I was totally engaged in her story. But the next time I looked up, I

161

couldn't see anyone from my group; everyone had disappeared. Remember, this was my second day in New York City.

I almost broke into tears. "Oh my word! Here I am in New York City, and everyone has left me!"

At the next stop, I got off the subway and changed sides because I thought I must have missed my group by just a stop or two. So I jumped on the next subway car that arrived. When I looked at the screen as the doors were closing, it said, "Express Bus." By now, I was really freaking out. I remembered my mom's warnings. "You have to always look relaxed; never sweat anything. Thieves are always looking for people to prey on."

Thinking about the thieves who might be targeting women who looked freaked out, who looked scared, or who were sweating, I started to let my mind run wild. I did not know where we were staying. I did not even know anyone's phone number. And this was before cell phones were available! So I did the only thing I knew to do. I said, "Oh Lord, I desperately need Your help."

The Express Bus only stopped once every ten stops. I was panicking on the inside and trying to remain calm on the outside. Slowly, I rose from my seat, while holding on to the seat handles for balance. I walked to the map on the side of the car and tried to reason, thinking, *I don't have a clue where I am. I don't know what color line to be on. I don't know what stop to get off. I don't know where the dorm is. We're staying at a Bible college dorm. But that's all I know.*

That is when a sweet voice came out of nowhere. I turned and saw a young woman approaching me. She said, "Hi. Are you okay? Do you need some help?"

I almost cried, "Yes. Yes I do!" Then I began rambling quickly. "I am with a group of missionaries from college. We're here for our first couple of days in New York City to spend the summer working with the homeless. I got off at the wrong stop and crossed over...." With a raised hand, she politely stopped my rambling. "Okay. Let me ask you some questions. Can I have you get out a piece of paper and a pen?"

I instantly wondered, *Does this woman know I have short-term memory loss and am severely directionally challenged?*

She continued saying, "I want to have you write some things down. You're staying in some campus dorms. Do you remember a neon pizza parlor sign on the corner?"

"Yes, I think I do, but in New York City, there's a neon pizza sign on almost every corner."

"Okay. Do you remember a firehouse? Do you remember fire engines going off in the middle of the night and feeling like they were right across the street from you?"

"Yes. Yes I do remember fire engines starting and waking me up in the middle of the night." My heart was pounding with hope!

"Good. Let's look at the map. I want you to write something down when we get to the next stop. I'm getting off there, too, so I'm going to walk you over. You need to wait for the Green Line. Take the Green Line, and write '36th Street.' When you get off at 36th Street, walk up the stairs. You'll take a left, go to the first street, and you'll see the pizza parlor. You'll take a right there. And your dorm should be on the right, across the street from the fire station."

I'm thinking, *God, how can this be happening? How can this be?*

When we got off at the next stop, she did what she said she'd do and walked me across the station. She waited while I wrote everything down, and then we waited until the Green Line subway came. I wanted to get this woman's phone number, name, and email address, so I could send her a thank you note.

But when I turned back, there was no one there. The only thing on my left hand side was a cement wall. Just a moment ago, she had been standing between me and the wall. Now, she was gone.

I asked people near me. "Did you see the woman who was standing beside me?"

One person after another said, "No. There was no one with you. You were by yourself."

Confused, I gathered my senses and began following her directions to the "T" and didn't make one wrong turn after that. Then I realized God had sent me an angel who led me back to my temporary home. I was never so thankful to see my bed that night. From this point on, I was sure to know the director's name, where we were staying, and the phone number.

I shared my story with three or four young women in our group who said, "Kelly, we had no idea." And they probably didn't. By 1990, the majority of my seventeen facial surgeries had been completed. Many people could tell that my right eye looked significantly different from my left eye, but by that time, I looked a whole lot more *normal*. I did not use a cane because no one had told me I was "legally blind" because I possessed less than twenty percent field of vision. Actually, it was twelve years before I went to see an eye doctor, and when I did, she screamed, "Oh my word! You are legally blind!"

It was twenty years after the accident before I began using a cane. But after this subway incident, all of the college student missionaries were divided into small groups. I was assigned to the group with Darryl Bridges, who became my guardian angel, and Mitzi Baines, who became my right and left arms. Neither of them let me out of their sights for the rest of the summer.

Chapter Twenty Nine

Blessings Received

The Lord replied, "My presence will go with you
and I will give you rest."
Exodus 33:14

There were fifty two students on the Crusade for Christ
summer mission trip, coming from all parts of the country to our
central meeting place – New York City. After I got lost the
second night, Darryl Bridges became my guardian angel. He was
a nice guy and one of those guys, who just brightened any room
or any conversation with his presence. As an extrovert like me –
outgoing and the life of the party – Darryl and I shared many
similarities.

As I mentioned, we were split into small groups, each group
having five or six members. Darryl, whose home was Florida,
would be the team leader, and Mitzi Baines would be the co-
leader. These two precious people were college students, each
having his and her own stories like the rest of us. Darryl had
been a big-time football player on a scholarship at the University
of Florida until he sustained a bad injury during his freshmen
year. Unfortunately he couldn't play any longer so the college
stripped him of his scholarship. Even though he was deflated
because of this injury, he'd always say, "Jesus is going to use
this." Darryl was an encourager and so much in love with Jesus;

his optimism was contagious, so we easily became friends. Mitzi had come from a dysfunctional family where her parents divorced. As a result, she struggled with a feeling of never measuring up and became bulimic when she was a tween. She'd overcome it through the power of God. She had such a sweet smile of acceptance; you knew she really cared about you. Mitizi was so talented and gave unselfishly to others. She exemplified Philippians 2:3-5: "Do nothing out of selfish ambition or vain conceit. Rather, in humility value others above yourselves, not looking to your own interests but each of you to the interests of the others. In your relationships with one another, have the same mindset as Christ Jesus."

One day when our group went to the streets to witness, we met a homeless man who couldn't walk or move his legs at all, and one leg appeared to be two inches shorter than the other leg. He was begging for money, like in the *New Testament*, by extending a plate in each passer-bye's direction.

When Darryl asked him, "Would you mind if we prayed for you?" The crippled man didn't hesitate. He asked, "Would you? Would you please pray for me?"

Darryl smiled. "Sure we will, but when we do, you have to be ready to receive what God has in store for you. If God wants you to walk, you'll have to walk."

Darryl prayed first; Mitzi prayed next; and then I prayed, "God, I know what you have done in my life, having healed me beyond anyone's belief that I could be healed. Here I am in New York City, living my life large praying for this man to walk."

Next, Darryl prayed, "God, if there is any way to let this man walk, we will give you all the glory and all the praise. Let him be fully used by you."

The cripple man stood up with Darryl supporting him on one side and Mitzi supporting him on the other. We watched in

166

amazement and thanksgiving as this man took his first steps. I'd witnessed God's miracles. Wet tears the size of dimes were streaming down this man's dirty face. He kept saying, "I never ever considered I could walk. I never thought I'd walk."

Darryl, stunned and elated, stared into his eyes. "Well sir, you must have had some kind of faith. God rewards people of faith."

The man nodded. "Oh, I believe in Jesus."

"Well, Jesus did this for you," Darryl assured him.

This was the first of many miracles we witnessed during that summer.

———————

One of my favorite organizations to work at during the summer in New York was the Time Square Homeless Shelter, which was blessed to have Billy as its leader. Before the shelter would welcome any of the homeless in for the day, Billy would gather all the volunteers together and preach a short sermon.

I'll never forget the time when he said, "You are standing in the gateway to hell. There are going to be men and women coming in here who may walk out of here and overdose before they go to bed tonight. They may be shot or involved in a gang war. Your job is to tell them what they need to know: *Jesus is alive. Jesus is the only way. And they need Jesus if they want eternal life.*"

Billy told it like it was. He laid it out, point blank. His audiences always had wide eyes. We loved this man who had given up a six figure job and everything he owned to come to Times Square and become the director of this homeless shelter. He lived in a one-bedroom shack down the street. He was the real deal, and I just felt so much gratitude in my heart that I was able to witness how he spent his life's journey.

Chapter Thirty

Amazing Grace

*Come to me, all you that are weary and are
carrying heavy burdens, and I will give you rest.*
Matthew 11:28 NRS

God was present and definitely alive in the Big Apple that
summer! As missionaries with Campus Crusade for Christ, we
worked with nine of the biggest ministry centers in the City. We
rode the subway to the respective sites to pray, to make lots of
peanut butter and jelly sandwiches, to feed, and to counsel with
the homeless population. I established personal relationships
with many, some of whom, I will never see again until I arrive at
heaven's gates.

A favorite memory was going to the Bowery Mission where
people could get back their dignity and self-respect. It's a very
successful program even today. The Mission was a place that
literally took men and women off the streets, cleaned them up,
gave them a bed to sleep in, assigned them responsibilities to
perform at the mission, kept them in Chapel three times a day,
kept them in Bible study two times a day, and took them out to
witness to others about Jesus every other day. Our roles were to
help with their church services, lead their devotionals, and be
their support systems as we accompanied them on their
witnessing trips. This was very serious work. I remember feeling
honored when I was able to participate. God used my

experiences at the Bowery Mission to plant seeds in my heart about the baptism of the Holy Spirit. Until you attend a service with over five hundred people singing "Amazing Grace," most of them men with deep, baritone voices, you haven't arrived. The ratio of participants was ten men to every woman. Their singing is remembered as one of the most incredible and moving experiences of my life. It will stay with me forever. My only regret is that I didn't record it; the singing was truly *amazing.*

During this summer of service, I decided to surrender my life to Christian service. Even though the homeless had been immersed into a new Christian way of living, they were "all about Jesus." Without a doubt, I learned more from them than they could ever learn from me. Their life stories were unbelievable. I enjoyed hearing where they had been and where they had come from before finding Jesus. And one such profound testimony I heard was Vinnie's, whom I met at the Bowery Mission.

Vinnie was an Italian gentleman, who was full of Jesus. He'd preach to a chair if it wasn't sitting on all four legs correctly. Except for the realization of God's omnipotence, omnipresence, and omniscience, Vinnie's testimony is hard to believe.

He had grown up in the "not so nice" part of New York City with parents who were constantly strung out on drugs. Vinnie entered into the same lifestyle, becoming a cocaine addict and an alcoholic. Because of his addictions, he lost everything and everybody. Needles were shared with whoever had drugs. After getting wasted, he'd find refuge beside a trash bin or inside a dumpster at some unknown restaurant and fall asleep.

But no matter where he ended up, he'd be awakened by two men who worked at the Bowery Mission. Their names were Phil and Tony. They'd "just happen to walk behind the restaurant" and discover him. Never once did they condemn him; instead, they would help him up from the bin or out of the dumpster and say, "Vinnie, baby! We've been looking for you. Come with us."

With Vinnie accompanying them, they'd return to the Bowery Mission where he'd get a shower, a fresh change of clothes, and a hot meal. Once safe and sound, he'd stay for their church service. Shortly afterward, he'd leave and was back to his old lifestyle. Vinnie recognized the truth, but the "pull of the street life was too strong." Vinnie said, "It is stronger than anything I've ever known."

But once again, Phil and Tony would "happen to walk behind another restaurant" and find him beside another trash bin or inside another dumpster. They even found him in the sewers or in crack houses. Somehow, they always appeared where he was and bring him back to the Bowery. Vinnie firmly believed that God sent them each time.

One night after Vinnie had been brought, he became paranoid and miserable, as many heavy drug users become.

He said, "I was just tired. I was ready to end it all, so I decided to commit suicide. My plans were to jump in front of the next subway coming in, and I even had chosen the spot where I was going to jump. I knew when I was going to do it and how I was going to do it. The subways are where a lot of people in the City commit suicide."

So a determined Vinnie walked down the stairs of the subway to the appointed spot on the platform and waited for the next train to end it all.

"I just didn't want to live this way anymore. So here I was, standing in the subway pit, ready to jump onto the tracks, and guess what happened? Yes! You're right! I heard two familiar voices."

"Yo, Vinnie! What's going down?" the two men yelled. "God sent us to find you today because He wanted us to come and give you hope."

Phil and Tony just happened to walk down those stairs at the exact second I was going to jump. Without a doubt, I know it was God who had sent Phil and Tony to rescue me. That is when I gave up believing in *coincidences* and began believing in *God incidences*. I knew that day was different from all the others because I was getting ready to end my life. I wasn't sure exactly what I believed about God even though I'd heard good things, but I hadn't seen many good things, but it had to be God who sent Phil and Tony to save me."

So they grabbed him, hugged him, and took him by the arms, leading him down the street and into the Bowery. The men helped him with a hot shower, clean clothes, a hot meal, and then he heard the *message*.

"It was no message like I'd heard before. I'd sat through dozens of services just like this one, but this time, when the altar call was given, I went up with a sincere heart; I wanted to change from the inside out. I went down front and lay prostrate on the floor with my arms, hands, and fingers outstretched. I cried out to God like I'd never done before."

"I cried, 'God, if you're really real, I desperately need You. I know I've messed up my life, and I'm tired of doing it on my own... I need You. I know it was You who sent Phil and Tony to save my life. And now I surrender my life to you. I cry out to You. I want to stay in the program here. I can't make it on my own. I can't make it out there on the streets.'"

So the Bowery Mission accepted Vinnie and brought him into the program. While going through detox, he experienced the shakes and watched little purple men climbing the walls. "If people tell you getting out of addiction is easy, they are lying. It was awful. But I got through it." He went through the Christian-based Alcoholics Anonymous.

Vinnie began reading the Bible. He attended services two times each day and attended the small men's group Bible studies. The people at the Bowery recognized that Vinnie had something different than hundreds of men who had been through the program: This man found joy easily and had a passion for telling others about Jesus. When he was slightly more grounded, he realized the awesomeness of God by uncovering his gift: evangelism. Therefore, Vinnie began witnessing outside on the streets.

The Bowery had gotten him into the Word and fed him scriptures 24/7. As a result, Vinnie had fallen in love with Jesus. And the Bowery didn't refer to our Savior as a *higher power.* They called Him who He is -- *Jesus Christ.*

Once Vinnie adopted his own saying, you'd hear his deep voice bellow, "Who loves you? Jesus! That's right! Jesus loves you." His beloved saying became one of the highlights of my day.

Before the summer was over, Vinnie confided in me. "Kelly, I can't believe I don't have AIDS. I can't tell you how many dirty needles I used to shoot up. There were no clean veins in my arms because I had shot up so much."

His shared testimony ended when he told me how a permanent job as counselor had opened at the Bowery, and he'd gotten it. His job was to counsel other men in the program and keep them on the straight and narrow path. And he ended up marrying a lovely woman.

To this day, I've never met anyone with more passion for spreading God's love. Vinnie had taken lots of detours and dead ends, but he'd done a one-eighty and started his journey anew.

Vinnie and his testimony taught me many things. I've listed just a few:

- Accept people where they are. Love them regardless.
- Do not judge. There is only one who can judge, and it is not you.
- Realize "But by the grace of God go I." How easily it could be me on the streets.
- Realize the homeless have names and are real people; they are Ken who used to be a U.S. mailman, or Susie who graduated from college and was laid off by the bank. My point is these people are the same as you and me. Not all the homeless are drug addicts and low-lifers.
- Live a "no compromise" lifestyle. Live for Him.

Three months after I left New York City, I learned that Vinnie had been diagnosed with the dreaded AIDS. I telephoned him, and the first question he asked me was, "Who loves you, Kelly?" I beamed, and before I could answer, he did it for me. "Jesus! That's right! Jesus loves you, Kelly!"

We had a good conversation, reciting the many things we shared in common. Both of us had experienced what it was like to have had a lot and had it taken away. And we both agreed that Jesus had replaced our losses with better blessings than we could have imagined.

Sadly, three months after our phone call, Vinnie's wife called to say he had passed away. I realized what a blessing our last conversation had been, and I knew in my heart what he was doing in heaven at that very moment: singing "Amazing Grace" in between shouting a praise that had once been a question, "Who loves us? Jesus does! That's right! Jesus loves us!"

"But if it weren't for God...!"

Chapter Thirty One

Seeds

And the Peace of God, which transcends all understanding,
will guard your hearts and your minds in Christ Jesus.
Philippians 4:7

With three-fourths of the summer over, we left New York City for a week long camp for inner-city kids. It was a three hour bus drive to Camp Comanche; this camp not only taught about Jesus, but it taught the kids that Jesus loved to have fun. Upon arrival, everyone on our team had the opportunity to bunk with someone else. Because I was interested in becoming a counselor, and there was a position available, I offered to bunk with Teresa, who was a full-timer, working with kids all summer long. Surprisingly, she became another sower of curiosity seeds for me.

As we prepared for bed, nonchalantly Teresa asked, "Kelly, have you ever been baptized by the Holy Spirit?"

The first time I ever heard of being baptized by the Holy Spirit was while I attended the University of Georgia. A friend of a friend had invited me to her church – an African-American church. In the middle of the service, a lady, who was sitting three people from me, began spewing out these words that made no sense – it was like a different language.

A Stranger to Myself

When I'd returned home that day, I called my good friend, Harold, who was a freshman at Auburn University. After I told him about the woman, he said, "Kelly, get out your Bible."

So I did. Harold led me to several verses in Acts and 2 Thessalonians.

"Kelly, if it happened in the Word of God, it can happen today because God is the same yesterday, today, and forever."

Even though I was curious, I pushed my questions and any interest to the back of my mind without realizing little seeds had already been sown.

But I heard myself stammering in answer to Teresa's question, "No, no, no, I haven't."

She smiled expectantly and stared into my wide eyes. "Well, you know, it's not anything spooky," she said with a laugh.

Teresa explained to me that it was a different way of communicating with God. All I'd ever known was how to communicate in the English language. Teresa said the Holy Spirit had no language. The Holy Spirit understood even the cries of our hearts – even the utterances from our mouths.

This all sounded wonderful but very overwhelming at the time.

"I can pray with you right now if you want," she offered. Her smile was genuine. "We can pray for you to receive the baptism of the Holy Spirit."

I honestly didn't understand what was holding me back. Even though I was intrigued and knew that I wanted to turn all of my life over to God, I hesitated.

"No. Thank you very much, but no," I replied, "I'm not ready yet."

Teresa had a sweetness about her and was a great listener. There is no question that God meant for me to meet Teresa and

175

to have her explain the baptism of the Holy Spirit. And it was His plan for her to offer prayer. When most people are first exposed, they, too, are not ready yet. I was thankful my new roommate respected my response and dropped the topic. But I replayed her questions in my mind over the following months. That's when I began to pray relentlessly for more understanding. You might say that my prayer tears began to water the little curiosity seeds and made them grow.

A few days later, I received my acceptance letter to begin my Master's Degree studies in the Rehabilitation Counseling Program at Auburn University in the fall. This was totally a *God thing*.

Chapter Thirty Two

Baptism of the Holy Spirit

The Lord is close to the brokenhearted.
and saves those who are crushed in spirit.
Psalm 34:18

Later, while I attended Auburn University for my Master's Degree, friends from my dorm invited me to attend a spirit-filled Pentecostal church. I just loved the church because when I wanted to raise my hands or dance in the aisles, I could. The church's way of worship was very much *alive*. As a result of our continued attendance, we subsequently received an invitation to dine at Pastor Michael's and his wife, Charmaine's, house. They were a precious couple who had an amazing story. I didn't know it then, but everyone at their dinner had been praying for months and months that I'd be ready to accept the baptism of the Holy Spirit that night.

After a delicious meal was thoroughly enjoyed by everyone, Pastor Michael led me through the Word of God and showed me verse by verse why God wanted us to have this gift. He said, "Kelly, it's like going from unleaded gas to premium gas – super powered gas. Once you get hold of God's Holy Spirit, you never want to go back to that unleaded gas again." His analogy made sense; he made something that seemed overwhelming and complicated easier to understand.

By the time he was finished, I was begging, "Please pray for me! Please pray over me! I want to be baptized in the Holy Spirit."

I had been reminded of the promise I had made to God when I was listening to one of Vinnie's stories in New York City. He told a story of a good man named Sam who had lived a good life, but he never did anything extraordinary. When Sam passed away and got to the pearly gates, Saint Peter greeted him and welcomed him to heaven. Saint Peter said, "We're so glad you're here. Let me give you a tour of heaven." He showed Sam the streets of gold and the calm seas, but Sam kept noticing a warehouse building off to the right, and he finally asked, "What is that huge warehouse doing in heaven?" Saint Peter tried to distract him by pointing to the silver-winged angels that were flying around and singing hymns. But Sam remained curious about the warehouse. Finally, an exasperated Saint Peter replied, "I didn't want to have to show you the warehouse on your first day in heaven, but here we go." Peter walked over to the warehouse and opened the door. Sam saw the most beautiful riches and sparkling gems he'd ever seen. Saint Peter said, "These could have been yours." Sam was confused. "These were the blessings that God had for you on Earth, but you never asked for them." By the end of Vinnie's story, I had made a vow that my warehouse would be empty when I arrived in heaven. I wanted all the treasures God intended for me to have, including baptism of the Holy Spirit.

When Charmaine and another woman placed their hands on me and Pastor Michael led us in prayer, it was like an eruption came from the center of my body. There is a verse in the Bible that talks about it coming from the lower belly. When he asked me to sing, "Jesus Loves Me," I did. Next, he told me to sing it in a prayer language, and I did. It just flowed.

Once I received the baptism of the Holy Spirit, I was so elated and joyful. My soul was bursting with the Spirit. I couldn't stop speaking in my prayer language. I couldn't go to sleep.

Once you receive this baptism, you can ask God what words you're saying, and He will pour the answers or the interpretation into your heart. Previously, my prayers had lasted thirty minutes at the most. But going forward, my prayers began lasting for hours. And even then, I felt like I was quitting too soon because God was right there in my midst. The *use of tongues* requires an interpreter in a church setting – a public setting. You cannot fake it because it doesn't work. And remember, it is a gift from God.

These are the things that Harold had explained to me months earlier. He'd had the baptism of the Holy Spirit for many years. Harold and I had become close because he was one of my friends from high school who had stuck by me after the accident. But I still find it confusing as to why I had called him months earlier other than I was freaking out from hearing the woman speak in tongues. I know now I was led to call him and have him explain things to me because he was more advanced in his Christian walk than I.

With 20/20 hindsight, I knew God had used the woman who spoke in tongues, Harold, Charmaine, Pastor Michael, and Teresa to plant the seeds of the Holy Spirit in my heart.

⚜

Just the other day, I was reading in my journal from my first days as a graduate student at Auburn. Two weeks after I had gone through my orientation, my girlfriend had telephoned me and was shouting into the phone, "Kelly, turn on your radio!" It was always on 93.7 FM – *The Joy FM.*

That's when I heard a young man narrating how he had been confused about whether or not God wanted him to go into the Rehabilitation Master's Program. He had gone back and forth and was plagued with doubt. Even when he'd attended the Program's orientation, he was still questioning it. The young man had sat next to a young woman, who began telling him her story. She had been in a terrible car and truck accident that had shattered every bone in her face. She'd lost most of her vision and had even had a blood clot the size of a grapefruit lodged in her brain. He concluded by saying, "Right then and there I knew God had me exactly where I needed to be."

"Wow," was all I could say at the time. I was humbled by God's use of my story to help this young man make a major decision in his life.

I finished my first quarter at Auburn with two A's and one B -- not bad for a girl who was told she "should never attempt college again." So let me pass along this advice. If it is God's destiny for you, you will succeed!

As John Calvin once said, "However many blessings we expect from God, His infinite liberality will always exceed all our wishes and our thoughts."

Chapter Thirty Three

Ski for Light

For we live by faith, not by sight.
2 Corinthians 5:7

It's important that I tell you about another inspiring week that changed my life forever. It is the week I spent at Ski for Light (SFL). My father was out riding his hand-cycle at a park in Atlanta, Georgia, when he noticed a couple on a tandem bike. He thought the woman on the back looked as if she may be blind, so he introduced himself to them. He learned the woman's name was Suzanne, and her husband's name was Joe. Their chance meeting began a wonderful friendship.

While conversing, Dad shared my story, which he so often did, and told them that I was legally blind. Well, as it turned out, Suzanne was on the Board of Directors of SFL and couldn't wait to send Dad more information about SFL to share with me.

Full of enthusiasm and excitement, Dad called me that same day. I listened and scratched down her phone number and the Web site address for SFL.org. I sat on these notes for about a week or two until Dad called to remind me that I'd promised to search the Web for this organization's information.

I finally did and found the organization's motto is "Just because you have a disability doesn't mean you cannot live a fulfilling life." Volunteers unselfishly give the SFL participants the time of their lives during the organization's *big event*, which

181

is one week of cross-country skiing at different locations. The organization focuses on assisting people, who are blind, visually impaired, and mobility impaired, to get unique physical exercise and to provide an opportunity for great socialization. There is something supernatural that happens when a group of people get together that have to live by faith instead of by their sight.

Well, the next thing I knew, I was preparing to go on a week-long cross-country skiing trip to Granby, Colorado, with 250 people that I'd never met. I packed 90 percent ski clothes and 10 percent everyday clothes because I thought it was all about the skiing. Boy, was I wrong! The week was about fellowship, the sharing of stories, and a lot of laughter. And as for skiing, there were two to three trails open to people with disabilities.

You might be curious as to how skiing is handled for people who are blind or visually impaired. There are two sets of tracks parallel to each other. A *guide* skis in the left track, while the participant skis in the right track. For my situation (I see nothing on the left but have a small window on the right), my guide would ski on the right side, a little in front of me, with me on the left track.

The guide to whom I was assigned was Kathy, who owned a log cabin building company in Michigan. She was a great guide who had been volunteering for over twenty years, so Kathy had a lot of experience in teaching totally blind people how to cross-country ski. My experience in down-hill skiing was great but very little translated to cross-country skiing. After about the twenty-fifth fall my first day, I learned that cross-country skiing was going to be a greater challenge than down-hill skiing. Many of my challenges resulted from my lack of balance. I struggled, but by the third day, I'd found my *groove* and hit my *glide*. It became more enjoyable. Don't get me wrong; I still struggled, and even to this day, I struggle with gentle down-hills. That is where I get nervous and find myself leaning back, but whenever you lean back and straighten your legs, watch out! There is about to be a wipe out!

What shocked me was that the skiing was only an excuse to get you to attend a week-long party! There was a happy hour at four o'clock in the hot tub that started right after the trails closed. Afterward, you went back to your room and got showered and dressed for dinner. We ate dinner every night in one of the grand ballrooms with everyone sharing the happenings of the day. Then we'd head to someone's room for drinks until it was time for the dance. I barely drank at the time, so this was alarming to my system. But I was thrilled to become a VIP (Visually Impaired Person) of the SFL organization.

During my first year, I met Terry Gerber the second night at the dance. Did I mention that I *love* to dance? They were playing my favorite dance music from the '80s. And yes, you've guessed it. I'm a survivor of the *disco era*. The disk jockey even had a *smoke machine* that emitted large amounts of smoke onto the dance floor. That night I was leaving the floor when the smoke machine went off. When the smoke cleared, there was a six foot, four inch man with one of the sweetest smiles standing before me. He asked me to dance.

Afterward, as we talked, I learned that Terry had a lot in common with Dad. Terry was participating in *two* Iron Men triathlons a year and, otherwise, running marathons in between for the fun of it. An Iron Men triathlon is where you swim over two miles in the ocean, bike over 150 miles, and then run a full marathon. So with our shared passion for exercising, Terry and I *hit it off* immediately; I mean, we skipped flickers and went to fireworks as I quickly discovered his beautiful heart – one of the most beautiful hearts I'd ever known inside a most adoring man.

We were two young adults, one living in Phoenix, Arizona, and one living in Charlotte, N.C., in the throes of infatuation; as a result, we became two passionate friends who found each other on this winding road called life.

Over the course of a year, we realized that distance and timing got in the way. God was taking us into different directions, but we knew we would be forever friends.

Chapter Thirty Four

A Journey of Faith

...while we wait for the blessed hope – the appearing of the
glory of our great God and Savior, Jesus Christ . . . .
Titus 2:13

Close to completing my Master's Degree at Auburn, I was
thoroughly enjoying my internship at Roosevelt Warm Springs
Rehabilitation Center. At the time, I lived in a house with six
other rehab professional women, who were physical therapists,
speech therapists, or occupational therapists. This proved to be a
much more pleasant situation than the sorority house had been.
The other six residents and I quickly became friends – especially
Patty. She was also in the internship program and what you
would call *wild* --a *wild child* throwback from the sixties. Patty
loved to laugh and tell terrific stories. She was a larger lady than
me -- probably fifty pounds overweight.

On Friday, while we were suffering from high temperatures
caused by our self-diagnosed cabin fever and spring fever, Patty,
Sarah (another friend), and I decided to go to Destin Beach for
the weekend, a mere eight hours away. (Isn't youth grand?)
Somehow, in the midst of sheer excitement and joy, we threw a
few clothes and our swimsuits into three suitcases and headed
towards sunshine, freedom, and fun. Patty and Sarah understood
that I seldom drove, but we were going to be using my car since
it was the nicest and big enough to fit the three of us and our

luggage in comfortably, so they alternated the responsibility of maneuvering my car down the crowded lanes of the highway towards Destin Beach.

We were tired when we finally arrived Friday night, so we bought fast-food before checking into a small mom and pop motel. The décor was from the sixties, with lots of pinks and turquoise, but it appeared clean, and that's all that mattered to our meager wallets. Like goddesses, we spent Saturday lazily basking on colorful beach towels in the steaming sun until we were french-fried a crispy pink and brown on both sides of our bodies. Uninhibited by the current fear of skin cancer, we still subscribed to lots of sunrays and baby oil mixed with peroxide to hasten our tans. On Saturday night, without much hesitation, we decided a good meal was deserved, so we located a half-empty / half-full seafood restaurant on the ocean. I ordered broiled salmon, and they ordered shrimp scampi. The food tasted scrumptious! Afterward, we traveled from club to club, dancing to the beats of the different genres like prisoners on the loose for one night. I refrained from drinking too much alcohol because my loss of vision caused me to have loss of balance. Even though I no longer took some of the stronger medications, if I had two drinks, it looked like I'd had ten drinks. So I behaved myself and drank light, while they drank mixed drinks. We left the last club around 2:00 a.m., eager to sink our heads onto cool, pillows.

Around 3:00 a.m., my two companions began vomiting, evidently from alcohol poisoning. No matter how much they puked, they couldn't stop. I became anxious every time I heard another heave and the toilet flush because I grasped the unwavering truth facing us: Today was Sunday. We had to drive all day just to get back in time for our 9:00 a.m. Monday internships.

A Stranger to Myself

Once the vomiting stalled for a little while, Patty and Sarah kept asking each other, "Are you going to drive home because I can't?"

Miserably, because I was the only one not puking, I whispered aloud, "Okay God. It's just you and me." So it was decided. And consider this, the girls had to be feeling so weak and nauseated, or they never would have agreed to ride with me.

Dreading the drive, I knew it would take eight hours if I travelled the highways, but to be safe, I decided to drive the entire trip on the expressways and two lane backroads connecting little towns. We had to stop and pull over every ten miles to let one of the girls puke. I sat sentry to a dwindling roll of paper towels. Throughout the slow-paced trip, I prayed and thanked God for every mile we gained toward home. My knuckles were splotchy white and my wrists were cramping from gripping the steering wheel so tightly. My neck was sore and stiff from turning my head every second to see ahead and to the sides. Somehow, without the invention of a personal GPS, I was connecting the dots on the map. God was guiding me. The girls were exhausted and asleep by the time I parked the car in front of our house. Elated to be home safe, I told myself, "I can do this! I can drive after all!"

The girls' puke-laced breath stunk as they groaned and passed me, tugging at their suitcases. I watched as they stumbled to their separate bedrooms. Relieved they were no longer my responsibility, I hastened into my room to call my parents. My pride was bubbling over! On a scale of one and ten, my self-esteem and confidence had been boosted ten points.

"Guess what I just did?" I announced. "I drove all the way from Destin Beach to Roosevelt Springs."

During our internship, I led Patty to Christ. After we graduated with our Master's Degrees, our roads diverged with her moving to a new city, finding a job, and attending a fantastic church that nurtured her. Patty was a born leader, so I wasn't surprised when she began teaching a Bible study class soon afterward. Our paths haven't crossed in a few years, but I'd love to know what one of my best converts was doing with her journey of faith.

Chapter Thirty Five

Focus on the Lord

We have this hope as an anchor for the soul, firm and secure.
Hebrews 6:19a

Of course, I was disappointed with myself when I failed the theories part of my comprehensive final exam for my Master's Degree. I had worked hard and done well in the program. My graduating GPA was a 3.8 GPA on a 4.0 scale. And indeed, I'd studied for my theories, but I had used my old study habits, going over them several times, which doesn't work for people with my kind of brain injuries. So when Dr. Byrd, recommended I work with Dr. Couch over the summer, I agreed. This became one of the most life-changing summers I've ever lived.

I couldn't remember how to get from point A to point B, which is how most people are able to perform, so Dr. Couch taught me a new technique. I learned how to go from point A to point G to point K to point L to point Z and then back to point B to get to a destination. Also, to improve my memory, I had to create crazy stories, and the crazier the story, the easier I could remember things. One story was about a truck with each wheel representing a different point of the behavior theory, the hood representing something else, and the bed of the truck representing something else.

At the end of the summer, I arrived at Dr. Byrd's office to retake the theory part of the exam and found that he and Dr.

Couch were eager to begin. Dr. Byrd had printed eight cards with the names of the eight theories. I'd pick one, and he'd ask me questions about that theory. Boom! Boom! Boom! Then I'd pick another card, and he'd ask me questions about that theory. Boom! Boom! Boom!

Dr. Byrd was impressed. "Kelly, I cannot believe how well you've done! You have aced this part of the test."

Dr. Couch was delighted. "Keith, ask her another one." He was showing off, and so was I. Then I took the written part, passed it, and earned my Master's Degree. My life had been blessed with another of God's miracles.

Looking back, I had been devastated after failing one out of ten parts of my oral exam. I can remember sitting on my couch, and the tears streaming down my face. After what seemed like a long time, I remember God speaking to my heart saying, "You need to praise me."

At first, I ignored His voice with the excuse, "God can't you see I'm having a major pity party?"

Then, as always, God repeated Himself with a stronger nudge, "You need to praise me…." I can remember it like it was yesterday.

I relented and automatically my hands lifted from my lap and through the tears came the most pitiful version of "Jesus Loves Me" you have ever heard. When I finished, strangely I noticed my tears had slowed, and I felt that old familiar nudge to sing it again. So I did. This time it came out stronger and louder, and I noticed the second time around there were no tears.

What is the moral of this story? When you are lost in the darkest despair, listen to that still small voice because God is right with you, trying to bring you out of the darkness. Take your eyes off yourself (which is exactly where the enemy wants you), and focus on the Lord. The Lord does not need our praise. He is a perfect parent. He knows that if we praise Him, it is impossible for us to drown in our self-pity. I learned a huge lesson that day, one which I carry forward and share with as many people as possible. My life had been blessed with another of God's miraculous lessons.

Chapter Thirty Six

Rebound

...and because he was a tentmaker as they were,
he stayed and worked with them.
Acts 18:3

Here I was, a graduate from Auburn University with a Master's Degree in Rehabilitation Counseling. After passing my next hurdle, which was the national certification for rehab counselors (CRC), I imagined neuro rehab centers lining up, waiting to hire me. But after six months of job hunting and having to move back home with my parents, I was ready to move almost anywhere to get a job. God opened a door -- the Walk to Emmaus Community.

At one of the monthly gatherings, I was told that the man giving the fourth day talk (the Walk lasts three days, and every day after is considered your fourth day). This man was the CEO of one of the largest rehab centers in the nation, which was based in Atlanta. Not surprising, when Emmaus meets, Emmaus eats, so after the meeting and during fellowship time, I made a beeline to meet Rick, who listened to the shortened version of my story. As I concluded, he handed me his business card and told me to set up a meeting with him the following week.

Rod, Jr., who now towered my 5'8" frame, drove me to the meeting. Rick displayed amazing compassion as he listened to the lengthened version of my story and heard why God wanted to use me in the field of rehabilitation. Unfortunately, he explained he didn't have any current openings. But he led me to a crowded room filled with filing cabinets and explained the top two cabinets were filled with neuro rehab centers' contact information, and I was welcome to any and all information in them. I recognized the big job ahead, so I recruited my brother, who was patiently waiting in the car. We began copying rehab center names, phone numbers, and contact names – a gold mine of information.

During the next two weeks, I methodically went down the list, calling one rehab at a time to see if there were openings. After receiving fifty two polite "Nos," God convicted me to persist. When I called the fifty third center, the 1-800 number led me through a series of prompts before I spoke with a real person.

She said, "I'm sorry, but we don't have any positions available. But wait, we may have an opening at Rebound in Troy, Ohio. Have you ever heard of Troy, Ohio?"

"No," I said as my hopes mounted. As desperate as I was for an opportunity, it might as well have been in Siberia, but it didn't matter. I was going for it.

One thing led to another, and Dr. Bill Smith interviewed me twice over the phone. He sounded like one of the nicest men I had ever met in the rehab world. Next, he offered to fly me to Ohio for an in-person interview. As it turned out, Troy was a small town outside of Dayton. I immediately fell in love with the people, small town atmosphere, and Dr. Bill and his wife, Johanna Smith.

When Dr. Bill made me a great job offer, I accepted, becoming a Rehabilitation Counselor at Rebound Neurological for people with brain injuries, aneurisms, and strokes. As you'll recall, these are called *acquired brain injuries* (ABI). And Dr.

Bill Smith would be my first fantastic supervisor. He and Johanna invited me to stay with them the first week or so until I was able to find an apartment, get the utilities turned on, and buy furniture. What an incredible opportunity God had given me!

This wonderful Jewish couple graciously entertained me in their home the entire week. It's important to note that Bill and Johanna were intellects. At night, Bill would retire, leaving Johanna and me to sit for hours and discuss my life long questions about the Jewish tradition. One such question was how do Jews pay for their sins today? They no longer sacrificed animals, so how did they come back into a good standing with the Lord? Johanna always began with a thirty minute explanation of Jewish traditions. Then after my questions had been answered, I would explain the Gospel to her.

It was fascinating to learn about the traditions of her faith and why the Jewish people believed as they did. And I continuously reminded her that I worshipped a Jewish man. His name is Jesus Christ.

My brother, Rod, Jr. was getting married the weekend before my employer requested me to report to work. Timing couldn't be more perfect with another *God incident* occurring. Aunt Nancy and cousin, Dougie, were driving from Michigan to the South for the wedding. Dougie was Rod's best friend and was going to serve as one of Rod's groomsmen. So Dougie wholeheartedly agreed to drive me and my car to Ohio, with my aunt following in her car.

We'd always lived away from our family in Michigan, so on the drive to Ohio, I spent time with my cousin, who was a medical student at the University of Michigan. As someone I'd always admired, I'd really never gotten to know him. His sister and I were one or two years apart, so we'd hung around together. The drive afforded me the opportunity to share my faith walk with Doug. He had always believed in God but had never taken the first step to have a personal relationship with the Lord until that trip. Doug was open-minded and receptive to hearing my story; we talked the entire trip, he willingly shared his own ideals. At one of the rest areas, Dougie and I bowed our heads, and he repeated the Salvation Prayer with me. Praise the Lord! Another star is born.

Upon arrival to Ohio, Doug carefully parked my car in the Smiths' driveway. Unfortunately, with more driving ahead, Aunt Nancy and Doug immediately waved goodbye and said, "Kelly, best of luck to you. We hate to leave you like this, but we have to get home."

Ready to begin my next adventure, I stayed with Bill and Johanna while I began working at the facility and searched for an affordable apartment. As Bill and I drove to and from the facility, he'd provide me with a list of suggestions for a place to live. The following day, I'd drive to one complex after another viewing potential apartments.

Eventually, I discovered a beautiful complex about two football fields from I-75. There were four apartment buildings in the complex, formed like a quad that went from A to D. As soon as I saw the vacant apartment on the second floor that was for rent, I knew this was where I wanted to live. I could look out the back door and see the highway. And driving on the interstate is where I felt the safest because I didn't have to worry about oncoming cars and surprises coming from the left as long as I drove in the left-hand lane. The facility was fifteen miles away and located right off the interstate, so driving to and from work would be easy enough.

After I signed the rental contract, Mom came to Ohio pulling an orange U-Haul trailer with her car. Bless my mother's golden heart! She had never let me down and still supported most of my decisions. Mom and I unloaded everything that we could handle, but there were some heavy furniture pieces we knew we couldn't lift. She and I hoisted the bed's headboard and footboard and the mattress up two flight of stairs before we succumbed to asking for assistance from two men who were sitting and watching everything we did as they drank their Friday night beers. Evidently, we had been their evening entertainment; otherwise, it seemed incredible that they hadn't already offered to help. But realizing the china cabinet would be too heavy for us, we had no choice.

So Mom asked, "Will you help us? Even though we're strong women, we don't think we can lift the china cabinet."

Without hesitation, they replied, "Oh sure! We'll be glad to."

Finally, the trailer was empty, so Mom and I drove to the nearest U-Haul dealer to return it. The owner of the U-Haul dealership combination gas station was named Randy. I made an unexpected discovery: Red necks don't always live in the South; they are all over the country. With experience living up North and down South, I can attest there are just as many *recky-neckies* in both areas of the country.

Immediately, Randy made an offer. "Well, being new to the area, you probably need someone to take you around and show you some stuff, don't ya?"

"I probably will." I replied.

Mom was staring.

He continued. "Where are you living now?"

"I live in Winterhaven," I replied.

Mom was still staring.

He said, "Oh. I think I know where that is? What street are you on?"

Mom was more than staring.

Even though he was getting a little too personal, I was flattered. Even so, I declined to tell him. But he knew the kind of car I drove, and a week later, he showed up in my driveway. It was scary and funny at the same time.

So *recky neckie* Randy visited several times, taking me out and showing me the town, but he always wanted to come back home to my couch. It had been eight long years since a man had been attracted to me; his attention was nice.

The apartment complex was overrun with people my age, so it was easy to make new friends as we hung out at the pool during the two and a half months of Ohio summer. One Saturday morning, as the sun worshipper in me allowed the sun to bake my already tanned legs, I reflected on my decision to accept the job at Rebound Neurological. I hadn't known anyone except the Smiths. I didn't have my parents to rely on. I didn't have Ellen or Rod, Jr. to help me. I was all alone – except for God. I didn't have a counselor at a student health center to visit when issues occurred.

With God's help, I had accomplished so much. I was a highly respected professional, working a full time job with a new life. Bill and Johanna had accepted me as part of their family, it was a great display of what God intended in the Christian community. The world teaches us to hate people of different religions. Isis and the radical Islamic movement only teach division and strong animosity toward anyone different from them. My relationship with the Smiths was the opposite and ran deep through Jesus's veins. The Smiths and I embraced our similarities, as well as our dissimilarities.

The next year would be a huge faith growth one for me. My faith sky-rocketed as I realized my life had been sheltered before this move. That's when I began to live again.

Chapter Thirty Seven

Ginghamsburg Church

Be very careful, then, how you live – not as unwise but as wise,
making the most of every opportunity, because the days are evil.
Ephesians 5:15-16

One day, when I was getting my cable vision connected, I stopped for lunch at my favorite fast food restaurant. The cashier was happily talking to each customer in the long line facing her. She seemed full of joy, so when I finally got to her, I asked, "Are you a Christian?"

To which she replied, "Yes, I am." She could have been on an advertisement for a teeth whitening company.

Happily, I stated, "I just moved to Ohio from Georgia. Will you be my first friend?"

Without hesitation, she laughed and said, "Of course I will. I'll write down my name and phone number on your receipt. Call me anytime. I'd love to invite you to my church."

Almost instantly, we became friends, and true to her word, she took me to her church the following Sunday. Realizing that attending this church fulltime would be a bit of a drive for me, she said, "Kelly, I know another church I want to take you to next Sunday. It will be closer for you and an easier drive. I'll go with you," which she did.

A Stranger to Myself

The church we attended the following Sunday was Ginghamsburg Church, a mega church located in Tipp City, Ohio, a suburb thirteen miles north of Dayton, Ohio. It hostsnearly 5,000 people of all ages on its campuses each week and is currently the fourth-largest United Methodist church in the United States. It has repeatedly been named one of the most influential churches in America.

Upon entering the double doors of the sanctuary, I immediately experienced the same sense of peace and belonging as I did when I attended the first meeting at Campus Crusade for Christ. God wrapped His arms around me once again. The Pastor Mike Slaughter was the dynamic minister there. Even today, I still love to hear his sermons. And his unbelievable preaching wasn't all -- this church had the most rocking music I'd ever heard, but at the same time, it was true Worship Songs. They sang a lot of Brooklyn Tabernacle Choir and Israel Houghton's music. I fell in love with the church and joined the singles' group.

Almost immediately, I was asked to lead a Bible Study class and invited to get involved in other leadership activities. This is where I first met Ben, a patient, gentle, sweet man, who lived in my same apartment complex, one street over. Ben was attractive and had a ten-year old daughter, Stacy.

The following Saturday, I was pleasantly surprised to find Ben at the pool with Stacy, so I began a conversation. One thing I'd learned was that some men suffer from shyness or have been hurt by women, so you have to hit them over the head with a two by four to let them know you're interested in them. I told Ben and Stacy about my accident and recovery. I had them sitting on the edge of their beach towels with every word I spoke; they seemed fascinated and touched by the story.

199

I can't remember how Ben and I began dating, but I'm sure I made the first move by inviting him over to assemble a table that I'd purchased at Lowe's. I'm one of those women who are not equipped with handyman skills, Ben politely came over and fixed my table. I gave him many compliments. A friend once told me, "Every man I've ever known has a fragile ego," which I've found to be validated numerous times. So when Ben finally asked me out, I was ecstatic.

That night before our date, *recky neckie* Randy, whom I hadn't heard from in a while, called to ask, "Kelly, can I come over tonight? I'm in your neck of the woods."

Relieved, I said, "I'm sorry, Randy, but you need to keep travelling to a different neck of the woods. I've met someone new, so it won't work anymore."

It wasn't long before Ben and I had fallen in love. The Lord knows any man for whom I'm interested has to have patience with me and my forgetful memory. So I put all men through tests, even Ben, but my test for Ben was unintentional and inadvertent at the time. He had purchased passes for us to King's Island, so we could spend one day a week at the amusement park. He liked riding the roller coasters almost as much as I did. We went to King's Island for another day of sun and fun, on the way home, I realized I'd forgotten my bathing suit. So he turned around and drove the hour back to the Island to get my suit, never chastising me or saying anything remotely indicative that he was aggravated. He'd passed that initial test and would continue to pass many tests. Every time he came over, I'd have a new list of items I'd lost that he'd help me find. It was quite humorous, and he loved the challenge.

When I awoke, I thought of Ben. When I drove to work, I thought of Ben. When I was at work, I thought of being with Ben. When I was driving home, I thought of Ben. So during one of my quiet times, God convicted my heart with a message. It was that I cared more about spending time with Ben than I did with Him. That took me back, so I knew I needed to find balance. I blamed my obsession with Ben on being starved for male attention.

Ben had been married twice before, which was a concern for me. Ben shared that Stacy's mother, Dee, had divorced him because she claimed he was physically, mentally, and verbally abusing her, but Ben denied all of the accusations. Ben did admit one incident for which he was embarrassed. He and Dee had been painting a room while she was pregnant. She'd gotten him so mad that he accidentally pushed her down. Regrettably, he knew the baby risked being injured. Thank goodness nothing happened to the unborn. And even though he didn't mention his first wife much, there were implied undercurrents of some abuse in that relationship, too. Concerned, I gave Ben another test to ruffle his feathers to see if he'd become abusive. When he didn't, I was satisfied.

Dee worked as a cashier at the Kroger store around the corner from my house. She was a beautiful, sweet woman. She was always kind to me. On many afternoons, I would stop for groceries at the end of my daily run, heading to her line to catch up and find out about Stacy.

I couldn't wait for Mom to meet Ben because among her many attributes, Mom has a gift of discernment about people. I purposely shared little information before I brought him home. During our visit, Ben was friendly, appropriate, and yearned to be accepted by my parents. On our last night there, he whispered, "I'm waiting for you to say that you're ready to get married. When you do, I'll have that ring at your door within the hour." And to be thoroughly honest with me about his intentions, Ben confided he'd had a vasectomy after Stacy's birth.

When we returned to Ohio, I called Mom to inquire about her impression of Ben. I wasn't prepared for her answer.

"Kelly, he reminds me of a pot that is getting ready to boil over."

I thought, "Oh my word! Wow! Mom discerned that in a short amount of time."

I knew I needed to talk to Dee. The manager at Kroger shared when Dee usually took her afternoon break, so I called Dee the next day to ask if we could meet during that time. She agreed.

We went outside to drink cups of coffee; it was then I stared into her eyes and pleaded, "Dee I need to know the truth. Ben denies there was any abuse in your relationship, but I know you're a Christian and won't lie. How bad was it?"

She took a sip of her latte before replying. "Kelly, I wish I could tell you different 'cause I really like you. Stacy loves you, and I think you're a fantastic influence in her life, but I have to be honest with you." I waited while she drank more coffee. "Yes. The abuse was real, and it happened quite often. Home became a place I didn't like being because of the control Ben had over me."

"Why did it start?" I asked. My heart had dropped six inches.

"I have no idea – none. But once we were married, his super-controlling behavior kept increasing. I couldn't go anywhere or do anything without him questioning me." She stared into her empty cup and shrugged her shoulders apologetically.

I knew she was telling the truth. Lately, Ben's and my phone conversations went something like this:

(Ben) "Where did you go after church last night?"

(Me) "I stopped at Target."

(Ben) "Oh really? Who did you see there?"

(Me) "I ran into Joey."

(Ben) "What did Joey have to say? What did ya'll talk about?"

(Me) "I'm tired of your third degree. I live a busy life and don't like giving a report to anyone on where I go or who I see."

Of course, he didn't like my mouthing off to him, so after talking with Mom and Dee, I decided he was too much of a risk to marry. And another thing that I truly regretted was I'd allowed myself to sleep with him. As a young woman, I'd been starved for physical affection.

After I broke it off with Ben, I missed him so badly. I endured many days of sitting by the phone and crying my heart out, refraining from picking up the receiver or walking to his street to say, "I miss you so much; I've got to have you."

After confiding my temptations to a friend, she said, "Kelly, it's like this. When you put a piece of tape on a freshly painted wall and rip it off immediately, it comes off with a lot of paint. When you put another piece on and rip it off, it comes off with less paint. And when you put on yet another piece and rip it off, even less paint comes off. Finally, when you apply a strip and rip it off, hardly any paint is on it. That piece of tape is like sin. The first time you fall into sin, you're really sorry. You cry; you beg God for forgiveness; you declare it will never happen again. Then it happens again. Then you let out one or two tears and promise God it will never happen again. You put the tape back on the wall. When it does happen again, you become immune to God's voice, hearing it less and less. Eventually, you don't hear His voice.

It's the nature of how God has made us as human beings. Even though my body physically craved Ben's, I couldn't and wouldn't go there anymore. Being with Ben physically was living in sin. Intercourse had clouded my judgment and impeded my decisions. God taught me from this experience why it is important to wait and keep the marriage bed pure.

Chapter Thirty Eight

Endings and Beginnings

But everything exposed by the light becomes visible -
and everything that is illuminated becomes a light.
Ephesians 5: 13-14

In the three and a half short years I lived in Ohio, I had my share of fender- benders – five to be exact. They all could have been avoided if I had had adequate vision. I could be parking in a lot and a car would come out of the left. Actually, most of them occurred when I was trying to take left-hand turns. Even though I looked both ways, when you are missing peripheral vision, you miss out on a lot. So I began looking both ways and saying a prayer, "God protect me," before pulling out. But still, someone would slam into me. Today, as a passenger, when the driver takes a left-hand turn, I still experience full body tremors because I have flashbacks from those days.

It was my first Sunday singing in the Ginghamsburg Church choir, and I had just finished having a celebratory lunch with the singles' group. I was heading home on I-75 (where I felt the safest driving) with the Brooklyn Tabernacle Choir playing at top volume on my car stereo. I observed that they had nothing on our choir, which was fantastic. One hand was on the wheel, and the other hand was raised in praises to God. It was a beautiful day, and the sun roof was open. I was so high on God, it felt like I was riding on *Cloud Number Nine.*

205

Even though the speed limit was 60 m.p.h., the car in front was travelling 55 m.p.h., so, I decided to change lanes. I put on my blinker, checked my mirrors, and started to switch lanes, but I failed to look over my right shoulder as I normally did. Unfortunately, a little Toyota truck was in my *blind spot*, and thank God, the driver drove tractor-trailers for a living. As an experienced defensive driver, he saw me coming over but had no place to go with a concrete wall beside him on the right shoulder. I drove straight into him, striking the front fender of his car. His wife was beside him and their six year-old son, was sitting in the back seat of the vehicle. If he had not been able to stop the car as he did, they would have smacked the wall hard, and the accident could have had tragic results.

I remember stopping my car and removing the special glasses I wore because I didn't want anyone to know I was visually impaired. Actually, I threw them on the floor while jumping out of the car. The driver jumped out of his car at the same time, lifting his arms and closed fists in anger and disgust.

"What in the hell are you doing?" He yelled. He was angry because his greatest treasures were riding in that car.

At his harshness and my own terror, I began crying and praying aloud, "God please don't let anybody be hurt!" I ran back to the car with tears pouring down my cheeks. I can't imagine what my face looked like, but the moment he heard my cries and realized my terror that I'd hurt someone, his anger left him.

Finding courage, I ran back toward him. "Please don't let anybody be hurt. God help them. Is everybody okay?"

He said, "Ma'am. We're fine. But are you okay? Ma'am, please calm down. We're fine. It's okay. We're okay." His voice had changed from anger to compassion. "We're fine. We're okay. Are you okay?"

A Stranger to Myself

"No, I mean yes! No, I'm not okay. No, I'm not all right. Is your son okay?" I was extremely confused and still terrified.

"Yes, ma'am. My son is fine."

"Can I see him? Can I make sure he is okay?" I cried. The tears kept coming.

His wife brought the child out of the car, and all I could do was hug the woman. "I'm so thankful that you all are okay," I said choking down my fears and tears.

A passer-bye had called 9-1-1. Earlier, I had been riding on *Cloud Number Nine* and thought nothing could bring me down – that is, until I heard the dreaded metal on metal sound. And then the cloud was stripped away and the world came crashing toward me. This accident occurred half a mile from taking the exit for my apartment.

Trying to make conversation and calm down, I sobbed, "I just sang my first Sunday in the choir at church. I was feeling so good; I didn't imagine anything could go wrong. I'm sorry."

"Ma'am, what church do you go to?" the man asked. He must have been trying to calm me down, too.

"I attend the best church ever. It's called Ginghamsburg Church. It's off Exit 73 in Tipp City."

"You know, we've been wanting to find a good church," the wife stated. "Maybe we should try Ginghamsburg Church."

"I'd love it if you would. I'd love for you to be my guest there."

My attention was diverted as a police car parked in front of my car. I voluntarily told the officer what I'd done and began crying again.

"Ma'am, don't be so hard on yourself. This is the most common type of accident. I probably investigate five or six of these a week. Calm down. Don't be so hard on yourself."

I stuttered in response. "I just sang in the choir for the first time today. I was so full of God, I thought nothing bad could touch me."

"What church do you go to?" he asked. This was an interesting question. Maybe he was trying to calm me down, too.

My tears stopped. "I go to the best church ever. It's called Ginghamsburg Church, off Exit 73 in Tipp City."

"Do you know you're the third person who has told me about Ginghamsburg Church? I'm going to have to try it out."

"I would love for you to come. Please be my guest next Sunday."

He smiled. "Maybe I'll come sometime. We're finished here. Will you be okay driving home?"

"Yes, thank you."

"Good day, then." He tipped his hat.

After getting back into the driver's seat, I began the longest drive of my life. It may as well have been one hundred miles back to my apartment. Still terrified, I pulled onto the highway and drove five miles under the speed limit.

When I entered the front door, I hung my keys on a rack and said, "Lord, I'm done driving." Without an idea of how to get to and from work, I promised Him I wasn't ever going to drive again. Then I went to my room, knelt beside the bed, and began wailing, sobbing, and thanking God that no one had been killed or seriously injured.

"I could have done to somebody else what was done to me," I cried.

It would be hard to live, knowing I had destroyed someone's face or put someone in a coma or created a blood clot in someone's brain. I couldn't fathom how the man who hit me slept at night. There is no evidence that he ever came or called the hospital to check on my condition.

A Stranger to Myself

I'll never know how long I prayed that night; maybe it was twenty minutes or forty-five minutes, but when the phone rang, I was in no shape to answer it. But the answering machine did. It was my friend, Chuck Townsend, from Ginghamsburg Church.

"Kelly, if you're there, please pick up. I need you to answer the phone if you're there. Please pick up. God impressed on my heart to get on my face and cry out for your safety. I've been praying for you for the last hour and forty-five minutes. God would not release me from praying for you. I need to know you are okay and safe."

An hour and thirty-five minutes ago was when the accident had happened. Of course, while he continued leaving his message, I picked up the receiver and the tears began again. "Chuck, the family I hit may be alive today because of you. God heard your prayers. I know there were angels all around my vehicle and all around the vehicle I hit. I probably shouldn't be here today. I know I shouldn't. Chuck, I'm giving up driving. I'm not driving anymore."

Chuck said, "Kelly, we have a hallelujah service tonight at church. I'll come by around 5:30. The service doesn't start until 6:30, but I'll be there around 5:30, so we can talk."

"Thanks, Chuck. I'd like that."

That night at the hallelujah service, there were about three hundred people in the audience. Those services have a big draw. During that service, I shared my testimony about what the Lord had done for me and the family I'd hit that day. After the meeting was over, Chuck drove me home. He parked, got out, and came around the car to open my door like a gentleman does. When he opened it, he said, "Kelly, what time do you want me here in the morning?"

"Chuck! Chuck! Are you serious?" I cried in delight.

"Yes, Kelly," he said with a smile. "I'm going to be the best chauffeur that you've ever had as long as I can do it." Chuck was unemployed at the time.

"I have to be at work at 8:00."

So at 7:45 the next morning, Chuck pulled into my driveway, parked his car, and came in, so I could give him my car keys. He became my first driver and treated me like a queen. From that day forward, I never opened my own car door.

Several nights later, I had a dream. Usually, because I'm a heavy sleeper, I don't recall my dreams, but God gave me a dream about the accident. In the dream, there were thousands of angels' wings pressing against the man's vehicle to keep it from slamming into the concrete wall.

The next Sunday, I had unbelievable surprises. Not only did the couple I hit visit the church, but so did the investigating police officer. I met them in the vestibule, so we could sit by each other. They raised their hands, and we praised the Lord together. And on the following Sunday, the police officer returned, bringing three of his buddies with him.

Did I mention we serve an awesome God? It turned out the couple loved the Church's children's program. The wife quickly found a place to serve in the pre-school department, and the husband found his ministry in our new Youth Center. He began leading a Sunday school class for sixteen – seventeen year-old young men.

Chapter Thirty Nine

Pernell

*In that day people will throw away to the moles and bats their
idols of silver and idols of gold, which they made to worship.*
Isaiah 2:20

Three months later, Chuck accepted a job offer to run a
camp in a nearby state, so my friend, Pernell, who I knew from
the single's group at church, became my second chauffeur.
Chuck had introduced us in the single's group, informing me that
Pernell and his parents attended a smaller church where his
parents were staff members who cleaned the church. Because the
church didn't have a singles' group, Pernell had begun coming to
Ginghamsburg Church.

Chuck trained Pernell to be my chauffeur. He said, "When
Kelly comes out of her house, you need to help her down the
steps. Then open the car door and help her get inside. Make sure
her dress and coat are tucked in. Ask her if everything is okay,
and when she tells you, 'Yes,' you close the door. Then you run
to your door and get in. Whenever you get to the gas station, the
grocery store, or her place of work, you may need to remind
Kelly to stay where she is. You jump out of the car, run around,
open her door, give her your hand, and help her get out. Pernell,
this is very important. You have a very special job. You're

211

taking care of one of God's most precious angels." What can I say? Chuck was great.

I had to be at work at 8:00 a.m. each day, so Pernell drove to my house and parked his car beside the garage. Then he'd back my car out and leave it running to warm up. Finally, he'd knock on my door, saying, "Kelly, your chariot awaits." There was always a big smile on his face.

As it turned out, Pernell had a mental illness called Schizophrenia. As in most cases, the disease did not manifest until Pernell was a junior in high school. Schizophrenia effects men seven to one and usually does not show up until ages 18 – 25. According to the U.S. National Library of Medicine, "Schizophrenia is a mental disorder often characterized by abnormal social behavior and failure to recognize what is real. Common symptoms include false beliefs, unclear or confused thinking, and reduced social engagement and emotional expression." It was unclear as to what had triggered his, but with proper medication, you'd never know anything was wrong with him.

When I first visited his home, Pernell and his parents invited me into a special room where they displayed all his running medals and trophies. Whenever Pernell talked, he talked from his high school days because they were the only times when he felt like somebody.

Our pastor was a very charismatic minister, who would shout from the pulpit if he got excited or passionate about God's message. On one Sunday, Pernell wrote me a note: "Kelly, is he mad at me?" I whispered, "No. He's just very passionate about what he's talking about. Try to shut off that voice in your head and pay attention to his words."

Once when we were driving on the interstate in the middle of winter and listening to a Christian radio station, Pernell seemed quieter than normal. So I asked him, "Is everything okay."

He shook his head no. Finally, he said, "Kelly, can you hear the man yelling in the car beside us?"

"No, Pernell," I responded. "And you can't hear him, either. It's in the middle of winter, and all the windows are up. Why? Do you think you hear him?"

He nodded his head affirmatively.

"What is he saying to you?" I was curious.

He shook his head no. "I can't say, Kelly. It's too bad to say to a Christian lady like you." Pernell's heart was precious and almost child-like.

I said, "Pernell, this is a delusion; it's not happening. Your mental disorder is talking now. I'm sorry you have to live like this. It has to be awful."

Afterward, I telephoned his mother, who was his lifeline, and relayed the event.

She took him to the doctor and got his medications changed. The prescription he'd been on since high school had lost its effect; his body was immune to it.

When Pernell went to the movies to see *A Beautiful Mind,* he immediately telephoned me and excitedly announced, "Kelly, I have to take you to see a movie because they finally got it right!"

One of many funny stories happened in the middle of winter. I walked out of the hospital and waited outside at the curb. Pernell started up the engine immediately and drove up, putting the car in park. He jumped out of the car to open up my door. As I walked past three or four nurses, who were standing outside in the bitter cold on a smoke break, I pulled my long, red coat closer to me. He offered me his hand and said, "Madame."

One of the nurses called after me. "What do you have that I don't have to get this kind of treatment?"

I looked directly at her and said, "When you've got it, you've got it," I smiled. "Thank you, Pernell."

After he helped me get in, he proudly ran around the car, wearing a huge smile on his face as we drove away. That was one of his proudest moments.

Prior to driving for me, I'd realized at church how embarrassed Pernell would become during social functions when someone asked him, "What do you do for a living, Pernell?"

He'd look down toward the ground, rub his foot with the other foot, and say, "I, uh, I, uh, I have a hand – a handicap and am on disability."

Politely, they would probe, "Oh? Tell me more about that."

But he had a hard time with this and had learned to make no response. Slowly, the person would understand and soon disappear. People just didn't know how to relate to him.

When Chuck had solicited Pernell to drive for me, he'd blessed him with a job opportunity and responsibilities he could excel at. I loved hearing him answer that awkward question he'd say, "I'm a full time chauffeur. I'm a driver. I take care of the woman over there." Then he'd point in my direction.

Even though I only paid him $20 or $25 a week, which is nothing, he was so proud. I was talking to Ellen about Pernell one day and mentioned how much I was paying him. She got so indignant, thinking that I was taking advantage of Pernell.

"Kelly! It's terrible that you pay him so little."

"I promise, Ellen. He doesn't do it for the money. He does it because he loves to serve and finds satisfaction from doing it."

The week before, Pernell had shared his gratitude for the job and said I'd added so much to his life. I was grateful for Pernell, who took me not only to work, but to the grocery store, to get my nails done, and to friends' houses where he'd disappear for two or three hours. He loved his job because he had a purpose. The worst time of the day for Pernell was between 12:00 p.m. and 3:00 p.m., when he experienced most of his delusions and hallucinations. But his job driving for me was his utmost priority and because he wanted to be extremely safe, he napped during this time with a shower following. Then he'd come to get me at 4:00 p.m., so this schedule worked out perfectly.

One year on his birthday, I bought him a card and placed a check in it for double the normal amount. When he arrived that morning, I met him at the door with a cupcake and sang "Happy Birthday" to him. When he opened his card, he read the verse and removed the check. He exclaimed, "Kelly! You don't have to pay me a dime more. You know I would do this job for free. I don't do this for the money. I do it because I now have a best friend. I have somebody that values me and makes me feel like I'm somebody. There is no amount of money that can be paid for that."

Sometime between his birthday and the following Saturday, I went to Walmart and bought one of the biggest stuffed bears that I could find. It had a red bow on it. I stuffed it into a huge gift bag and tied it with a string. The next time Pernell came over, I said, "Okay. Are you ready for your real birthday present now?"

I gave him the bear, and you'd have thought I'd given him a brand new car. He smiled from ear to ear, and his eyes danced with joy. "Oh, Kelly. I love him!" Then he gave me a big hug. "This is the best gift I've ever had." Pernell still has that stuffed bear to this day.

I made sure Pernell never had a dull weekend by including him on outings with my friends. He had only one desire, and that was to be accepted -- just like I had. Acceptance is something we all need.

Pernell drove for me until the day I moved to Charlotte. He was so sad when I left Ohio.

After driving for me, Pernell began volunteering for a food bank by stocking the shelves and carrying out the purchases for folks. I believe one of my spiritual gifts is working with people who have disabilities. I always try to validate them and accept them right where they are. To treat people as I would like to be treated – the Golden Rule -- works every time.

When you help other people realize their value, they can become the persons God intended them to be. But this world does such a good job of beating people down all the time and making them feel insignificant and powerless. All it takes is one person believing in you to change your world. Pernell realized the value of knowing God. Just like me, he knew he couldn't get out of bed in the morning without God being by his side. His faith was strong. He knew who he belonged to and that he had a purpose. Until I came along with my needs, he had always struggled with his purpose, but driving for me had given him a purpose and a meaning for his life. But as always, I was the one who felt blessed.

I believe one of the things I learned from Pernell was unconditional love. He loved me in my good, bad, and ugly states and put me on an undeserving pedestal. He was a mirror that reflected what I had grown to know: acceptance is important. He helped me to see the beauty in the simple things of life.

Chapter Forty

Paul

So, if you think you are standing firm, be careful that you don't fall! No temptation has seized you except what is common to man. And God is faithful; he will not let you be tempted beyond what you can bear. But when you are tempted, he will also provide a way out so that you can endure it.
1 Corinthians 10:12-13

The city had experienced a vicious snow storm one Sunday night when Pernell was still driving for me. He didn't like to drive in bad weather, so he wasn't going to drive me to work the next day. I was worried about how I'd get there when Paul telephoned me and said, "Kelly, I'm coming over to get you. Stay where you are." That's when our friendship solidified.

I'd met Paul while I was leading a Bible Study class at Ginghamsburg United Methodist Church. Paul was confined to a wheelchair, the result of an automobile accident when he was sixteen years old; he was now forty. His father had been driving the family from Ohio to Florida, and when they were driving through Gainesville, Florida, a young lady and her toddler child crossed the center line and ran head on into them. No one ever knew the reason, but tragically, his aunt had died instantly, his grandmother had been severely injured, and Paul had experienced a thoracic five and six break in his spinal cord. He was paralyzed from his chest down.

Unfortunately, Paul also suffered from denial. He had never accepted his disability, refusing to get a handicapped placard or license plate because he didn't consider himself "handicapped." Whenever he drove to the grocery store, he'd park in a normal parking space. Many times, he'd exit the store only to find that someone had parked too close, hindering him from getting into his car, so he'd have to wait for the customer to return and leave.

During my residency in Ohio, sleeping for me was still an issue. It was not as bad as the first three years, but I still experienced severe insomnia. When I had a night where my brain would not shut off, I wished there was someone to talk to. Women process things verbally, whereas men have to get alone to process their thoughts. So when Paul ended a visit with the invitation, "Kelly, if you can't sleep during the night, call me because I don't sleep anyway. It's no big deal for me to talk anytime." I began calling my new best friend without feeling guilty because he didn't work; he currently was on disability even though he didn't consider himself disabled. Isn't that ironic? He'd listen to me and in a clever way, relate what I was going through to a Bible verse and once again, take my thoughts off myself and focus them back on God. He read and studied his Bible four to five hours each day. I could give him the first part of a Bible verse, and he could finish it along with the chapter and verse. When it came to the Word of God, he was brilliant. During our conversations, he'd always tell me a joke or two and then pray for me, and then I'd fall into a deep sleep. Paul's dry sense of humor was a riot and made me laugh hysterically.

Unbeknownst to me, Paul had been pursuing me relentlessly during our two years as best friends and secretly hoped that making me laugh and removing my challenges would win my affections. Paul got tired of sitting at home and got a part-time job in a bait shop. One day as he was rolling around, straightening up the shelves, he noticed something sparkling on the floor. He rolled over to it, reached down, and to his amazement, picked up a diamond ring. Paul wondered, "God, could this be the ring I'm supposed to give Kelly?" Because no one had inquired about it or had returned to claim it, he took it home and placed it on his dresser. Each day, he prayed over the ring. "Please let Kelly realize that I'm the only man for her."

When Paul entered a race for a City Council position, I became his greatest campaign cheerleader even though he lived in a different part of Dayton, and I couldn't vote for him. On the night of the election, we attended church and returned to my home to watch the results on television. When I saw that he'd come in second to last place, I wanted to crawl under my sofa out of sheer embarrassment for him. At the same time, I was perplexed. How could he have been that unfavorable? How could he have lost so badly? Had the county people discovered something about his character that I didn't know?

But on that Tuesday night, my compassion for his disappointment outweighed any questions swirling in my brain, so I leaned forward to hug him. That's when it happened – our first kiss. After a quick making out session, before Paul left that night, I had a very serious discussion with him about his smoking. But like all of us, Paul had some issues. The main one was that he smoked cigarettes and carried the packs in his front shirt pocket. Respectfully, he had never smoked around me or smelled of smoke, being careful to cleanse himself of the smell. As our relationship had matured to an engagement, I shared my feelings with him.

"Paul, there is something that I must talk to you about. I've never smoked a cigarette in my life or ever had the urge to smoke. I've never been around cigarette smoke, and I don't think it is something I can allow in my life. I'm just being honest with you and letting you know that if you want this relationship to continue, I'll need to know that you will quit smoking."

He quickly brushed aside my comments by downplaying the fact he smoked. "Well, I just have one or two a day; it's not like I'm a habitual chain smoker." Needless to say, I read his reply as a promise that relieved my troubled soul.

On the following Sunday, Paul led me into the prayer room at church. This is when he relayed the events of finding the ring on the floor of the bait shop and how he'd been praying over the ring for eight months. Afterward, he extended a jewelry box and presented me with the ring as he began proposing.

My heart was overflowing with love and happiness. "Paul, I've never been as sure about a decision as I am now. I will marry you." Both delight and relief showed on his face as he released a long sigh. Then we laughed and hugged each other in a tight grasp.

Paul quickly injected his possessiveness and responsibility for me. He loved that he could take care of me and especially enjoyed the times whenever I got sick. He'd come to my apartment, bring food to eat, cook my meals, make freshly squeezed orange juice, rub my back, and ensure I had medicine. He treated me like a queen. Sometimes, he'd insist that I take my meals in bed. Paul treated me wonderfully.

Dad really liked Paul because of their shared bond of being in wheelchairs. Dad immediately took my fiancé under his wing and couldn't wait to educate him on the many opportunities available for people who were wheelchair bound. Dad even gave him one of his old racing chairs -- the first one Paul had ever owned. Paul's physician was old school and had informed him that if he had a catheter, it would diminish his fertility, so he'd never gotten a catheter. Of course, this was incorrect.

I've always felt strongly about counseling because counselors can see a lot more than what we can see, so we immediately began meeting once a week with Mark, a Christian counselor who worked in our church's counseling center. Mark had actually counseled with Paul's brother and his wife during the demise of their marriage, so he was even more familiar with the family's background. After our first session was over, Mark walked behind Paul's wheelchair to push him as a courtesy. I'll never forget Paul's non-verbal response to this innocent gesture. My fiancé whipped around, and if looks could kill, Mark would have been dead, a victim of good manners. His strong reaction communicated plenty: Paul had never dealt with being labeled "disabled" or "handicapped."

For our next session, Mark carefully probed Paul about his reaction. There was uncomfortable silence in the room as he looked perplexed in response to his pointed questions.

I gently butted in, offering my assistance to downplay the questions. "Paul, I'm disabled. You're disabled, too."

"No, I'm not," he stubbornly replied.

"Yes, you are," I argued. "You can't walk independently. A disability isn't like having a *Scarlet A* on your chest. A disability is something that we've had happen to us so that God can glorify himself through our disability."

But his stubbornness was strong and had been ingrained a long time ago; he didn't view it that way. It actually took a long time for me to convince him of that. Fortunately, Dad came to the rescue again and convinced Paul to get a disability placard, so he could park his car in wider spaces. I already had one, which we had been using most of the time.

As the wedding date quickly approached, Mom flew to Ohio to spend a week with me. It was an exciting time for us as we marveled over God's blessings and how just a few years earlier, no one would have thought that I'd survive the accident, much less plan a wedding. Delighted to be together, Mom and I spent the week interviewing caterers, choosing the bridesmaids' dresses that would be custom made, and meeting with the pastor to determine the order of service. Mom and Paul decided they'd handle the selection of a nice hotel for housing our out of town wedding guests, while I was working. It delighted me that they were spending quality time together and getting to know each other, while handling this important task. And I knew my mother would make the right choice regardless. Unfortunately, with lots of *things to do* marked off our long list, the week ended much too soon, and Paul and I found ourselves reluctantly taking Mom to the airport. At the gate, we kissed and hugged each other goodbye. Life seemed good.

One weekend shortly afterward, we were driving down the interstate when Paul pulled off the highway and parked the car in a rest area. When he didn't make a move to get out, I turned towards him to see what was wrong. That's when I saw that he was lighting a marijuana joint and extending it to me.

"Here, Kelly. Take a draw. I'm not feeling well. Smoke a joint with me. I'm sure it'll make us both feel better."

I was shocked. "You smoke marijuana? Paul, didn't you know when I said I didn't want you smoking cigarettes that included smoking marijuana? What is wrong with you?"

He looked dejected, but I didn't care. Then the dejection turned to – what? Surprise?

"You know I've cut back on nicotine, and you know that caused me to have huge welts all over my body."

I did know; he was telling the truth. I'd seen the red splotches all over his exposed skin when he'd taken me to the Sizzler Steakhouse. The itching was miserable; he'd even used his steak knife to scratch his back.

"I need this joint for my pain. It's the only thing that works." Was he trying to validate his use? He went on further to say, "Sometimes when I'm reading my Bible, the pain is so bad that I smoke a joint. That doesn't make me a bad person, Kelly."

I was dumbfounded. He'd never said anything about his discomfort or pain. I think it had more to do with the high than his pain level. What was even scarier is that after he smoked, he wanted to continue driving while high.

"Please take me home, Paul," I was disappointed and crying. "I have a lot of praying to do. I think we need to postpone our wedding for a while."

Grudgingly, he ground the joint in the ashtray and took me home. Without another word, I exited the idling car and entered my apartment, closing the door and Paul behind me.

Over the next few days, I prayed and fasted incessantly for God's discernment. I knew God would lead me to the right decision regarding our marriage. My doubts and fears about his addiction to marijuana led me to counsel with Mark alone. During our meeting, I confided in him. "Mark, I don't think I want to go through with this wedding."

Mark looked relieved. "Kelly, as a counselor I'm supposed to stay unbiased and not take sides or be in either person's favor, but I'm sorry. I have to break those rules this time and tell you that you are making the wisest decision."

Astounded, I somehow comprehended that my counselor was advising me to run, not walk, but run away from Paul. I now knew God's answer, so I asked Mark to assist me in preparing the words I needed to say to Paul. It seemed cold and shallow to deliver my decision over the phone, but that is where I felt the safest. Mark agreed. Patiently, he helped me draft the exact words I was to say to Paul. Mark wisely advised me to keep it short and to the point. When I returned home that night, I was prepared for his call when it came.

Without hesitation and fortified, I said, "Paul, I guess you have noticed I've had doubts when I postponed the wedding. My doubts that we can make this marriage work are greater than my feelings for you. I'm sorry, but I must say goodbye."

There was silence on the other end of the line. Then he finally said, "Okay. If that's the way you want it, Kelly."

"Yes. That's the way I want it."

There was a loud click on the other end.

Our song had once been "You're Just Too Good to be True" by Frankie Valli and the Four Seasons. Three days later, I arrived home from work to hear a wrathful message. Paul was singing our song, replacing the lovely lyrics with hateful lyrics and phrases. He said I thought I was too good for him, and he wasn't worthy of my love because he was trash compared to what I thought I was entitled. He said I could kiss his *you-know-what*. It was a terrible ditty that made ugly what could have been a precious memory. All our months together were instantly reduced to zilch.

There is a grieving process we all go through when a relationship ends, and anger is one step in that difficult process. I'd expected he'd be hurt and angry. So I quickly hit the delete button and decided to move forward with my life.

Once my composure returned, I telephoned my parents to break the sad news. That's when I learned more about my parents' absolute desire for my happiness and their unwavering faith in God. My parents received instant relief after months of praying.

My mother said, "Kelly, when I boarded the plane and finally sat down in my assigned seat, I couldn't stop the tears. They were flowing all the way from Dayton to Atlanta. When your dad picked me up, I was crying so hard I could barely speak. I was finally able to blurt out, 'Kelly is making a huge mistake!'"

That night, my mother reported various facts about Paul, starting with, "He does not live the same way we do."

Dad asked, "Marilyn, what's wrong?"

That's when she started crying again and told him, "I'm so afraid Kelly is making a huge mistake. Paul is not who she thinks she's marrying. Paul has deceived Kelly and not shown his true self." In just a short week, Mom had learned enough about Paul to form an impression.

"He does not live the same way we do. His filthy car was a huge flag, and his house smelled like a pack of cigarettes. I ran my finger over his TV screen and came away with a finger laden with ashes. And the stale cigarette smoke and language bothered me."

Dad and Mom had decided not to say anything to me. Instead, they got on their knees and prayed for God's wisdom, revelation, and intervention. And He did not fail them or me.

When I look back on my relationship with Paul, I realized a lot of good had come out of it. Jesus in his infinite wisdom knew I needed to feel beautiful inside and out. Paul helped me to realize that I did in fact need the help of others. Paul had always insisted on driving me and was so disappointed when I didn't call him for a ride. I'm sure Paul would have preferred if I had never driven again. Wisely, he was careful not to say that because he knew I would have labeled him as too controlling. He was a good man, and I believe he truly loved me. He taught me to be more patient with myself when I would get frustrated

225

because I was having difficulty with a co-worker or a church member. He'd listen first and then ask, "Do you want me to just listen and pray for you, or do you want to pray and see what God has to say through me?"

Paul also helped me to mature as a Christian. He was knowledgeable about the Bible, and I was always going to him with a scripture I didn't understand or needing an example for our Bible study group. I believe he truly cared about me, and I pray he sees how his life was blessed and how he, too, matured through our relationship. Hopefully, I assisted him in healing and in recognizing that his disability is not a curse but an open door to be used by our heavenly Father.

Chapter Forty One

The Truth Shall Set You Free

See to it that no one takes you captive through hollow and deceptive philosophy, which depends on human tradition and the elemental spiritual forces of this world rather than on Christ.
Colossians 2:8

When I told God Almighty years before that I was locking the key to a secret in my soul, I knew the huge chains were still wrapped around the box that was double-pad-locked in my conscience and heart. Even though my Priest had assured me that God had forgiven me, I didn't realize that as long as the box still existed, the pain of what had happened to me, and the shame of what I'd done existed too. So faithful to my self-promise, the high school spring break secret had remained hush-hush for many years – through the accident and long recuperation, the undergraduate years, the Master's degree years, and my first job and move to Ohio. The truth of the matter is even though I had been given mercy and forgiveness by the Most High, I had never forgiven myself. My conscience and my heart housed the raw wound that I kept applying a makeshift salve to, but the wound could never heal. That is, not until I learned how to forgive myself. And the sadness was I didn't know how. But never doubt this: God always has a way – and a plan.

Brenda was one of my closest friends in Ohio and an incredible believer in Jesus Christ. She and I enjoyed many girls'

227

nights out because we loved each other's company, becoming almost inseparable. One night after having dinner at our favorite restaurant, Brenda shared about a time in her life when she was not walking with God. Intrigued, I listened as she continued bearing her soul. She had fallen, much like I had with Ben, into a sexual relationship with a man.

"When I found out I was pregnant, Kelly, it was awful. I was ashamed and confused and didn't know what to do or where to turn. When I told my boyfriend, he acted shocked that I hadn't prevented the pregnancy. He blamed me and wanted no part of the situation. He definitely didn't plan to be a father."

"His words cut me in half when he said, 'I can't accept a huge responsibility like this in my life now.' His career was blossoming. I realized he'd only used me for sex – not love like I'd hoped."

While she talked, tears formed in my eyes; I couldn't swallow the lump in my throat. We'd lived the same nightmare and worn the same shoes. Sadly, my intuition told me how Brenda's story was going to end before she even continued her story.

"So, I had an abortion," she mumbled. Immediately, she hung her head. My hand grabbed her shaking hands. I wore the shame and guilt, too. That's when I unlocked the box. After I shared the horrible details of my rape and my regrettable decision to have an abortion, I experienced a momentary epiphany. Having Brenda as a friend was no accident: God had predestined this friendship, so our wounds could heal.

Our experiences reminded me of what I'd heard on a *Focus on the Family* radio broadcast years earlier. A young preacher was saying, "Young men give women love to get sex; women give men sex to get love. It is usually a woman, who is left heartbroken and alone."

A Stranger to Myself

I'd gotten involved in the "Chrysalis Walk," which is similar to the "Walk to Emmaus," but its targeted audience is high school aged youth, not adults, and its presentations, given by clergy and lay speakers, are different: Two of the presentations are the "single-hood talk" and the "marriage talk." I had been honored to participate in the upcoming "Chrysalis Walk" as a table leader for a group of six or seven girls and would be giving the "single-hood talk."

Every lay speaker previews his/her talk before the team members to receive constructive feedback as the members are instructed to pretend they are young women to anticipate potential questions a teenage girl might ask. After agreeing to be a table leader and presenter, I hung up the phone receiver and heard God's voice, loud and clear, "Kelly, it's time."

I tried to be coy with God and asked, *Time? Time for what, Lord?*

His response was firm. "You know what I'm talking about. It's time to let your dark secret out."

Oh no, Lord. Not that, I pleaded. *You can't mean that! Not the a-ab-abortion.* I could barely say the shameful word.

His response was simply, "Yes, it is time."

So I have to ask, "Have you ever tried to tell the Lord, 'No?' If so, you know it doesn't work well."

Now, I'd given seven presentations by this time on various subjects. I had been told I was a good orator. Developing my speeches had been easy. But this time, I was struggling with the outline the leaders had provided. It should have been easy enough to complete the blanks with personal stories or examples; unfortunately, I found myself agonizing over the computer's keyboard. I fought back God's voice because I knew what I'd hear: "Kelly, it is time." But for me, it was NOT time.

On Friday night (the only overnight stay of the preparatory meetings before the actual weekend retreat began), I was the last speaker of the night. As I stood to present, I heard God's voice repeating his familiar command loudly and clearly, "Kelly, it is time." Dismissing His voice yet again, I began reading my notes. But His voice got louder. "Kelly, it is time." I continued, blatantly ignoring God's mighty voice. Can you imagine my nerve? When I was one paragraph away from the end of my pitiful "single-hood talk," I heard it again, only more forceful: "KELLY, IT IS TIME!"

Finally, succumbing to His will, I flung my papers to the floor and responded aloud, "Okay, Lord. You win!" There was no stopping when I heard my voice announce, "Let me tell you about Kurt."

The chains disintegrated as my secret erupted. The leaders heard how Kurt had been my world back during my teen-age years. They heard how he'd professed his love many times. They heard how he'd promised his love would never end. They heard how he'd tried to persuade me into having sex to prove my love. They heard about my friends, the "goody, two shoes girls," who'd surrendered to the temptations to hold onto boyfriends. They heard how I'd been curious about intimacy but vowed to wait until my wedding night as my parents had done. And they heard how Kurt had forcefully stolen my virginity from me. With hot tears flowing and emotions rolling rampant, I poured out my shame, my guilt, and my self-condemnation. I'd begun by talking about the accident and ended by talking about the rape and abortion.

No longer a prisoner of Satan's, I had emerged as an emancipated woman. The past eleven years of wearing the heavy shackles of shame and guilt were over as they lay behind me on the wooden floor of that conference room. As John 8:32 says,

"Then you will know the truth, and the truth will set you free." What a prisoner I'd been because of Satan's conniving subtlety. He'd convinced me to hide behind the mask of a good Christian woman and deny the shame that was eating my soul inside out. He'd lied that people would condemn me and hate me if they knew my truth. He'd persuaded me to stay silent, or my witness for Christ would be ruined. I was no longer fooled because my eyes were no longer blind. The truth is God wanted to use my experience for His glory.

The audience was dumbfounded. As I stood there at the podium, you could have heard a pin drop. Finally, a team member asked a riveting question: "Did I think the accident was a punishment for having had an abortion a year earlier?" My teachings had taught me how to answer the question.

"God does not work that way. I believe God forgave me when I went to confession."

And I was more prepared to answer that question when one of the young women asked it during the actual retreat weekend. I quoted her John 1:9: "If we confess our sins, he is faithful and just and will forgive us our sins and purify us from all unrighteousness." Then I said, "God forgave me that Saturday, but the critical thing was I'd never forgiven myself. And in Psalm 103, we're told 'the Lord is compassionate and gracious, slow to anger, abounding in love. He will not always accuse, nor will He harbor His anger forever; He does not treat us as our sins deserve or repay us according to our iniquities.'"

For as high as the heavens are above the earth, so great is his love for those who fear him; as far as the east is from the west, so far has he removed our transgressions from us.

"We all deserve hell, but God forgives us. Does anybody know why we're not told He removes our sins as far as the north is from the south?"

231

I was met by blank stares.

"Because there is a north pole and south pole, which means there is an ending point. Think about it. If you begin walking east, you'll go forever east, and if you start going west, you'll go forever west. That means your sins will never meet up with God or you again!" It was such a joy to see a room full of thirty to forty women all have an epiphany moment at the same time. They got it!

There was a long line of young women waiting to speak with me in the Chapel. The leaders said they'd never seen a line so long, but I'll never forget meeting Candace that night. She said she'd just found out she was pregnant the day before the retreat and thanked me for sharing my story because she had planned to schedule an abortion after the weekend. Now, she planned to keep the baby and give it up for adoption. We hugged, cried, prayed, and praised God for her decision. I shared my telephone number with her, so we could talk if things got tough. Praise the Lord; a life had been spared!

I also met three girls who had had abortions. I counseled with each girl, assuring her of God's love and forgiveness.

That night my table group and I slept soundly on the cement floor. I'd never experienced a better night's sleep! Many women had been set free.

Chapter Forty Two

God's Direction

For He will command his angels concerning you to guard
you in all your ways; they will lift you up in their hands,
so that you will not strike your foot against a stone.
Psalm 91:11-12

It turned out that due to insurance cut backs and new laws, our patient load at Rebound dropped from thirty to two or three patients. Dr. Smith informed me that Rebound would be shutting its doors in another month and to use my time wisely with the low patient ratio. Basically, he was telling me to look for another job.

The next door God opened for me was a chaplaincy internship out of Miami Valley Hospital. There were only five people in my class, and four of them were placed in a hospital setting. The leader of our group specifically asked me how I felt about my rotation being at a nursing home. I was immediately thrilled, as I'd always loved working with the elderly. As I started the job, I learned so much about loss and growing older. I fell in love with these wonderful elders who had wisdom that I could glean.

One of my favorite things was to walk from room to room and just say, "Tell me a story." And before I knew it, an hour had passed, and I was still enthralled. Through this internship, God taught me how to deal with death. One responsibility was to be on call one night each week. Sure enough, more weeks than not, I would be called to the hospital to sit with an elderly person or the family of an elderly person. I sat on the deathbed of many saints who went home.

We only have two choices for eternity: heaven or hell. And praise the Lord, God allowed me to lead many into salvation; their homecomings changed for eternity. After the person passed, I learned to invite the family in to stay with him/her. Even though the spirit is no longer there, I would say to them, "What would you like to tell him? This is your time to say what you need to say." Many nights I spent caressing a family member's back with my hand as she wept over her mother or father who had just passed. God used me to help that family member to bring closure to the relationship. I also learned how important it is to say what we need to say to the people who have made a difference in our lives and to the people who have sacrificed so much to give us the lives we have. I learned to have an attitude of gratitude for the people I have in my life and to say what needs to be said now and not to wait until it is too late.

But during that semester, I realized that chaplaincy was not a good fit for me because God gave me abundant energy. Instead of being that soft-spoken angel sitting by a bedside, I was more inclined to participate in sing-alongs. But the internship opened my eyes to a new mission field: Elder care. I felt certain this is where the Lord wanted me to be, and I received affirmation when a nursing home executive director called me. Kimberly had gotten my name from Rebound. She was with Springmeade Nursing and Rehabilitation Center in Tipp City, Ohio. We hit it off immediately.

She explained, "The home is in disarray; we're losing residents and staff members, and the families are up in arms with the care their family members are receiving." I couldn't believe the job she offered me.

"We need someone to come in and be our ambassador of goodwill. Your job is to walk from room to room and uplift the residents. Spread joy. Ask them how their care is going. Work with the families to ensure all parties are pleased. You can bring stories to read."

But the most important thing Kimberly told me was this: "We're a Christian-based home, so you have freewill to talk about Jesus and to pray with the residents."

I accepted with a hearty, "Well, I'm your woman!"

I became the director of provider relations, which never made sense to me. I preferred the name, "Director of Love." And who is love? Jesus! God had given me a perfectly-suited job. He had taken me full circle. Was I really the same girl whom the sorority sisters had shunned and hid in the back room during sorority rush because they were embarrassed about my appearance? Would I really be in the forefront of this public relations department?

I could relate to many of the elderly's stories because we shared something in common: We had lost a lot. Most of the women and men I met had lost children, spouses, homes, independence, and some, their memories. I started collecting funny stories off the internet about elderly people. One such story I remember was on the AARP site about a lady that saw five gentlemen, "My Five New Boyfriends!" I will paraphrase the author's words as closely as I can.

I am seeing five gentlemen every day. As soon as I wake up, Will Power helps me get out of bed. Then I go to see John. Then Charlie Horse comes along, and when he is here, he takes a lot of my time and attention. When he leaves, Arthur Ritis shows up and stays the rest of the day. He doesn't like to stay in one place very long, so he takes me from joint to joint. After such a busy day, I'm really tired and glad to go to bed with Ben Gay. What a life! Oh yes, I'm flirting with Al Zymer.

I'd always get smiles and chuckles out of that story. The important thing was I was meeting people where they were at and actively listening to their rich heritage. Who could've imagined my new calling would be in the elderly care-giving business? The five or six other directors and I did our jobs so well, it only took two years to get the home in better condition and reach our goals. But because I was not dispensing pills or providing physical therapy, guess who got cut during the next year's budget cut? They gave me a very generous separation package and thanked me profusely for all of my hard work. And then God had other plans for me.

By this time, Ellen had married Ken, and they had one son, Jack. Rod, Jr. had married Kathy, and they had one daughter, Kaylin. They all lived in Charlotte, North Carolina, and had begun their custom homes building business, Bannister Homes, Inc., and I was getting wearisome of Ellen and Kathy calling me once a week to inform me they knew I was not living where God wanted me to live.

I'd say, "Oh, has He spoken to you? Do you have a direct line to God that I'm not privileged to have, because He hasn't called me yet."

But then they'd argue, "I know you're not where God wants you to be because you have a little four-year old nephew that needs his Aunt KK." (My niece Kaylin had given me this title when she was a toddler and could not pronounce Aunt Kelly, and it always came out as Aunt KK). Ellen and Kathy were clever in using their children as ammunition and left me sobbing after each call because of their guilt trip and longing to leave on the next plane to see my nephew and niece.

A Stranger to Myself

So when my job at Springmeade ended, after much prayer, God gave me the go ahead to move. It seemed each time I saw my niece and nephew during the holidays or on occasional trips home, they seemed to have grown inches. I love them so much, so I didn't want to miss out on their childhood and teenage years.

Chapter Forty Three

Held Accountable

I can do all this through him who gives me strength.
Philippians 4:13

We do not achieve anything without God's help, and most of the time, He chooses to use a person or a family to do just that. Since I did not have family anywhere in Ohio, other than the Smiths, God gave me the Richards to be my second adoptive family.

Linda Richards was the Director of the Counseling Center at Ginghamsburg Church. Her ministry is on the front lines, helping people find their way. Linda had been in full-time Christian work for many years, and I was blessed when she became my counselor, friend, and mentor. One of Linda's great joys is telling the story of how we met.

Linda:

It was a drenching Tuesday night, and I was excited to be leading a wonderful new class called "Boundaries," which followed the book, *Boundaries -- When to Say Yes, How to Say No to Take Control of Your Life* by Henry Cloud and John Townsend. I began the class the same as always by asking the participants to do some deep-breathing, meditative relaxation

238

techniques. They were getting into the depths of their techniques when all of a sudden, all we could hear was STOMP, STOMP, STOMP at the top of the stairs, followed by a door being flung open. In walks this young lady who appeared more like a drowned rat and who had lost her way.

She asked, "Is this the 'Boundaries' class?"

Even though I had just closed the roster (meaning no more new people would be added), I took pity on her and couldn't turn her away. And I'm glad because my compassionate act began a life-long friendship with Kelly.

Kelly:

I could tell the class leader had taken pity on me by the way her eyes softened. She invited me in, asked me to remove my wet coat, and continued the introduction for her class. In no time at all, we became good friends, and Linda invited me to join her on Wednesday mornings at 6:30 a.m. at the Bob Evans Restaurant. That is where the Walk to Emmaus Reunion Group met each week. These meetings stemmed from the need for the Walk to Emmaus movement for leaders in the church to have small group training sessions to learn more about accountability and to receive encouragement. These meetings became a highlight for my week.

When I had slipped into sin with Ben, I confessed my sins to God first and then to this Reunion Group, so they could hold me accountable and encourage me to never do it again. Ben and I didn't want to displease God, but we had struggled with the temptation to be intimate. And when we succumbed to the sexual temptation, I brought what I'd done to the next Wednesday meeting. They listened benevolently as I confessed my story. I met no condemnation. Instead, they wrapped me in a blanket of

239

understanding and love, but they also told me the truth. I had to stop this behavior because God had so much more in store for me. I asked them, especially Linda, to keep me accountable and to find scriptures for me to hold onto. This is the only way I'd be free from this sin.

They required me to give them a report each week about my thoughts, my purity, and ended by asking me some tough questions. This is what I needed to support my times of trial, and God had used these people to keep me uplifted, accountable, and encouraged.

Because I was the new person on the totem pole at Rebound, I usually was stuck working the holidays because the facility never closed its doors. On one particular Thanksgiving, Linda asked, "Kelly, what are you doing for Thanksgiving?"

I responded, "Working the morning shift, but I get off at 2:00."

"Great," she responded, "Because we are eating at 3:00. Why don't you come over after you get off work and eat with us?"

That is how our friendship deepened, and I got to know Linda's husband, Mark. From that point on, I always had a place at their table for any holiday meal when I was unable to go home to Atlanta. The Richards introduced me to Evelyn Rhoades, who graciously volunteered to drive me to the breakfast Reunion Group meetings after I quit driving. Evelyn was a colorful lady, in her late eighties, and was a profound prayer warrior in our church.

Later, when I made the decision to move back to the South, I announced this at our Wednesday meeting. I explained how much I missed my family and asked for advice on how to turn in my notice at work, how to hire a moving company, and how to schedule a date for moving. God was so good to me in that He supplied my every need.

The movers were scheduled; the date for me to move was set. I was excited about my decision, and that is when the phone rang. It was my friend, Nancy, telling me she had been accepted on the next Walk to Emmaus, and I had been designated as her sponsor! Well, this was such an important thing, so I took a step of faith and decided to postpone my move for a month. At the next Wednesday meeting, I announced my dilemma. Linda spoke to Mark and without hesitation, I was invited to stay at their home after the movers took my stuff to Charlotte. This was a wonderful gift for me and a tremendous sacrifice for them.

Every morning, I'd come down the stairs and be welcomed by a fresh pot of coffee and a smiling Mark, who became my short order breakfast cook, making me eggs for breakfast. Linda, a fantastic cook, made me healthy lunches and the best dinners I'd eaten since moving to Troy. We spent the mornings laughing and sharing anecdotes. Mark loved an audience for his corny jokes and stories, so I was grateful to be one. And in addition to this huge blessing, I inherited an additional chauffeur – Mark, who was retired from Chrysler Automobiles. He said I was an easy person to be around because I loved to laugh. I am so full of joy, it is easy to let it spill over. I'll forever be indebted to the Richards. They are true Christian people in every sense of the word, for the love and support they have given me. In the same way I will never be able to repay Jesus for all He's done for me.

I am living proof that our God will make a way wherever there seems to be no way. Isn't God good or what? A scripture that has helped me in my journey of faith is Philippians 3:19, which says, "For My God shall supply ALL of my needs, according to His riches and glory in Jesus Christ." If you are lonely right now, cry out to God for a special friend or family.

Don't waste another second. There are plenty of other people out there looking for you. One of the best teachings from my Mom when I didn't have many friends was that to have a friend, you have to be a friend. The world does not revolve around me and my problems. Try asking someone you meet, "Is there anything I can pray about for you?" I bet you will get positive responses. Remind him/her that no prayer is too trivial. If it is important to him/her, then it is important to God. Whatever is shared, do not tell them you will pray for them before you go to bed. Instead, pray for him/her right then and there.

Now, not everyone is comfortable praying aloud, and I wasn't either in the beginning. So I began praying for others in my personal quiet time. I got a notebook and dated each page. Then I would write down my daily prayers, including the people who had given me specific prayer requests. Then I'd add my own prayer requests, grab me a favorite flavored coffee, and sit in a comfortable chair. That's when I'd begin my conversation with Jesus, just as if He were sitting in front of me. Gradually, I gained confidence and became comfortable praying aloud in front of others.

Another thing I began doing was reading scriptures aloud. Whenever a verse "jumped off the page at me," I'd write it in my notebook and try to memorize it. This is another nugget for someone who is not to comfortable praying aloud.

Because of the love and acceptance I received while living in Ohio, I regained my confidence and realization that Jesus was enough. I regained security in knowing He was all I needed. During my journey of knowing myself and accepting who I am, I've had certain limitations that aren't easy to live with. But with the help of Jesus, I have come to realize that I truly can do all things through Christ who strengthens me.

A Stranger to Myself

You won't believe the next part of God's story. The Richards's son, Mark, Jr., and his wife, Kristin, moved to Charlotte, N.C. after college, so Mark and Linda decided to move south too. Now we all live about twenty miles apart and get together often. I can never convey my gratitude for their friendship. I love you dearly, Ohio mom and dad.

"But I would be no one if not for God...!"

Chapter Forty Four

Rocky Roads

*If you say, "The Lord is my refuge," and you make the
Most High your dwelling, no harm will overtake you,
no disaster will come near your tent.
For he will command his angels concerning you
to guard you in all your ways;
they will lift you up in their hands,
so that you will not strike your foot against a stone.
Psalm 91: 9-12*

You never quite understand why the road gets rocky at
different times and why you have to traverse hilly ground. When
we sometimes feel sorry for ourselves and that our lives are
harder than anyone else's, that's when you meet a person like
Tom. It's strange how one person shares something with another
person and that person shares with another person. In the end,
people realize you have a common connection -- perhaps a
divine intervention. That's what happened when my sister met
Tom's mother, Monet.

Ellen and Monet were volunteering in the infant nursery at
church one Sunday. To pass the time while the babies were
quiet, Monet began telling Ellen about her son, Tom, who had
had a debilitating brain tumor in 1985 (the same year I had my
accident). Ellen listened, but she couldn't believe her ears. As

Monet continued talking about the challenges Tom experiences each day, Ellen could no longer hold her tongue. She began telling Monet about my story and the similarities we shared. Excitement mounted, and these two well-meaning matchmakers decided we should be introduced to each other.

When I met Tom, he stood six feet, four inches tall and was a husky man, weighing in at 250 pounds. He was diagnosed with a malignant brain tumor that was the size of a grown man's fist and lodged directly in the center of his brain, affecting his balance. The doctors said it was inoperable, and he'd probably not live more than six months, but his mother, a registered nurse with a Ph.D. in Nursing, refused to accept this prognosis – one more example of how a person's quality of life is based on his/her support system. Family is the best support system and advocate in times of illness or need.

Monet never gave up, taking him to different neurosurgeons until number seventeen or eighteen asked, "What do we have to lose? Let's operate!"

Blessedly, the tumor was successfully removed, but the removal damaged his balance, leaving him with significant challenges. Whenever he walks, he looks like the town drunk. Because of our brain injuries, we both have short term memory loss and significant organizational challenges. Tom jokes about our "CRS disease." The nice definition stands for "Can't Remember Something!"

A few years after we met, Tom began running with a new goal to finish a full marathon. I unsuccessfully recommended he be content running a half-marathon (13.1 miles), which would be quite an accomplishment because he could barely walk without stumbling. So I invited Tom to my second Skiing for Light (SFL), where he was blessed to have Terry assigned as his guide. This would be Terry's second year guiding as the SFL personnel were impressed with his abilities. And it made perfect sense. Terry was a natural athlete, the only six foot, four inch man volunteering, and the only one big enough to handle someone like Tom.

Tom lacked insight to his challenges and insisted he could ski, so Terry tried him on skis. Plan A was squelched quickly when Tom wasn't able to align himself in the ski tracks, which was messing up the tracks for other skiers so on to Plan B.

In cross-country skiing, you stand with your skis on, so Tom skied in what is called a "sit-ski," which is a recumbent sled into which they strapped Tom's legs and trunk into. He was given special poles to propel himself. The first time Terry took Tom around the little 5K track, Tom fell over in his sled close to fifty times – tough work for Terry. When a person on a sit-ski falls over, he/she are dead weight, causing the guide great difficulties and strength to lift and replace him/her on the track.

After a long morning, Tom and Terry appeared for lunch. Jeff, the leader of the Mobility Impaired People (MIPs), realized Terry needed another guide to assist with Tom so for the next three days, he had two guides: Terry and Bill. On the last day of SFL, there is always an exciting festive race. Tom made it around the 5K track without falling once! So in the end, if there had been an award given for having the biggest heart, determination to succeed, and the most improved, Tom would have been the recipient.

After we returned from Skiing for Light, Tom and I agreed we were serious about training for a marathon. Terry was our biggest cheerleader, encouraging us to shape up and train. I returned home one Sunday afternoon from a church-sponsored weekend in Myrtle Beach. The nice couple I'd travelled with dropped me off around 4:00. The weather was perfect, so I threw on my running shoes for a long run. That evening I ran 2.5 hours across the many city streets of Charlotte. I'd been employed at the drug store for two weeks, so when I finished my run, I jogged into the store to get my work schedule for the next two weeks. Afterward, I walked to the passenger light and pressed the "walk" button at the main thoroughfare of Providence Road.

I stared at the light until it turned green and began walking, not thinking to look to the left. Besides, crossing these roads was a familiar feat. As it turned out, an elderly gentleman was turning left from Laurel Avenue onto the same road I was crossing. Unfortunately, for me, he was dusting fish eggs from his sweater as he made the turn. I didn't see the car, but I felt it as it slammed into my left knee and threw me up and forward into the air. My limp body landed on the car's hood before bouncing like a rag doll onto the hood ornament, then the bumper, and lastly the pavement. I never lost consciousness.

A barrage of panicked, high-pitched voices assaulted my acute hearing, "Call an ambulance!" "Somebody help her!" A geyser of blood pumped rhythmically as my shaky fingers located a huge gash on my right temple. The pavement was the hardest thing I'd ever felt. That's when I looked toward the sky and asked, "Can someone put a pillow under my head? Can someone stop this excruciating pain?" At the time, I didn't remember the pavement from 1985, but I'm sure my mended bones and tired body were thinking, "Oh no. Not again!"

According to Eckerd's assistant manager, once he'd heard the impact and sirens, he ran outside to see what had happened. He said a man jumped out of a silver Lexus and ran to me. He held me, crying, "Please be okay! Please be okay! I didn't mean to hurt you."

I have no memory of this, but the assistant manager said, "I guided the man to the corner where I calmed him. He was weeping over you and crying hysterically, 'I can't believe I hit this poor woman!'"

Fortunately, there was a fire station across the street from Eckerd's. Ten firemen surrounded me, each asking what they could do to help me. They said when I opened my eyes, I asked, "Wow! Is this what you have to do to get the attention of ten good-looking guys?" They laughed at my comment, but the Sergeant cautioned me. "Lie still, ma'am, and don't speak. It's important that you lie still. We're getting help for you."

But one of the other guys said, "No. Let her talk, Sarge. She's telling the truth."

To my right was a young lady kneeling beside me. She asked, "Is there anyone I can call for you?"

Normally, I always keep a cell phone with my family's numbers for times like this. When I returned from the beach, my cell phone battery was almost dead, so I'd left it home, charging. Somehow, I remembered Rod, Jr. and Kathy's number and told her. She left a message on their answering machine, which is checked once a week, if then. I remembered my parents' number in Atlanta, so she called them.

When Mom answered the phone, the woman said, "Mrs. Spence, your daughter is here. She's been struck by a vehicle. We're waiting for an ambulance now."

Of course, when my mother heard this stranger's voice and her message, she almost collapsed. She ran to tell Dad, and he said, "There's no way she can make it through another serious injury like the first one." My parents entered panic mode and telephoned Ellen's and Rod Jr.'s cell phones.

Meanwhile, as the EMTs placed me on the stretcher and rolled me into the ambulance, God gave me Psalm 91:11-12: "For He will command his angels concerning you to guard you in all your ways; they will lift you up in their hands, so that you will not strike your foot against a stone." But my version was, "So thy head will not hit any harder against the pavement."

He gave me these verses because they were so real to me. The moment I felt the impact to my knee, I flew into the air, but when I came down toward the hood, I felt hundreds of hands underneath me, bracing my fall. When I bounced to the bumper, I felt the hands again. Even though I hit the pavement hard, I'm sure they cushioned me against that impact, too.

While in the ambulance, the EMT called the hospital, announcing the estimated arrival time. "Female patient has a large hematoma over her right eye."

I argued with him. "No, sir. This isn't a large one. A large hematoma is the one I had twenty-three years ago. It was the size of a grapefruit. This is nothing compared to that one."

He replied, "Ma'am, just lie quietly; we're getting you there as soon as possible."

"Okay," I mumbled, thinking, "I'd better shut up." But instead, I recited the Twenty-Third Psalm aloud. He was respectful and bowed his head and prayed with me. Why was I arguing with an EMT? It seems hilarious now! Sometimes, laughter is needed when you're in the midst of trials.

Ellen arrived at the hospital before the ambulance. She tried to find me by asking a nurse. "I'm sorry, but there's no one admitted by that name." That's when Ellen saw an EMT carrying bloody running shoes. She ran to him, grabbed his arm, and asked, "Where's the woman who belongs to those shoes?"

The man motioned. "We're about to bring her in."

Ellen said I was in hysterics when they rolled me in. Somehow, my mind had traveled back twenty-three years. I was in Atlanta. "Oh God. Please don't let me die. Please, please, God."

I remember when Ellen grabbed my hand and said calmly, "Kelly, you're going to be okay. This is not the first accident."

"Ellen, I asked, "Is there a cut above my eye?"

"No," she replied. "I'd call it a gash."

"Will they sew me up?"

"I'm sure they will," she said while patting my hand.

After Ellen talked with the doctor and knew the extent of my injuries, she called Mom immediately. "Kelly is going to be okay. She's possibly broken her left knee, but she's okay. There is a gash above her eye."

Mom and Dad were relieved it wasn't worse. In a few minutes, Mom was in the car driving the four hours to Charlotte.

When the good-looking doctor who sutured my gash announced they were going to release me at 3:30 a.m., Ellen was appalled and furious. "Don't you realize this woman has had a severe brain injury in the past? You're going to send her home where she lives alone? Well, I'm not going to let her be by herself."

So my sister took me home where she checked on me every hour on the hour.

* * *

Terry had tried calling me the night I was hit by the Lexus. He'd left a message: "Kelly, I just felt a strong urge that I needed to call you. I hope you are okay."

Those well-wishes might have been what had saved me from being permanently injured – again. But somehow, God had forgotten to guard my two front teeth. I hit the pavement so hard with my two front teeth that I scraped the enamel from them. As a result, I now have veneers. My teeth were paper thin.

My friend, Hal, called after he'd heard about the accident. "Kelly, are there any angels left to look after me because God seems to need them all to look after you?"

A Journey of Giving and Belonging

Chapter Forty Five

The Marathon

*When Jesus spoke again to the people, he said, I am the light of
the world. Whoever follows me will never walk in darkness,
but will have the light of life.*
John 8:12

After my marathon training had been interrupted by the
silver Lexus accident for five months, setting a goal to run even
a half marathon was overwhelming. The problem was that every
time I put on my running shoes and started on my familiar route,
a vehicle was sure to turn from the left onto a street I was about
to cross, narrowly missing me. Immediately, I'd go into a full
blown panic attack right then and there on the sidewalk. It was
scary for me to run alone. That's when God sent Sherri into my
life.

Sherri and I met at a single's function at church. She
seemed nice and grounded in the Lord, so I asked her for a ride
home. I didn't know at the time, that Sherri had misgivings. She
later confessed to me that her initial thoughts were, *Uh oh.
Watch out, because this could be trouble. With your busy
schedule, you don't have time to take this woman home every
week. What if she's one of those "needy singles" who loves a
compassionate ear to unload her hardships?*

A Stranger to Myself

After several weeks, we'd developed a closer friendship, so I shared my running troubles with her. Immediately, she offered, "Kelly. I'll start running with you."

In disbelief, I stammered, "Will you really?"

We set up a schedule where we'd meet at my house at 7:00 a.m. on Mondays, Wednesdays, and Fridays. Sherri began encouraging me and sharing with me what the Lord had taught her during quiet times. Whatever topic we talked about, Sherri was always turning it back to what the Bible said about it. I eagerly anticipated our running times.

We set our goal to be ready to run in the Thunder Road Half Marathon on November 18. Training was going well and both of our spiritual lives were soaring. Sherri became my prayer partner and closest friend. It had seemed that most of my friends always needed something from me, but not Sherri. She was a giver.

One night, I invited her to a sleep over because we were rising early to go on a retreat together. She knew that I struggled with locking myself out of my apartment because I could never remember where I'd put my keys. Sherri arrived that night carrying a lock box. It was exactly the type that realtors use whenever they sell homes. I was so delighted with this and wondered why I'd never thought of it before. When I tried to pay her for it, Sherri just smiled.

"You can't pay for a gift." That is a true friend.

Tom's training also was interrupted during the most critical time. One month before our big race, he had a staph infection. No one knew what caused them, but they were painful. However, not even a staph infection could deter Tom. He was determined even though Terry, who had arrived two days before the race, and I were doing our best to discourage him from running a full marathon. In the end, we gave up because there was no turning back for Tom.

On the day of the race, we were excited. My true victory was being in good shape to run this marathon. I'd spent five months in rehabilitation and had overcome panic attacks brought on by running alone. My friend Sherri offered to run with me, and Tonya, a trainer at my church, gave up much of her time to work with me and would only accept $50 a month for payment. Tonya pushed me through my fear of running with minimal vision. It was nothing short of another miracle performed by God.

So, Tom, Sherri, and I had trained hard; Sherri and I were running the half marathon, and Tom was running the full marathon – 26.2 miles. We went to the Race Expo on the day prior to the race and got lots of free stuff. We even picked up a new pair of running shoes at a low price. Terry and I still were trying to talk Tom out of running the full marathon, but there was no budging Tom; his mind was made up.

When race day came, we awoke to a temperature below freezing – a whopping eighteen degrees outside, but we felt ready. I wondered about Terry's reaction to the weather. So we dressed in layers and began the race with about two thousand other runners. We kept it light and humorous, ever mindful of our goal to finish under two and a half hours. Sherri was ten years younger than me and a much more accomplished athlete, but she was committed to seeing me finish the race. So when I wanted to walk up a hill, guess who also walked up the hill? Sherri! Terry begrudgingly slowed down to a snail's pace jog.

We crossed the finish line at exactly two hours, twenty eight minutes, and thirty two seconds. What a feat! We'd had a blast! And Tom finished the whole marathon – a true accomplishment.

Completing a half-marathon became a highlight of my life. I was so thankful to Sherri, Terry, Tom, and Tonya, who God had used to infuse me with hope and determination.

Chapter Forty Six

Fish Eggs

The Lord is my shepherd; I shall not want. He maketh me to lie down in green pastures; He leadeth me beside the still waters. He restoreth my soul; He leadeth me in the paths of righteousness for his name's sake. Yea, though I walk through the valley of the shadow of death, I will fear no evil; for thou art with me; thy rod and thy staff they comfort me. Thou prepares a table before me in the presence of mine enemies; thou anointest my head with oil; my cup runneth over. Surely goodness and mercy shall follow me all the days of my life; and I will dwell in the house of the Lord forever.

Psalm 23 KJV

A year after the silver Lexus accident, I started thinking, "You know, that man had to feel awful about what happened. If I'd had peripheral vision, we could have avoided the whole thing."

So I telephoned my attorney's office to obtain the man's name and phone number. Then I called his home and asked, "Is James there?"

The sweet Southern female voice said, "I'm sorry. There is no James who lives here."

I continued. "Ma'am, was your husband driving a brand

new Lexus a year ago." She said, "Yes. Yes he was. Why?"

"Well, I'm the woman he hit. I just wanted to call and let him know I'm okay, and I'm as good as new. I am doing well now."

She quickly replied, "You mean Jonathan."

"I'm sorry to have used an incorrect first name. I never had the privilege of meeting him," I said.

Her voice lifted. "Oh, you're such a blessing to call. Do you know Jonathan still has sleepless nights because he wakes up with the horror of what happened?" She also shared that Jonathan had suffered an eye disease a year or so before the accident. He'd lost his left peripheral vision.

Imagine that! He'd had no chance of seeing me as I'd had no chance of seeing him. We'd been at the wrong place at the wrong time – or was it the right place at the right time? Happily, I left my contact information with her. Jonathan returned my call that night.

I answered and said, "Jonathan, thank you for calling me back. Maybe you and your wife and I can go to dinner one night because I think you need to see me, and I would like to share my story with you."

He explained, "I'm in the process of selling my plant store. I've decided to officially retire, and I have a lot going on. Why don't we meet in another week or two? My life is crazy right now with the sale and all. I do want to meet you."

Two weeks to the day after our first conversation, we made plans for dinner. Jonathan and his wife picked me up at my apartment, so we went to Red Rocks Restaurant, which is practically in my back yard. Mind you, his wife was driving. After we sat down, I looked at him and said, "Jonathan, I forgave you before the EMTs arrived."

He just stared, but I saw tears forming in his humble eyes. Clearly, he'd been touched by my words.

"Really, Kelly?" he asked. "You really forgave me that quickly? How? How could you do that? I've been beating myself up for the past year."

"I'm a Christian, a born again believer, Jonathan," I explained. "I realized that if I did not forgive you, Jesus would not be able to forgive me. And I came to realize that night how easily you could have been my own brother or sister or friend because we all get distracted when we're driving."

"Thank you," he said. His wife smiled and touched my hand.

"But I do have one question I just have to know," I said.

Their relaxed shoulders stiffened.

"What's up with the fish eggs? The report said you were brushing fish eggs off your sweater. So for the past year, I've imagined you eating caviar and crackers while driving." We all laughed.

"Kelly," he began. "I owned a garden shop, and we had a large aquarium on one wall. If you've ever owned a fish tank, you've realized that during April and May, the fish all lay their eggs in the coral and rocks. If you don't remove the eggs, the other fish will eat them. So I had been removing fish eggs from one tank and transferring them to another tank with no fish."

"Wow!" I exclaimed. "Oh, my goodness! Who would've ever thought that? I just thought you had some serious money and loved eating caviar. I'm sorry, but I'm planning to write a book, and this will be another chapter in it. By the way, you'll get your own copy with my personal signature."

As we talked and ate, Jonathan said he'd come to the hospital during the wee hours of the morning after the accident. He was so distraught, he couldn't sleep and was told I'd been released. In addition, he'd come to the Eckerd's store on a daily basis. He'd always ask, "Is Kelly back yet?" But because of confidentiality laws, the manager couldn't give him any information except, "No, she's still on leave."

He continued this daily visit for weeks, seeking solace for his troubled mind. His attorney informed him I was stable but he lived with the uncertainty of my condition – until his wife received my phone call.

"How could I blame you for the accident?" I asked. "Even though the light was green, I could have turned my head to be sure. Now, every time I cross a street, I do just that."

Over dessert, coffee, and friendly laughter, God had provided me with an opportunity to share my journey of faith with two nice people. So I did.

"But I would be no one if not for God…!"

Chapter Forty Seven

The Sit Ski

However, I consider my life worth nothing to me; my only aim is to finish the race and complete the task the Lord Jesus has given me--the task of testifying to the gospel of God's grace.
Acts 20:24

By my third year at SFL, I had learned to pack 80% party clothes and 20% ski clothes. It was more about the fellowship and having fun and less about the skiing. People were made to feel special because they could share their stories with others who could empathize with them.

Take Kirk, for example. He and his best friend, Willie, always skied and trained together because Kirk was on his way to becoming an Olympic athlete in cross-country skiing. They were closer than brothers – inseparable. Kirk always came in first place, winning the races time after time. He was incredible.

But they had a tragic car accident with Willie driving. Kirk was badly injured with resulting scars all over his face. He'd lost all vision. But Willie took an opposite approach from Lucy and her mother. Willie stayed at the hospital as often as possible. He accompanied Kirk to his physical therapy, occupational therapy, and all of his other medical appointments. He promised Kirk one thing: "I'm going to be your eyes. You can always count on me."

And Willie cared for Kirk like nobody's business. He was "Johnny on the spot" to accommodate all of Kirk's needs. Their friendship was incredibly profound. Seeing them in action was inspirational and amazing. During that trip, I often wished this could have been Lucy and me. I wanted to blame her mother, but she was just following the doctor's orders.

— ❦ —

Dad's and my accidents didn't stop our family from enjoying our week-long annual ski trips, so five years after Dad's accident, we'd resumed our trips to Winter Park, Colorado, where we had skied during our high school years when no one in our family knew what a disability was. On this occasion, we returned to the Winter Park Ski Resort in the Rockies, which we'd learned years earlier was the world's headquarters for helping skiers with disabilities to ski. We'd always been impressed when we'd see a skier wearing a neon orange vest with the words, *Blind Skier* or when we'd see an amputee skiing on one leg. These skiers were remarkable and had impressed our innocent minds. Somehow, we'd never considered that our family might one day have disabled members: a legally blind daughter who was also a sister with a brain injury that inhibited her from remembering what run she was on and a paraplegic husband and father.

The runs in Colorado can take forty-five minutes to ski from top to bottom of the mountain. One run can lead to another run and that run can lead to yet another run. A skier can be on six runs before arriving at the bottom. Because the part of my brain that is responsible for not getting lost is damaged, I have to ski with a guide that knows the mountain like the back of his/her hand and who can also keep up with me.

On this family trip, there were eleven of us because our family had grown. It was Mom and Dad; Rod Jr. and his wife,

260

Kathy; their two children, Kaylin and Trey; Ellen and her husband, Ken; their two children, Jack and Janie; and me. In the afternoon, we skied with dad. Now we were faster than Dad because he skied on a mono ski. When he first started skiing as a paraplegic, he wore a harness around his upper body with a trained guide and a tether, which the guide would pull if Dad was descending too fast. Dad didn't like wearing a harness and tether, and he didn't like having a guide. So it didn't take long before his natural athletic abilities emerged, and he was going down the green runs (easiest) by himself. Then came the blue runs (intermediate) and then the black runs (most difficult).

Mom, Ellen, and I were waiting for Dad underneath the chair lift lines at the bottom of the run. We were cheering and clapping loudly as he descended when two little boys and their mother were riding the lift to the top of the run. One of the little boys pointed at Dad on the mono ski and yelled, "Mommy, I want to do that. Mommy, can I do that? Please mommy?"

We all smiled and looked at each before bursting into loud laughter. We were all so tickled by his innocence and thinking Dad was privileged to be riding the mono ski and not on his own two legs. It was a precious moment and has since become a cherished memory.

Dad still had a blast skiing, and he always made it off the green runs. His guides with the harness and tether would quickly agree, "Yep, you're ready to get rid of this tether, and on to the blue runs you go."

I was so proud to be my dad's daughter.

Chapter Forty Eight

The Rods

But by the grace of God I am what I am, and his grace to me was not without effect. No, I worked harder than all of them--yet not I, but the grace of God that was with me.
1 Corinthians 15:10

Rod, Jr.:

Like my sisters before me, I had attended the University of Georgia. While in my junior year, I was returning from the tennis courts and made my way through the pool area (for obvious reasons). That's when I saw a gorgeous girl in a bikini. With twenty eight thousand students at UGA, I had instantly fallen in love with a girl from my home town! Kathy accepted my invitation to take her to a local comedy club, and the rest became history. Soon after college, we were married. This became my miracle number three.

We each got jobs in corporate America – me at Safeco Prison -- and while corporate America promoted continuing education for its employees, we took advantage of the opportunity and earned our MBAs at Mercer. The classes were free as long as you earned an A.

Even though my job at Safeco Prison seemed secure, within two years I was having entrepreneur ideas. Life was good; we were expecting our first child (Kaylin). But my ideas became frequent and weighed heavily on my mind. I reminded Kathy that my work location had barbed wire around the property. During my performance review, my manager congratulated me on underwriting the best book of business than anyone else had written in my division that year. But he warned me that I needed to stay awake during our weekly meetings.

My heart and soul desired something else, but I had no idea what I was supposed to do. I often thought about the building business. My family knew I was not satisfied in my work, so they all began praying for me. Kelly tells me that she had prayed for months that the Lord would make my career choice as clear as black is to white. Then the call came from my brother-in-law, Ken Smith. He had recently been laid off from his job of selling tools but had always dreamed of beginning his own business. He realized at 40-something, if he was ever going to start a business, he'd better do it now.

One night, the phone rang. It was Ken saying, "Rod, you may think I'm crazy, but what do you feel about us working together to start a custom home-building business?" His words were like the heavens opened up and the heavenly hosts began singing the Hallelujah Chorus! It resonated within my soul. I instantly knew this is what God wanted me to do with my life. And shortly afterward, Bannister Homes was birthed.

Most of our mistakes were made in the first two years while we traversed the huge learning curve of running our own business. But honestly! I was never happier. Our families became neighbors, living side by side. My nephew, Jack, who was four years old, used to run to our house each morning at 6:30 a.m. to ensure I was awake.

Shortly afterward, Kathy gave birth to our son, Trey, and Ellen gave birth to their daughter, Janie. I have four children because our kids are like siblings. The only benefit is that I don't have to pay for two of them.

Rod, Sr.:

Finally, at age sixty five, I decided to retire after working eighteen years for Rex Wallin as an estimator and project manager. Our three children and four grandchildren now lived in North Carolina, so Marilyn and I desired to live near our family. After we announced our decision to the kids, Bannister Homes came to our rescue. We updated the kitchen in our house in Marietta, Georgia, which was no easy task. The house sold shortly afterward, and our children brought a moving truck to bring us and our belongings to Charlotte.

We lived with Ellen's family for a year while our home was being built. Ellen and Ken even installed an elevator in their new home. Their big sacrifices were not lost on Marilyn and me.

As a result, our home is much better than I ever imagined it could be. And it has been a true blessing to watch our grandkids grow up in a city that we have learned to love. Church is a big part of our lives, and Marilyn and I are active in Bible Study classes.

I have tried to live a balanced lifestyle that includes time for God, family, work, and play – in that order.

Chapter Forty Nine

Circle of Friends

The Spirit you received does not make you slaves, so that you live in fear again, rather, the Spirit received brought about your adoption to sonship. And by Him, we cry, "Abba, Father." The Spirit himself testifies with our spirit that we are God's children.
Romans 8:15-16

My friend and ballroom dance partner, Al Jones, invited me to my first Circle of Friends meeting. Phil and Kathy Armstrong began Circle of Friends at Forest Hill Church on Park Road in Charlotte to honor their third child, Todd, who was born with a severe case of Cerebral Palsy. He'd always been in a wheelchair, never had fed himself, and never had been able to toilet himself. They wanted to create a safe place where Todd could feel God's acceptance and normalcy. So Circle of Friends was born with seven people in attendance. Ten years later, over three hundred people attend each Thursday night, and Todd has a new nickname because of his power chair with painted flames. He's called Todd Rocket. Attending Circle of Friends is the highlight of my week.

A full band with the most wonderful Christian musicians begins each meeting, and I have the privilege of signing for the band, which means I'm up front with them. Dave Hardman, a

265

wonderful musician and singer, is the leader of the band. He says I'm part of the band and that makes me happy. I'd rather hear this band play than pay $50 to see Bruno Mars at the Time Warner Arena. Dave, his wife, Heather, and son, Corin, moved to Charlotte from Nashville because Corin is autistic. His parents have showered him with love since the day he was born, so Corin has been shaped into a lover and a terrific young man.

I learned sign language during my undergraduate studies. It quickly became my favorite course, and while I attended church in Ohio, I was invited to sign for the praise and worship service. I'd gone several years without using this gift, and as you know, if you don't use it, you'll lose it. Fortunately, I was asked to sign for the band, but I'm not qualified yet to sign for a sermon. Usually, someone in the audience can fill in when I don't know a word. Another member signs for the worship service.

At Circle of Friends' meetings, you feel out of place if you don't have a disability. But I've said for years, "If you're breathing, you have a disability," meaning everyone has something wrong because we live in a fallen world. Some people are just better than others at hiding them. We all have scars from our past. At the meetings, there may be someone who has Turrets Syndrome, who occasionally says, "Damn," in the middle of a song or during Phil's twenty minute devotional. But it's okay. Everyone is accepted just as he/she is.

Love overflows at these meetings. Praise is free and uninhibited. People don't have reservations about raising their hands to God in praise or in singing at the top of their lungs. It's the most wonderful and amazing group I've ever come in contact with.

I can be standing up front, signing, and the music will be so good that at any given moment, tears will start running down my face because I can't believe how blessed my life is. If for nothing else, this group helps put my life into perspective. I can have the worst day; I can be yelled at all day long by my supervisor or feel like I've not done anything good, but when I attend these meetings, all of my problems fly out the door when I see the joy on these people's faces. Some of these precious people will never live independently, will never have a checking account, hold down a regular job, or drive a car, but the amount of joy that adorns each face during these meetings more than compensates for those things. Witnessing this pure bliss is one of the greatest privileges of my life.

I have learned more from Todd Rocket than anyone in the group. At the end of the night when we've helped take down the band's equipment, Todd always pulls me aside, and says, "Kelly, we need to pray." And with his precious heart, he prays for the needs of all of the people who attended that night.

Chapter Fifty

Joy Prom

*Rejoice greatly, O daughter of Zion; shout, O daughter of
Jerusalem: behold, thy King cometh unto thee: he is just, and
having salvation; lowly, and riding upon an ass,
and upon a colt the foal of an ass.*
Zechariah 9:9 KJV

A brilliant event that happens every April is the Joy Prom at
Carmel Baptist Church here in Charlotte. The church has been
hosting this Friday and Saturday night event for thirteen years.
This delightful occasion celebrates people with disabilities. The
dress code is marvelous with men dressed in tuxedos or their
best suits and women wearing lovely evening gowns. It's just
one of the best things you can imagine.

The Joy Prom initially was held on Friday nights, but they
quickly learned there were so many people who wanted to
attend, they had to add another night – extending it to Friday and
Saturday nights. Sadly, people's hearts are still broken as many
are turned down because registration fills up so quickly.

To host the Joy Prom, over 2000 volunteers are required for
Friday night and 2000 required for Saturday night. It's a big
production, with many retail stores, including Belks and David's
Bridal Shop, being generous to the participants. These stores
donate free dresses to the ladies attending the Prom. Nail and

hair salons also provide free services. When an attendee enters the red-carpeted foyer, a volunteer doorman, dressed in a dark tuxedo, greets him/her. Other guests and volunteers line the balcony above while the announcer says, "We'd like to announce that [name] is entering the building."

Another volunteer greets them, saying, "I'm so glad to meet you. Please come with me." The volunteer ushers the attendee to registration as the onlookers above clap and cheer. They even have people assigned to be the paparazzi and media, complete with cameras. I'm glad to be alive as I watch these people entering in wheelchairs or with walkers or seeing paraplegics or quadriplegics with huge smiles on their faces.

After registration, the youth volunteer asks, "What would you like to do now? Would you like to get a tiara?" The ladies are offered sparkles for their hair. A shoe shine stand is available for the men. It's an awesome event.

I have a dear friend, Kristin Saccardi, from my Circle of Friends who doesn't just remind me to sign up every year but calls and registers me for the event. She doesn't trust me to remember, and if you don't call within the first fifteen minutes on the registration date, you will not get a spot. Last year, Kristin informed me I'd gotten the very last spot!

My friends who attend Circle of Friends on Thursday nights consider this the highlight of their year. They are made to feel special and normal, like somebody, which they are.

Many people ask me why I think God allows people to have disabilities. I always direct them back to John 9 where Jesus is walking with his disciples and see a blind man on the side of the road begging. The disciples ask Jesus why this man was blind. Did his parents sin, or did he sin? In my words, Jesus said, "Hold the phone. Stop right there. This person was not born blind as a hindrance, but he was born blind, so he can bring even more glory to God than if he'd been born with sight."

My friends at Circle of Friends don't think of themselves as any different because they realize everyone has some disability or something wrong. No one's life is perfect, and they also know God allowed them to be disabled for a purpose and a reason. Everyone has an inspiring story of God's love.

Chapter Fifty One

Helping Others
A Father's Observation

The Lord is my light and my salvation; whom shall I fear? The Lord is the stronghold of my life; of whom shall I be afraid?
Psalm 27:1

Rod, Sr.:

One of the many things I admire about my daughter is her incessant drive to continue her path towards *normalcy*. Kelly's heart was broken many years ago when I told her that *normalcy* could possibly take five years or more. So instead of relinquishing control and allowing the calendar pages to dictate her life and time tables, she defiantly grabbed control, redefining the word *normalcy* for herself. And she set her own timetable, which became "when I can achieve" rather than when five years were over. Overcoming steep slopes while skiing, learning to ballroom dance, and continuing her impeccable tennis strokes made me proud of Kelly. But what I'm the proudest of is that Kelly surrendered her life to Christ after the accident, and with that submission, she asked God to use her life for His will. And our Father is doing it in many ways.

Kelly acquired licensing to become a Certified Nursing Assistant, so she could work with Alzheimer's patients and others with brain injuries. She signs for a praise and worship band at her church. She attends church regularly, getting involved in leadership opportunities such as teaching Bible Studies classes and working with youth in different organizations. She freely gives to everyone of herself; she takes every opportunity to praise God and to show others how much God loves them.

Kelly:

After Dad's injury, he began learning how to play tennis in a wheelchair, so I would volley with him. Immediately, he focused on me, noticing I was having trouble returning the tennis ball – not because of my tennis strokes – they were still perfect. My coordination and judgement of where the ball would land was a problem. As a result, I was taking stutter steps instead of full steps, which was frustrating and causing me to fall at times. My impaired vision struggled to tell my brain how close the ball was. So he suggested I allow the ball to bounce *twice* rather than once. And that helped my judgement to become more acute.

Dad's injury also gave him the opportunity to help many young people in wheelchairs to enjoy sports and have fun on the tennis court. For thirteen years following his injury, he helped run a wheelchair tennis clinic in Atlanta where kids with Cerebral Palsy, Spinal Bifida, and other spinal injuries learned the fun of playing tennis. Each year, some benefactor donated a sports chair to the most enthusiastic participant.

"Watching those kids as they gained confidence and began to have fun again was probably the most rewarding achievement of my life besides having my own three kids," he said.

Today, my family plays tennis year round (snow, sleet, rain, hot and cold) at Dilworth on Saturday mornings with a group of tennis lovers. Dad and I have the privilege of working with kids who participate in Special Olympics. It's delightful and inspirational to watch as they get so excited just to make contact with the ball, much less hitting it over the net.

Jon was one of the kids I worked with, and he can be described in one word: Precious. After volleying the ball several minutes, I applauded him and said,

"Jon, you did such a great job!" His response was immediate, "Yeah. I'm pretty great, ain't I?"

Then we tried to give each other a *high five*, but we had trouble locating each other's hands. So here's a tip I'll pass along: It's not a good idea to attempt *high fives* when the two participants are both legally blind. That's a funny, by the way.

Chapter Fifty Two

The Murrays

Hear my cry for help, my King and my God, for to you I pray. In the morning, LORD, you hear my voice; in the morning I lay my requests before you and wait expectantly.
Psalm 5: 2-3

The Murray family have become true blessings in our lives, like *family*, so when we were able to enjoy a short reunion, we were delighted. Walt had been my high school friend prior to the accident and remained my friend during the darkness of the sorority house days. And Walt had changed my life when he introduced me to Campus Crusade for Christ. I remember immediately feeling God's embrace as Walt had guided me down the stairs and introduced me to lots of his friends and acquaintances. He'd never turned his back on me.

George Murray had been Dad's friend and fellow runner in the Chattahoochee Road Runner prior to his accident. And he remained Dad's friend during the dark days of his hospitalization. George had come every evening to visit Dad and was instrumental in the gift of his first racing wheelchair. Dad always said, "George Murray will forever have a gold star beside his name in my book because I just needed to know I had a friend who cared."

Our *family reunion* occurred after Walt married and had children, as had Rod, Jr. and Ellen. Fortunately, my brother and sister-in-law own a lake house together with her parents near Clemson University. So we agreed on that location for our *family reunion.* Unfortunately, it turned out to be a cloudy day.

After we'd visited for hours and had eaten a bountiful and delicious lunch, I decided I wanted to get in a thirty minute run. I assured everyone that I'd be fine and back soon. Usually, I'd stay on the path, not turning right or left or detouring in any way. Because there were humongous hills, after a while, I couldn't remember where the house was. All the hills looked the same, and the sky was getting dark. Clouds were rolling in. Did I just feel a sprinkle of rain? I began to panic!

"Dear God, please help me find my way back to the house," I begged, almost in tears.

An hour after I'd left, Walt became concerned that I hadn't returned. He'd been watching the black clouds rolling in, so he asked Rod, Jr., "You know, Rod? Kelly's been gone for a while. Should I go look for her?"

My brother said, "No. She's just probably caught up with all the beauty and stuff. She's alright."

Because Rod didn't seem alarmed, Walt agreed to wait another twenty minutes. When I still hadn't returned, Walt announced, "I'm going to find her."

A truck was heading in my direction, so I felt intense relief penetrate my body. When it pulled up beside me, I saw the smiling face of my friend, Walt.

"Hey, Kelly!" he called. "Get in. I was out looking for firewood. Want to help me?"

"Sure I do!" I'd never been so happy to see anyone. It was just another time when God sent Walt to rescue me.

"But if it hadn't been for God...!"

Chapter Fifty Three

Starting Over

About Benjamin he said: "Let the beloved of the LORD rest secure in him, for he shields him all day long, and the one the LORD loves rests between his shoulders."
Deuteronomy 33:12

Dad has never let his confinement to a wheelchair stop him from being the adventure-seeker that he always had been. One of the exciting challenges Dad began participating in was the annual "Cycle to the Sea" during the third week in April. As a member of the ASAP (Adaptable Sport Athletic Program), which is a subsidiary out of CMS (Carolina Medical Systems) Dad was the oldest participant in the hand-cycle ride, which started in Monroe, North Carolina, and finished in Myrtle Beach, South Carolina -- 180 miles with over 70 miles traveled each day

Mom, Howard, and I would be onsite to meet the cyclists as they crossed the finish line in Myrtle Beach. Afterward, all the participants and their families and fans would meet at a large restaurant for a celebratory dinner. It never failed! These aged thirty or forty younger *bucks* would arrive complaining.

"Rod, we have bones to pick with you. We're half your age. We should be kicking you're butt on that course. We can't hold a candle to you. What's wrong with this picture? The only part of your chair we see is the back." Dad would just chuckle and say, "You'll have to train harder next year." The proud smile on his face was priceless and is engrained in my memory always.

Unfortunately, Dad suffered a shoulder injury and had to quit riding in the event. But he continues to go and support his friends for the send-off and the homecoming in Myrtle Beach.

———————

Our family planned another annual skiing trip to Breckinridge, Colorado, but this time, it was in honor of my parents' fiftieth wedding anniversary and was the week before Christmas, including Christmas Day. I was skiing with Dad our first morning and noticed he was off balance, especially on his left side. He was wavering, which he'd never done before and was definitely not his typical performance. He skied two more hours that day before announcing, "I'm done."

The next day, he skied another two hours and quit, and on the third day, he fell once, on his left side. That's when he announced, "I'm done." He never skied during the rest of the trip. Mom, who loves to ski, quit skiing that day, as well. I didn't think too much about it because they were 73 years old at the time, so it was easy to accept they were tiring and maybe quitting was not much of a sacrifice for either of them.

Unbeknownst to our family, Dad had seen Dr. Perry, a specialist, about his shoulder pain prior to the trip. The doctor had recommended that he stop his athletic prowls and take it easy. But Dad refuted him, saying, "When I go skiing, I'm going to ski and not hold back. So don't tell me that." Can we use the word *stubborn*? So Dr. Perry ordered an MRI, and the results would be available when we returned.

On the last day of our trip, I took a lesson from Carl, I didn't want to ski, because the rush had begun, and the mountain was busy. There were forty-five minutes to one hour lift lines, but because I wore a "Blind Skier" vest, I didn't have to wait for a lift and could have skied four times more than others. After the lesson was over, Mom and Dad invited me to come to the top of the mountain to meet them, and I was determined to take the bus by myself in this bumper to bumper traffic and seven degree weather. Graciously, Carl guided me to the front of the ski lodge and pointed to the bus stop. He told me to wait for the bus (green, yellow, or orange).

Proudly, I met my parents at the gondola, which we took to the top of the mountain where there was a cozy and warm restaurant. We watched in awe as crazy teens came off the Pike (horseshoe shaped) from the Olympics ten feet off the ground and landed on their snowboards. We enjoyed our meal and time together.

When we got back to Charlotte, I told Dad I was accompanying him and Mom for the MRI results. He was reluctant and declined, so I can only believe it was because he knew something bad was wrong and didn't want me to witness his reaction.

Dr. Perry, the specialist who'd seen me after the Lexus accident, entered the room with a chart in his hands. "Rod, you have a massive tear in the tendon that holds the muscle to the bone. We'll need to operate to correct it."

Later when my parents telephoned me to relay the diagnosis, I was astonished. "Dad, didn't you have a great amount of pain from this?"

But he's not a complainer and only said, "Well, when it hurt, it was my left hand. That's not my dominant hand, so I just did whatever I could with my right hand."

Mom told me that Dad's first question was about me. "How long will I be out because my daughter, Kelly, depends on me to drive her back and forth to work. I don't know who will get Kelly to work."

When mom told me that, I said, "Dad, I made it just fine the ten years before you moved to Charlotte, and I can make it the five or six months you're healing before you can drive again. Don't worry about me. Put your own health first."

So they scheduled the surgery for a Tuesday morning. But before they anesthetized Dad, Dr. Perry confided to Mom.

"Marilyn, I don't feel good about this surgery. I want to do one more microscopic look at the shoulder."

So they performed another microscopic look. A grim-faced Dr. Perry took Mom to the side and said, "Marilyn, there is no way I could improve your husband's shoulder. The surgery would only make it worse. He'd go through six months of therapy just to get it back to the same condition it is today. I don't advise having the surgery."

Mom thanked him, feeling grateful to God that Dr. Perry wasn't one of the surgeons who have the mentality that they can do anything.

When I talked with Dad later that afternoon, he was extremely disappointed. He had hoped the surgery would remove the pain, and he'd have his old shoulder back.

But after talking with many of his wheelchair buddies, he learned that many of them had experienced a similar surgery with bad results, so by the second day after the decision, Dad realized that Dr. Perry had done him a huge favor. He couldn't pour a cup of coffee with his left hand, and he had to learn to serve the tennis ball differently, but Dad can still lift his left arm above his head. And he's started back on his weight training. This goes to show you that with God, all things are possible.

Dad is my greatest hero.

"But if it had not been for God...!"

Chapter Fifty Four

Baskets of Blessings

Now Jabez was more honorable than his brothers, and his mother called his name Jabez, saying, "I gave birth to him in pain." And Jabez called on the God of Israel saying, "Oh, that You would bless me indeed, and enlarge my territory, that Your hand would be with me, and that You would keep me from evil, that I may not cause pain." So God granted him what he requested.
1 Chronicles 4: 9-10

I don't have to look far to find a role model. I've been blessed with wonderful parents and role models. If I had a million parents standing in front of me and God said I could only choose one set of parents, I would choose my mom and dad over and over again. God made them who they are; He knew what I'd need. I'm so glad they are mine.

"Women of Faith has been encouraging women since 1996 with compelling stories, laugh-out-loud humor, Bible teaching, heart-tugging music, rejuvenating worship, and more! Women of Faith events are produced by the world's largest producer of inspirational events for women, based in Plano, Texas. Through authentic connection with audiences, humor, and an atmosphere of encouragement and acceptance, world-class communicators deliver life-changing messages through high-quality programs in cities across North America". In previous years, Patsy

Claremont, Barbara Johnson, Amy Grant, and Marilyn Meberg have been guest speakers.

Once when Mom and I attended the event, she turned to me and said, "Kelly, you could do this. You could be one of these speakers for the Women of Faith."

Mom had always believed in me, so I was touched by her devotion and faith.

"You know, Mom," I agreed, "You're right. I can do this."

Unequivocally, she added, "Your story is no less powerful or inspirational than these women's stories."

And I hope God will open the door for me to speak at one of these events some day.

Chapter Fifty Five

My Coffee Loving Friend

Taste and see that the LORD is good;
blessed is the one who takes refuge in him.
Psalm 34: 8

Dr. Elaine Osborne Harris:

Kelly is like a breath of fresh air after a summer rain. After you talk to her or spend time with her, everything looks different. Colors are brighter, the sky is bluer, the world looks somehow better, and your problems seem to have somehow disappeared. Her outlook on life is like the antidote for a sad soul. To Kelly, each day is a blessing and has its own wonder and enchantment. I realize that from where she stands, each day is a blessing, and after her 1985 accident, each day is "icing on her cake."

Just ask Kelly, and she will tell you in no uncertain words. "Life is short. Eat dessert first!" Maybe this is not the best advice for a dieter, but it is the best advice for a perspective on living and enjoying life to its fullest.

I first met Kelly at a combined church singles outing for older singles if you consider thirty-something older. All of these events can be–well–interesting, depending on who attends. There are the younger folks and the older folks. And then there are the other folks that, for lack of a better way to put it, are single for a reason. For this particular outing, I arrived late with my friend, Audrey, because I'd learned that you might not want to attend without someone to talk to, if you catch my drift.

Most everyone had already arrived, so Audrey and I ended up sitting at a table with Kelly and two of her friends. I think the five of us talked more and laughed more than anyone else at the event. We immediately found common ground with our shared enjoyment for snow skiing; that was all it took. Kelly and I became fast friends and ski buddies. So I ask you this question: What visually impaired person wouldn't want a friend who skis AND drives? And besides, who wants to drive three hours alone to ski? The answer is no one.

Now, I need to explain that Kelly is an advanced skier. She learned how to ski prior to her accident, and after her rehabilitation, she renewed her love of skiing. However, I am not an advanced skier. I am an intermediate skier now, but when Kelly and I first began skiing together, I was a *low* intermediate skier. I tend to work my way down the mountain, making turns and being careful. But Kelly, well, she isn't like that. She points the skis south and just goes!

I am an optometrist with specialized training in working with visually impaired persons. I can teach and conduct sighted guides, which means I can help a visually impaired person walk safely and can teach his/her family member to do so, as well. I cannot teach someone to use a long cane. Now, imagine my interest and apprehension in skiing with someone who is visually impaired. The idea was awesome, while the reality was a little frightening.

Kelly also has a very poor sense of direction to add to the poor visual field. Those of you who have skied know that there are trail maps so that you know where you are on the mountain. Kelly likes to take her own ski guide. She calls the ski mountain folks to let them know she is coming and that she prefers to use her own guide. The ski mountain folks are to provide her with a guide, but she typically likes to use one of her friends to accompany her. And Kelly's guide is supposed to ski with her, keep her on the trails, and not let her get lost. This becomes hard when she skis faster than her guide and when that guide is me. But we work this out by agreeing to various meeting places along the way, and it's easy to find her because she has her very visible vest that identifies her. The vest says, "BLIND SKIER," and in small handwriting below, "Get out of my way!" As you can imagine, we get lots of questions about these words, which we gladly answer. Kelly also appreciates that I typically ski in a hot pink jacket that is easy for her to spot as well. One definite advantage is that we get to go to the front of the line, which on busy weekends is great! By the end of the day, everyone is very tired!

And Kelly is a patient teacher. She has helped me improve my turns and helped me gain confidence with my abilities. She will get in front of me and say, "Just look ten feet in front of yourself." This helps especially if the hill seems steep and my confidence is lagging ten feet behind. I can attest, though, that she is happy to broadcast to everyone that I assisted her with one thing in skiing: Getting back up after you fall. And for this "no small task," I am a pro! Kelly says she does not like to fall because she has a hard time getting back up. And she will ask before we get going too far, "Now, you take off which ski?"

Just in case you need to know, leave on the downhill ski; then when you get up, put on the uphill ski. I personally find it impossible to get up wearing both skis. One is perfect; then you can pop on the other ski. Now you're ready for more!

I think of our ski trips, which usually end up being a ski day; the most memorable part is the time we spend talking to and enjoying each other's company. Kelly is always eager to learn about what is going on in your life. She frequently breaks up the conversation with a quick (or not so quick) prayer. When Kelly prays, she has this quality about her prayer that seems to be a hot line to the Lord. Her prayers are not just petitions to the Lord. She prays with her whole body and focus. She literally seems to be wrestling in prayer. Kelly is a true prayer warrior. This is something that has to be experienced in order to completely understand. Kelly can burst into song, and with me she literally does so frequently. We sing praise songs, show tunes, silly songs -- all of them with animation and intensity. Kelly can barely hold herself back with praise songs; she signs what she can and sings with deep intensity because she is worshiping in song as often as possible and as much as she can.

Frequently, after our ski day, Kelly will proclaim, "This was the BEST day of skiing EVER!"

"But Kelly," I will reply, "You said that the last time, too." Oh, just to have so much wonder as she does for each day! We could all use this attitude more often than not.

I must apologize if I sound a little like a "mother hen," but my experience with the visually impaired is that safe travel is either done with a long cane when the individual is alone or with others, using a sighted guide. Kelly and I have grown to be in tune to each other, so when we are in a parking lot or other crowded or dark environment, I place my elbow in her way, and she immediately grabs it. We continue walking with no verbal exchange needed. When we first began venturing out, I asked Kelly why she didn't use the long cane she hooked to her purse.

"I only use it when I need it." Kelly's definition of needing and my definition of her needing the cane are different.

As I write this, I am reminded of a girls' sleepover we had. We watched the movie, *Mamma Mia*, which I love, but my husband refuses to watch because he considers it a *chick flick*. We laughed and sang during the entire movie. And to my amazement, Kelly asked to watch it again right after watching it the first time – this time with the captions on so we could sing along with the words. She says this is one of the benefits of her brain injury: She does not remember much about it the first time; she just enjoys it and immediately wants to watch it again!

Kelly loves her coffee. And I stress that she really loves her coffee. She does buy de-caffeinated and is happy to get a coffee anytime of the day; she seems to like mini-mart coffee the best. I'm not sure why this is, but Kelly will say "yes" to a coffee shop any time of the day.

I remember one trip when she wanted to get a beloved cup of coffee. She started across the parking lot without looking – just walking! Imagine my concern, as I yelled, "Kelly, wait!" I lectured her then about using the cane or walking with someone. She, of course, smiled and said she was fine. We have since come to an agreement that she will hold my elbow as we cross unsafe areas, such as streets or parking lots.

Kelly is famous for carrying her Styrofoam cups with lids that are full of coffee. I often find these lying about after she has come to visit, along with anything else she may have forgotten. I call her and tell her what has been left behind. Often her response is her usual, "Imagine that!" and you know she is smiling when she says it. That is her outlook; she laughs at herself and does not let challenges hinder her from doing what she wants to do.

The items left behind frequently include her cell phone, long white cane, handicap parking placard –the important items that she needs. I remember calling her cell one time, and someone else answered. The polite and helpful person explained to me that Kelly had left her phone at Kinko's. Fortunately, I was able to catch her by dialing another number to let her know where the phone was. She has left her cell phone at so many places. If that cell phone could talk, it could tell some good stories!

Kelly also loves the beach or any other trip she can take. If someone says they will take her somewhere, she is ready and out the door. Well, mostly, you could say she is ready, but she can put it all together pretty quickly when she needs to as long as she can find everything. This is another challenge of her injury: Organization. But she works it out. She uses her famous cell phone to set alarms for things that she needs to remember or to do.

Kelly is fun on road trips because of all the enjoyment she derives from going somewhere, anywhere, but she is very in tune with her driver and wants to make things as easy as she can for him because she knows she cannot help with the driving. She keeps the conversation going, ensures the driver has what he/she needs, and interestingly enough, wants to pump the gas! Who could ask for anything more? She says she does not get to pump gas that often, so she likes to do it whenever she has the opportunity. I think it also makes her happy that the gas stations are mostly mini-marts, so she can get her beloved decaffeinated coffee! On one such trip when we were heading to Charleston, S.C., Kelly read to me from a book she was reading to pass the time. She even used different voices for the different characters! Her "Southern" accent for the male was something considering she is from the North.

There is also the issue of the bathroom. Often, Kelly will tell me she needs to go to the bathroom, so after parking the car, I will either accompany her or ask if she needs me. Kelly has gotten lost on several occasions just going to the bathroom alone at ski slopes or other places, so I tell her if I don't see her in ten minutes, I'm coming for her. Many times she has gotten turned around or sidetracked and has been relieved to hear my voice calling, "Kelly! Kelly, are you in here?"

"Oh, Elaine. I'm so glad you're here. I was just thinking that I didn't remember how to get back."

Once when we were on an overnight ski trip, we were unloading the car and carrying things into the condominium where we were staying. I hadn't seen Kelly for several minutes, so I asked our companion to wait in the condominium while I went outside to find Kelly.

I couldn't find her anywhere, so I frantically began calling, "Kelly! Kelly!"

Immediately, she came rushing out of the wrong building with her obvious fear turning to instant relief. Since then, I have learned to ask if she knows where the restroom is located or where the car is located. Then I finish the conversation by saying, "Ten minutes! You have ten minutes," I state trying to look stern.

She instantly reads through my bravo and says, "Okay" with a smile.

Kelly has even gotten lost on ski slopes. On one occasion, I was on the easier slope, and Kelly was on the more advanced. She wasn't where I had anticipated that she would be, so I stopped and scanned for Kelly. Fortunately, Kelly stands out with the bright orange skier vest I saw her at the base of the hill, and she explained that she'd been frantic because she didn't know where she was. She'd begun to pray. Instantly, she was able to see my hot pink jacket.

"Elaine. You can never ever wear a different color jacket."

Since then, Kelly has received additional orientation and mobility lessons from a certified orientation and mobility instructor.

Her outlook on life has been so special to me. I think that is one of the reasons I married the man I did. He, like Kelly, had a life changing experience at the same age as Kelly. He had ulcerative colitis and had surgery to remove the damaged part of his colon. Unfortunately, he hemorrhaged several times after his surgery and was close to death. He has a similar outlook on life as Kelly. Each day is a bonus at this point. My husband and Kelly easily could have died during their ordeals, but they have come through with the help and grace of the Lord. Both of their perspectives have made my short scare that much easier to handle.

You see -- two months before we were to be married, I was diagnosed with breast cancer. Fortunately, it was caught early through a regular mammogram. I had a lumpectomy and radiation and have been fine after all my check-ups thus far. But I have to say the two of them made it easier for me because I knew my situation was scary, but it was nowhere near what the two of them had gone through. Yes, the surgery was no fun and coming back from our honeymoon to radiation was no picnic, but I had two examples of wonderful people who had taught me how to get through my situation. I could have gotten depressed and gotten mad at the Lord, but He had brought the two of them through much more serious and life-threatening times. I asked myself: "Why would He not get me through this temporary thing? Why would I react in an ungrateful way when the Lord could take care of much bigger problems than the one I had?" God is good – and He is good all the time.

For years, Kelly has wanted to write this book, and I know that with her organizational challenges, as well as her desire to live life, she was not able to make much progress. We talked about her getting parts to one friend or another for editing or meeting to work on the book. But Kelly believes, and I am getting there too, that we all have Divine appointments: A time when the Lord has set things in motion, and we need to recognize them for the opportunities that they are. This happened one morning in church.

I was talking to my friend, Sandi, who is an author and freelance writer and who was telling me about helping to write some memoirs for different people. It was like a light came on. Immediately, I spoke without talking to Kelly first. I asked Sandi if she would be interested in helping Kelly with her book, and she said she would! I had hoped things would work out. I know the Lord knew what He was doing as this dream of Kelly's has come true. Her dream has turned into a full-fledged manuscript and, ultimately, a book. And here I am writing a chapter for it. I could not be happier for my dear friend Kelly.

Chapter Fifty Six

The Love of My Life
Hallelujah Ending!

See, I am doing a new thing!
Now it springs up; do you not perceive it?
I am making a way in the wilderness
and streams in the wasteland.
Isaiah 43:19

Howard, My Husband:

Even though I'm an introverted accountant, I also possess a self-imposed extroverted side that includes activities like playing tennis and golf, watching other sports, discussing politics, and going to the theater. And one of the best things I did for myself – especially now in hindsight – was to take ballroom dancing classes. I put a lot of heart and soul into my lessons and became a good dancer if I say so myself. Afterward, I began attending community dances called "Socials for Singles," which were held in the basement of an Episcopalian Church in Charlotte. My purposes in attending these were to meet other people and keep my newly learned skills sharp. I was not seeking a companion or a long-time commitment. I soon discovered the dances were enjoyable and something I looked forward to attending whenever the church hosted one. That's where I first saw Kelly. I remember thinking she was a little strange as I observed her time after time happily dancing by herself or with other females. She didn't seem the least bit inhibited and displayed immeasurable energy. But her solo dances were few because many of the gentlemen kept her out on the dance floor "kicking up their heels" as you might say. Because she seemed *so different,* I wasn't the least bit interested in her.

After we'd been going to these dances for a couple of years, Kelly finally made it to my side of the room and asked me to dance. The more we danced together, the less strange she seemed and the more I liked her. I left that night with a new impression of Kelly; she seemed warm, fun, and attentive. She exuded such a positive disposition as she easily made everyone around her feel important.

On a different night, we danced to several songs before she offered me her phone number during the fifth dance. It's strange how I remember it was our fifth dance.

"I should give you my phone number, so we can practice our dances together sometime."

Delighted at her aggressiveness, I said, "Well, I don't see any negative in that. I'd like that very much."

When the song ended and we trailed away to dance with other partners, I found myself often glancing her way. It's not hard to notice her lovely figure and long, shapely legs. Surprisingly, I was disappointed when the social was over, and I saw her leave with another man! Kelly definitely was an intriguing woman and had piqued my interest. And she'd forgotten to give me her number! I ended up calling five people before I could track down her cell phone number.

A Stranger to Myself

Kelly:

Being the extrovert I am, I began taking ballroom classes every Monday night at a church not far from where I lived. The lessons were a huge bargain – only costing $5 each week. Where else could you get three hours of ballroom dancing, make new friends, and have a ball for that nominal fee? That's where I first saw Howard.

We'd seen each other and politely said "hello" and "how are you?" for about two years, but there seemed to be no interest on his part, and he wasn't the stereotypical male I usually noticed. Howard was twenty-five years older than me (a year and a half younger than my dad) and was an inch or two shorter than me. But our relationship began innocently when I finally approached him and invited him to dance. As you know, I've never met a stranger, so asking Howard to dance was no issue. I quickly discovered his great sense of humor and his quick one-liners. He knew intuitively when to land the punch line and regaled in my abundant and loud laughter.

"You're easy material," he said. Of course, I wasn't so sure about that and promised myself he wouldn't think so either.

Afterward, we began looking for each other at the weekend dances. During our conversations, I realized that Howard didn't know about my vision loss and inability to drive a car. He probably had wondered why I was always leaving the socials with different men. Somehow, men, not women, were always volunteering to drive me to and from the dances. Anyway, when I explained my dilemma, he quickly offered to drive me to the weekend dances. Because he was a perfect gentleman, he began insisting on paying my way to the dances. We began dating exclusively after I discovered he had a heart of gold and had accepted my many flaws and idiosyncrasies.

But when I learned he'd been married and divorced three times with his last marriage only lasting three months, I swallowed the lump in my throat that splashed in my stomach acid with ripples. I know what you must be thinking. "Girl! What were you thinking? How many red flags does one woman need? Why didn't you run?"

Simply, my response still is, "No one before Howard had ever shown me such unconditional love and adoration."

Howard:

I'll never forget that when we began dating, Obama was running for President for the first time. When we discussed my interest for his candidacy, Kelly seemed receptive, interested, and excitedly accompanied me to one of his local rallies, which introduced her to the world of politics and campaigns. On another occasion, we went to see the theater production of *Wicked*. We thoroughly enjoyed the colorful and vibrant musical. I was elated to find Kelly was interested in the activities I was passionate about -- dancing, politics, theater, and sports -- and that quickly won me over. She was fun and different from other women I'd known; I couldn't help myself. And besides that, she did have the most gorgeous legs I've ever seen.

I am blessed to have a dentist who is also my son. His dental practice is in South Carolina, so after Kelly and I became a "couple," I arranged for my son to provide Kelly with some much needed cosmetic dental work for a considerable discount. Kelly was beside herself with glee and continuously displayed her sincere gratitude to my son, who thought she was a delightful patient and a pleasure to work with. After the work was over, we thanked him again and headed back to North Carolina. On the way, we stopped at a gas station combo Dairy Queen.

A Stranger to Myself

Kelly was beaming with the day's blessings and was giggling. "Because your Dr. Son was so generous to me and gave me 100s of dollars of dental work for practically nothing, I'm going to buy your ice cream today. You can have anything you want. Let's splurge!"

When we entered the store, I allowed her to order for us. I can't remember anything except we enjoyed our ice cream over constant laughter and good natured ribbing. After we'd finished, we began driving the hour and a half home. Just as we pulled into the parking lot of her apartment complex, Kelly's face was stricken; she went into an immediate panic.

"Oh no! Howard! I've lost my purse. I can't find it! It's not here! I must have left it at the Dairy Queen. I think I hung it over the back of my chair."

It was easy to see she was terrified, so my job was to calm her. "Kelly, it's going to be okay. Let's go inside and call the Dairy Queen to see if it's still there. Try not to panic."

We located the number without any trouble; a lady answered.

"Yes, sir! We found it after ya'll left, and my manager locked it in her closet."

We were both relieved.

"Kelly," I said. "We'll go back and get it right now. I know you're tired and sleepy, but you can rest while I drive. Besides, I knew what I was getting into when I accepted the title of boyfriend. It's just part of the package – the good and the bad."

She seemed pleased. "Howard, are you sure? That's a lot of trouble. I'm so sorry to cause you this much trouble."

"Come on," I urged. "Let's get back in the car."

"Thanks. You're a sweetheart. Besides, I could really use a nap."

Kelly:

My heart sang the day I left my purse at the Dairy Queen in South Carolina because of Howard's understanding and compassion. He'd already earned brownie points for getting me dental work at a huge discount, but he earned many more that day for how he handled the situation. When we got back into the car and drove the hour and half back to Dairy Queen, we walked into the store and asked for the manager. An attractive lady appeared and introduced herself as Amy. As she was leading us to her locked closet, she asked, "I notice you had sticks attached to your purse. Can I ask why?"

"Those sticks unfold into a cane that I use to identify me as a legally blind person."

Then I shared a shortened version of my testimony, and while I was sharing, her eyes became glossy, so I stopped intuitively and asked, "You have a story, too, don't you?"

She nodded her head and told me she'd been in an automobile accident six months previously and was dealing with severe chronic pain in her back. Howard and I listened patiently. When she was finished, I asked if we could pray for her.

"Yes, please," she replied without hesitation.

I began by thanking God for bringing us back to the Dairy Queen and for His goodness. I thanked Him for His death on the cross and for His strength by which we are healed. I prayed for Jesus to reach down and touch Amy, healing her lower back, her ligaments, and tendons, and I ended by giving God all the glory and pledging that Amy, Howard, and I would never stop telling of His wondrous works.

When I looked up, Amy was crying. She wiped her eyes and blew her nose before saying, "I was raised in church, but over the years, I've fallen away. I believe God sent you both to remind me that He still loves me. Now, I'm even more determined to come back to Him and walk with Him."

At these words, we rejoiced.

When Howard and I returned to the car, he turned to me, took my hands in his, and said, "Kelly, Amy is why God had us leave your purse today. He knew Amy needed to be reminded that He still loves her."

I nodded in silence, thinking, "But for God!"

Another thing I appreciated about Howard during our early months was whenever we went to dinner, and I needed to visit the ladies' room, he'd walk with me and stand outside the door because he recognized my fear of being lost. After I'd emerge, he'd extend his elbow and escort me back to the table like a queen. Howard didn't risk me losing my way and becoming terrified.

Once we were on a day trip and stopped at a gas station. This gave me the opportunity to quench my coffee addiction, so Howard remained outside, pumping gas. My parents will tell you I like a little coffee with my cream and sugar, so whenever I'm at a gas station, I jump out to get the biggest cup of coffee I can find.

On this occasion, I walked around the store until I found the coffee dispenser. As I approached the cashier, he asked, "Ma'am, do you know that man out there?" pointing toward Howard.

"Yes," I replied. "He's my boyfriend."

"Oh, I was wondering. I couldn't help but notice he hasn't taken his eyes off you."

For some reason, the cashier's comments bothered me. Was Howard being too controlling? My heart said, "No. He's just being cautious." But to be sure, I prayed about it and sought the Lord's will. That was when He showed me that Howard was just being protective over me. Howard realized the minute I walked out of a gas station that I couldn't remember where the car was parked. So he watched me closely – not to control me or my actions – but to protect me from getting hit by another car.

Another reason why I fell so hard for Howard is because he was not afraid to pursue me. He made it clear when I decided to date him that I was number one in his life, which is such a wonderful feeling. It's easy to become addicted and submerged in that amount of devotion and attention. Fortunately, I had friends who'd met Howard and liked him and unfortunately, friends who didn't. It was terribly disappointing when some friends quickly judged him, misconstruing his attentiveness as being controlling or overbearing. They rejected him without spending five minutes to get to know the real Howard.

Sadly, two friends, who had considered me "their best friend," felt they knew better than me what was best. This meant constantly criticizing Howard and finding fault. They even convinced me he had a bad attitude. Because Howard and I had been spending lots of time together, they resented him for the time I wasn't spending with them.

Howard:

I was devastated when Kelly listened to some friends who ill-advised her, accusing me of being over-protective and controlling. Therefore, she broke off our relationship. After a week or so, she called me and apologetically asked if we could see each other again. This happened several times. I'd had enough. She had to learn to make her own decisions about what or who was good for her – not what others thought. And besides, my heart had been broken too many times. I was done. I vowed never to see her again. That is, until one night, when the phone rang. "Could it be Kelly?" Secretly, I longed for it to be her, but I resisted the urge to grab it and allowed it to ring once, twice, before answering it on the third ring.

"Kelly, is that you?"

"Yes." Then she burst into tears and said, "Howard, I have missed you so much! Can we have dinner and talk?"

"Sure," I said. My heart was pounding; I was relieved. This was the longest time she'd gone before calling me.

When we met that night for dinner, I displayed a protective and defensive stance, but I allowed her to pour her heart out to me. Personally, I needed it like salve for a wound.

"I've been such a fool," she confessed. "My life is miserable without you, Howie. Will you come back to me? Please? I'll never hurt you again. I love you."

"I've missed you, too," I admitted. "And when I'd start missing you, God would always direct me to pray for your happiness, Kelly. I truly want you to be happy. That's all I've ever wanted. And that is why I never called you when we'd break up. I knew what I wanted. I needed you to know. Believe me, I love you and want you to be happy."

"I know you love me. I've never doubted it." She dabbed at her tears with the linen napkin. "And after being with you for seven years, I know the good, the bad, and the ugly, just like you know the good, the bad, and the ugly about me. I want you back. Please come back to me."

My heart was elated. Her words literally grew tears and a huge lump in my throat.

"Why don't we celebrate getting back together by going on a trip?"

Happily, she agreed. "Where?"

"One of your favorite places – Myrtle Beach. We'll go to SOS (Shagging on the Sand, which is a twice a year festival in

Cherry Grove). I think shagging the weekend away is what the doctor ordered."

Kelly:

I was convinced I never wanted to lose this man again. Besides, my family loved Howard, and they saw how happy he made me, so in the end, I chose Howard over several friends. If he'd ever ask me, I was ready to make a life-long commitment to this man that I loved.

Our SOS trip that weekend at Myrtle Beach was so much fun. The streets were packed with shag lovers while authentic beach music and laughter permeated the air. Like the thousands of other beachcombers, we shagged Friday and Saturday nights away to the tunes of the Drifters, the Embers, and others. Sadly, Sunday morning arrived too soon, so while most of the dancers packed up and headed back to homes and jobs after an enjoyable weekend, we decided to stay one more night and go to Flo's, our favorite restaurant in Murrell's Inlet.

It was such a lovely night, and I was feeling romantic. As we walked along the boardwalk, arm in arm, I heard mellow music coming from a nearby tavern. I turned and grabbed Howard's hand in a dance pose, inviting him to dance as I'd done once before. He accepted. His impulsiveness and uninhibitedness made me feel like the most blessed woman in Murrell's Inlet. Unbeknownst to me, bystanders had stopped and were watching us dance. I heard whispered comments that we looked "so much in love." I began crying tears of thanksgiving for this accepting and resilient man whom I loved. To me, this was another sign that he was the man God had intended for me.

A few evenings later after our beach trip, Howard asked if I'd like to go and see a wonderful musical at Central Piedmont

Community College and have a late dinner afterwards. I readily agreed, feeling so European. When he arrived, I was wearing my best dress and a crocheted shawl. He looked handsome in his dark suit. We were heading out for a glorious night on the town, but I couldn't help but notice how nervous and fidgety he was during the play.

Howard:

After the musical, we drove to the Village Tavern, another favorite restaurant of ours. I parked the car, feeling exuberance and relief at finally being alone with Kelly. I took her hands in mine and began saying the words I'd rehearsed all afternoon.

"Kelly, you know I've never loved any woman as much as I love you. I don't want to spend another day away from you. I want to spend the rest of my life serving you and making you happy. So Kelly, will you marry me?" In the end, I said hardly anything the way I'd rehearsed it, but I was speaking from my heart. I pulled out a black velvet box from my suit pants' pocket and opened it. Thankfully, the parking lot lights performed their magic.

Kelly:

When he opened the box, there flashed the biggest diamond I'd ever seen; I thought my heart was going to jump out of my chest.

"Yes! Of course!" I beamed. "Yes, I'll marry you!" Then I grabbed him and laid a whopper of a kiss on his lips. He instantly repeated it, but this time with a slow, wet kiss that left me breathless.

As we walked into the restaurant, my mascaraed lashes were wet with joy and our smiles couldn't be erased from our faces. The restaurant staff immediately asked what the occasion was, and when we announced our engagement, they celebrated with us that night. Everything felt so right. It was perfect.

We couldn't wait to tell my parents and the rest of our families. So, we called my Mom and Dad and invited them to lunch the next day. They accepted, and we met at Brixx's Restaurant in downtown Charlotte. Because it was another glorious day, Howard asked for a table outside. When my parents arrived, Howard immediately graced my mother with a dozen red roses.

Howard:

After we'd finished eating our lunch at Brixx's in downtown Charlotte, I signaled to Kelly that I was about to stand. She gave me a sweet smile and a nod. So I cleared my throat, stood, and said, "There is something I wanted to ask Kelly in front of you." Dropping to one knee, I grabbed the velvet box in which I'd replaced the ring and offered the diamond to Kelly again. "Kelly, will you make me the happiest man alive by marrying me?"

"Of course, I'll marry you," she said smiling. Her mom's eyes were shining and brimming with tears.

Kelly:

My family readily welcomed Howard into the family, which was all the confirmation I needed. Ellen and Kathy couldn't have been happier for me and congratulated us with big hugs. Life was beautiful and God was good all the time.

A Stranger to Myself

During one of our marriage counseling sessions, Minister Dennis Livingston gave us some words of wisdom that I will never forget. He said, "Marriage is the most important relationship besides your relationship with God. If anything or any person threatens that relationship, they must go. You must hold this relationship dear."

Howard:

Kelly Spence made me the happiest man alive as she was escorted down the aisle of the church by her father in his wheelchair. Her mother beamed when she saw her daughter and husband approaching and stood with the rest of the audience of happy witnesses for this joyful event. On one side of the lavender and white adorned altar was her sister, her sister-in-law, and her two nieces. On the other side was her brother-in-law, her brother, and her two nephews. My son served as my best man.

Kelly's face was joyful -- every frown, every doubt, every tear she'd ever experienced was replaced by the most radiant smile I'd ever seen. She was beautiful in her white bridal gown, and as she walked toward me, I told myself, "There is no one like Kelly. I'm the luckiest man alive."

Kelly:

When I opened my eyes that Saturday morning, I groggily realized that I was in a different bed. I was in my parents' home where I'd lived for the past three months because my fiancé had moved into the townhouse that we'd share after our marriage. And then it hit me! My wedding day had finally arrived! This was the day when my life would change forever. I felt a little melancholy that this precious time with my parents was over.

God had blessed us with these three months as a time to celebrate and share some really meaningful times that I would not trade for the world.

I stretched and lingered in bed, remembering our wedding rehearsal the night before followed by dinner at my sister's home. Howard had catered the meal from our friend, Linda Hidelsman, who runs a restaurant and catering business out of the YMCA. Linda's food was incredibly delicious! What a joyful night it had been! Dad began the night by toasting Howard and me. He shared how I had been as a little girl and how I'd grown into a woman. Mom welcomed Howard into the family with sweet humor saying, "You realize you can't give her back, right?" And after seven years of courtship, Howard assured her he had no intentions of giving me back.

Then we received toasts from our collective brothers and sisters, nephews and nieces. Jack, my oldest nephew, recited a beautiful and somewhat humorous poem. While he was speaking, tears stung my eyes. His life was about to change, too. Jack would soon head to the University of South Carolina on a swimming scholarship. I was so proud of him. My Aunt Nan and Cousin Doug had made the long drive from Michigan, along with many of my aunts and uncles. We were saddened that Howard's son, Brian, and his wife, Leslie, were not able to make the trip to Charlotte.

This seemed surreal. Was it the alarm clock or the beating of my heart? Regardless, I was ready to start this day with every intention of savoring each beautiful moment. My engagement had been one of the best times of my life. Ellen, Kathy, and Nonie had given me a grand bridal shower and bachelorette party where we played silly games like making lingerie out of toilet paper and danced (just girls) at a club named "Bubbles." Your imaginations can have fun envisioning those antics. Everything was planned so tastefully; it was hard to imagine all the work that was done especially to spoil me. At the age of 48, I'd given my share of showers for girlfriends, and I'd been a bridesmaid in over twenty weddings. Now my wish was coming true. The fuss was about me this time. It was my turn.

I hurried to the kitchen because Dad was making his famous waffles and eggs. Aunt Nan emerged from my parents' other spare bedroom drawn by the smell of coffee. After breakfast, Aunt Nan and I went on a prayer and praise walk. My parents live across the street from the church, so we crossed the busy street so I could familiarize her with the huge property. We found a lot of activity at 10:00 a.m. when we arrived, so we remained respectful of the funeral that was being held and walked on the outskirts. As we laughed about childhood memories, I spied something on the ground. It was a $20 bill.

Aunt Nan said, "Kelly, He just keeps shining on you and blessing you."

I was beaming as I bent to pick it up. I'd never found a bill that large in my life. I decided to put it in the offering plate at church. Things were truly looking up. For months, I'd prayed for my wedding day to be on a beautiful sunny day, and God granted me that prayer. It was the end of the first week in March with just a little chill in the air. It was perfect!

I felt pretty and special, too, as Nan and I returned to my parents' home. On Thursday, Kelly, my step-daughter-to be, and I had gotten manicures and pedicures. I'd even gotten a spray tan. It was time to take a shower and get my hair done. Kathy had secured Cathy McNish with Natural Brides, Inc. to fix our hair. She proved to be amazing. But every time Mom's and my eyes met that day, we became glossy-eyed and looked away. I was going to wear the dress that Kathy, Ellen, and Mom had taken me to purchase two years before when Howard and I were supposed to have gotten married. That's when we both discovered that it had not been the right time.

Howard and I wanted our wedding to be drama free, so Ellen would be my Matron of Honor and Kathy would be my Bridesmaid. Howard asked Rod Jr. to be his Best Man, and Ken to be his Groomsman. We wanted all family members to have a part in the wedding, so we asked Kaylin (16) and Janie (14) to be our Junior Bridesmaids. We asked Jack (17) and Trey (15) to be our Junior Groomsmen. It was brilliant planning. I've never seen my nieces and nephews so excited; they'd put on their dresses and tuxedos and were giddy. When Mom and I arrived, there was a buzz of activity. Girls were running around being pestered by the boys. They were having fun.

Ellen and Kathy explained that I would be second to last in getting my hair and makeup done. And to keep anyone from passing out during the ceremony, sandwiches had been ordered. Ellen made sure I ate one of them, too. Finally, it was my turn. Cathy was such an amazing professional. Within minutes, she had my hair in a down/up do, held together by about thirty bobby pins, hidden carefully so no one could see them. She sprayed my hair and turned me around. I felt like a princess ready for her wedding day! I watched as she worked on my already beautiful mother. After a few minutes, Cathy had her looking absolutely stunning.

Ken Thomas, our photographer, met us at the church. He photographed me getting ready with my girls pretending to help me with my dress and jewelry. Mom and I shared sweet moments when she told me how proud she was of the woman I'd become.

Then as if by magic, it was time. The sanctuary was packed with almost every chair being filled. Talented Larry Greene was singing to the accompaniment of Debbie on the piano. Our wedding coordinator directed us as the music for the wedding party began. Suddenly, it was just Dad and me. He looked up at me from his chair. There were tears in his eyes. We hugged each other.

Then he asked, "Are you ready to do this, kid?"

I replied, "Yes, sir. Let's do it!"

The doors opened to the music of Twila Paris's, "How Beautiful." Some of the lyrics are "How beautiful are the hands that served the poor, the feet that walked the long dusty roads." Toward the end of the song, it speaks of "How beautiful will the bride (us) be when our Groom (Jesus) comes for us." The song ends with "How beautiful is the body of Christ."

Emotions overwhelmed me. Tears streamed down my face as I walked down the aisle beside my father's wheelchair. I looked into all the different faces of the people who had helped me in so many ways. These people were truly my family.

The ceremony was by no means boring. You'd have thought Pastor Greg Baker and I had practiced a comedy routine. As Dad walked me to the altar, Pastor Baker welcomed everyone. Somehow I thought that he'd forgotten to have Dad give me away. He began praying, then talking, and then praying again, so I felt the responsibility of reminding him. After I did, he looked at Dad and say, "Boy, she really wants to get rid of you!" Everyone cracked up. A little later in the ceremony, the pastor stated, "Howard and Kelly, as we discussed in our counseling sessions, life will not always be this easy."

"There will be some difficult times...." At that, I gasped aloud, grabbed my dress, and pretended like I was heading for the door with an expression of "I'm out of here!" Again, everyone laughed at the joke.

In reality, I'm sure there will be more difficult times. When there are, Howard and I will pray one of our familiar prayers,

"Lord, we believe you can use us more as a team than you can individually. Here we are, Lord. Use us."

Our reception was fun. We ate delicious food, danced for four hours straight, and cut the cake. There was so much love in the air as the night drew to an end.

I asked Howard, "Should we ask the DJ if he can stay for another hour? Look at how much fun everyone is still having."

Without a moment's hesitation, my husband replied, "The night isn't over for us yet. We still have plans." And we did. We spent that night at a SouthPark hotel, overlooking downtown Charlotte. It was lovely. On the following morning, we left for our week-long honeymoon in the Dominican Republic, Punta Cana. It was a paradise!

It's been six months of marriage, and it was definitely worth the wait. The man I married is the same gentleman who opens my door for me and brings me coffee in bed. I'm so blessed.

Never give up on your dreams. Never settle for less than His best. We serve such a good God. "Take delight in the Lord, and He will give you the desires of your heart" (Psalm 37:4).

No man or woman was ever intended to be an island; we need each other. If it hadn't been for the body of Christ walking beside me every step of the way, I would not have survived. There were many who said, "I will help you." They were assisting God in His plan for my life.

There is no way I could have traveled to Europe, traveled to Israel on a pilgrimage of the Holy Land, and participated in mission trips in New York and Panama City Beach, Florida, if it hadn't been for saints (believers of Jesus).

While in my valley of despair, I'd never imagine saying this, but I'm so thankful God chose me to be involved in the horrific accident that changed my life. It is a better life than it would ever have been. I have purpose.

A Stranger to Myself

Do you realize how many people will never know that God has a purpose for their lives? I'm sorry for them. God chose me to go through these challenges because He knows more than I do. He knew my inner strength and my capabilities. He knew I would walk with Him every day of my life.

Am I perfect? Absolutely not! Not even close, but I am forgiven. But if it hadn't been for God, I would still be a stranger to myself.

Epilogue

I am with you and will watch over you wherever you go,
and I will bring you back to this land.
I will not leave you until I've done what I promised you.
Genesis 28: 15

I was listening to Joel Osteen, a television preacher out of Dallas, Texas, on September 21, 2008. He told a story of a man who lived in a hut on an island. The man was a sculptor. He was taking a walk one day by a plantation where the wealthiest man on the island lived. He noticed there were a few tree stumps dug up, along with some cut up wood. He went up to the man's door and knocked.

When the man answered, he asked how he might be able to purchase one of his stumps. The wealthy man looked at the sculptor with a puzzled look and responded, "They are not for sale; they are just broken down old trees." The man asked the wealthy man if he would mind if he could buy one. The man replied, "Buy it? I'll give it to you. That will be one less I will have to throw away."

So the man strapped one of the stumps to his back and carried it home. He brought it in and placed it in the middle of the hut. He spent the next couple of hours walking around the stump. Joel Osteen stated, "The man thought there was something in it that needed to be freed." Then he carefully started chipping away at the stump with such precision and

310

detail. It was like watching the hand of the Master working. The detail was stunning. Before he knew it, it took the shape of a beautiful eagle. It was incredibly majestic, so beautiful with its wings outstretched. The man then placed it on a stand on the front porch looking out to the dirt road.

A couple of weeks passed by and the rich plantation owner was on a walk on the island when he saw this magnificent eagle. He walked up to the stand and was in complete awe at the beauty. He walked around it and noticed the intricate detail. The rich man searched until he found the sculptor. He did not even recognize the sculptor. He asked him, "I want to buy this. How much will you sell it to me for?" The man smiled and said, "I'm sorry, but it is not for sale." The man insisted that he sell it to him. He said, "Name your price; how does $500 sound?"

The sculptor, quite surprised by the large offer, agreed and sold it to the plantation owner for $500. It was more money than the man ever had. The wealthy man paid him cash right then and there. As the man was leaving with his prized purchase, the sculptor proudly called to the rich man and said, "Do you realize you just paid me $500 for the same wood that you gave me for nothing just weeks ago?" The next day the sculptor walked by the plantation and saw a sign by the woodpile that read: "Tree trunks for sale -- $500."

Pastor Osteen's message of that story was that old sculptor could see something in that old stump that other people could not see. The plantation owner thought the wood was worthless, flawed, and of no value. The sculptor saw it as a masterpiece. That is exactly what God saw in my broken down, shattered life.

During the early years after the accident, I could not see an end to my heart's pain. All I saw was dark depression, rejection, and heartache. I barely had the strength to get out of bed in the mornings, but God saw a masterpiece that needed a lot of chipping away. I needed my pride, my ego, and my self-reliance to be chipped away. It all had to go. Today, I would not be half the person I am if I had never gone through those valleys. I would not have nearly the closeness to my Heavenly Father that I do today had I never had to rely on Him like I still do. My hind-sight vision tells me that I needed every valley to mold me into the masterpiece I am today. Believe me, it is a life-long process, and He is still chipping, carving, and even doing some pruning to this very day, and I am sure it will continue until the day I am laid in the ground.

I often ask myself, "How does one undergo such struggle and pain? Is it not more than one should have to take?"

When I thought life was too hard, and I felt like the weight was too much, I would always think of Joni Eareckson Tada and all she has had to go through, and how to this day, she has an army of eight women that show up at her doorstep every morning to get her bathed, dressed, and make-up applied. I am humbled by all the things God has allowed to come back to me. For example, dressing myself, cooking for myself, and being able to pay my own bills. These are just a few I'm grateful for. It takes me much longer to get ready; I may not look as perfect as I once did, but my priorities are different. I have matured more. Now it is more important for me to read my Bible in the morning than fix every hair on my head so it looks "perfect." My clothes may not be the hip new fashion, but I have peace. I at least had the hope that things would get better and my life would find a sense of "normal" for me again. I will be forever humbled by Joni's strength and inspiration.

Final Thoughts

How do you forgive? Where do you start? What if you have never met the person that almost took your life? How could I hate someone I have never met or seen? How could I place blame when they called it an "accident"? The very definition of the word means "an unfortunate happening that occurs unintentionally and usually results in harm, injury, damage, or loss; casualty; mishap."

It turned out the driver of the truck that hit Lucy and me was a man who had been convicted of three DUIs (Driving Under the Influence), and it was later discovered that this same man had a warrant out for his arrest for another DUI in Alabama. He was a man already on the run.

The accident had happened right after his lunch hour (about 1:15 p.m.), so I assumed and could almost guarantee that he had been drinking. At that time, DUI laws were not as severe as they are today. You would basically get your wrists slapped, and you were free. My mother was very upset to learn the police had failed to give this man a "Breathalyzer Test" to see what his blood alcohol level was at the time of the accident.

But somehow, I'd forgiven the man; nothing would ever change the outcome. It was what it was. We are to do for others what Jesus did for us. Continuing to place blame would do nothing for me.

Once when Mom and I were driving alone, I asked her if she'd ever gotten angry with God for what had happened to our family. She amazed me with her response.

"Why would I be angry with God, Kelly? I've lived my life long enough to know that bad things do happen to good people. So, why would I be angry with God?"

I meekly replied, "Supposedly, because He's in control of everything. I know I've been through my anger with God. I've raised my fists at Him and shouted profanities out at Him and fought with Him."

But God had seen beneath all of that and saw the pain of a young girl whose life had been shattered.

She nodded and said, "I think He allows people to get angry, Kelly."

I thank God He allowed me to take my anger out on Him and not out on my family members.

Do you need to forgive yourself for anything God has already wiped clean? Are you having a hard time letting something go? Does the devil have you believing that you caused it? Hear me clearly. It is not your fault! And Jesus's blood has paid for it all. The blood of Jesus covers all past sins, present sins, and future sins.

Has someone hurt you? Do you need to forgive someone? I didn't say you needed to forget what was done or how you were hurt. If you don't forgive the person, you are really holding yourself captive and putting on a layer of chains. Ask Jesus to help you forgive that person. He will help you. Here are some simple steps to freedom that was shared with me by one of my mentors, Brenda Livingston. She guided me through a similar process.

Thank Jesus for loving you enough to die on a cross for you. Confess (say aloud) to Him what the issue is and ask for forgiveness. (Admit or state that you are at fault in some way). It is very important for you to say it verbally because the moment you speak, Satan will lose his power over you.

A Stranger to Myself

Say, "I forgive myself for _____."

Forgive anyone who has hurt you.

Give Jesus all of your pain, shame, anger. Ask Jesus to replace this pain with peace, joy, or _____.

Jesus wants to replace your pain with peace. He wants to replace your shame with self-respect and confidence. He wants to replace your anger with laughter and joy. He wants to replace your self-denigration with a newfound love for yourself. It is important for you to claim Jesus's gift and receive it from your Heavenly Father. He wants nothing more than to set you free.

Thank Jesus for setting you free.

Everyone is different and unique. When you go through this freedom process, allow God to meet you where you are, and allow Him to have His way.

What weaknesses do you possess? What special challenges do you have? Allow God to use them for His good.

I'm astonished at how far that I've come after having gone through so much. That is why I tell people my story, almost daily. I tell them it does me more good to hear it than it does for you to hear it because it's so easy for me to focus on the day-to-day struggles with short-term memory. "Where did I put that?" "What time was I supposed to be here?" "Where did I place my hair brush?" "Where is my phone?" "Where is my cup of coffee?"

Another lesson I've learned and tried to live by is to take it one day at a time. The "here and now" is the only thing we have control over. So I leave you with this quote that I love and received on my Walk to Emmaus. It goes like this:

"I am not the God of the past; my name is not 'I was.'
I am not the God of the future; my name is not 'I will be.'
I am the God of the present.
My name is 'I AM.'"

315

Kelly Spence Cain was born in Ann Arbor, Michigan, to Rod and Marilyn Spence. As avid and excellent athletes, they inspired her and two siblings to love competition and athletics as well. Kelly earned a degree in educational psychology from the University of Georgia and a master's degree in rehabilitation counseling from Auburn Univ.

Even though a tragic accident left her comatose and legally blind with a life-long brain injury, she enjoys tennis, ballroom dancing, snow-skiing, traveling, and public speaking.

Kelly recently married Howard, "the love of my life." They reside in Hernando, Florida.

Kelly would enjoy hearing from you:Godsmilebook@gmail.com

"God offered me a new life with more meaning, more beauty, and more promise than I could ever imagine possible. I've learned that everything happens for a reason; nothing is impossible with God. He is in the miracle-making business."
Kelly Spence Cain

Kelly Spence Cain

Sandi Huddleston-Edwards is a proud North Carolinian native where she has lived all of her life.

She earned an A.A. degree from Central Piedmont Community College and B.A. and M.A. degrees in English from the University of North Carolina at Charlotte.

Since retiring in 2012 from a 36 year career with Duke Energy, she now focuses on her two favorite passions: teaching and writing. For the past 16 years, Ms. Huddleston-Edwards has been an adjunct English instructor at Central Piedmont Community College, Montreat College, UNC-Charlotte, and Johnson & Wales University. She has been published in *Lake Norman Publications, Tarheel Wheels, and Reader's Digest.* She is the author of two novels, *Richard's Key* and *Roy's Sandman,* and a children's book, *The Guardian Angel.* She is in the process of writing two novels, a memoir, and two devotionals. "All glory goes to God."

In addition to teaching and writing, Ms. Huddleston-Edwards, a proud mother of three sons and four grandchildren, enjoys bike riding, reading, traveling, watching old movies, and spending time at Myrtle Beach with her husband, Barry, and their two Yorkshire Terriers, Maddie and Abbie. She and Barry reside in Huntersville where they are members of Ramah Presbyterian Church.

Sandi would enjoy hearing from you: authorsandi@gmail.com